DISPATCHES FROM THE FRONT ▼

DISPATCHES FROM THE FRONT

THEOLOGICAL ENGAGEMENTS WITH

THE SECULAR ▼ STANLEY HAUERWAS

Duke University Press   Durham and London   1994

TO ▼

ANN RICE

JIM LANGFORD

ALASDAIR MACINTYRE

TOM SHAFFER

CONTENTS ▼

It is the worst of times to be a Christian theologian; it is the best of times to be a Christian theologian. That both claims are true is apparent by the fact that most people in America, Christian and non-Christian alike, could care less whether this is a good or bad time to be a theologian. Theology is a ghetto activity as insulated and uninteresting as the Saturday religion pages of the local paper. God knows, it is hard to make God boring, but American Christians, aided and abetted by theologians, have accomplished that feat.

Yet I love theology since I find nothing more exciting than the subject of theology, that is, the truthful worship of God. Moreover, it is a wonderful time to be a theologian. No matter how hard theologians may try to be "good academics," they will be suspect among those who populate the more established "disciplines." The study of rocks by geologists is legitimate, but God just does not seem to be an appropriate subject to constitute a respectable discipline in the contemporary university. Which creates a wonderful opportunity for those of us who remain theologians. Since we are never going to make it as academics, or anything else, we might as well have fun.

By fun, I mean that we do not have to be constrained by the "normalizing" character of most academic subjects in the contemporary university. The university exists, and the academic disciplines that constitute it exist, to underwrite the presumption that the way things are is the way they have to be. Yet Christians are schooled by a discourse that trains us to recognize the contingent character of *what is*. Accordingly, theology not only must risk appearing funny, but it should risk being funny.

I have had a great deal of fun writing this book. I hope the reader will sense the fun or, perhaps better, the joy that being a theologian gives me. Theology or, better, God is so entertaining. Thus, I hope many readers will be entertained. That is, I hope they will discover, as I discover now and then, how wonderful it is to be creatures of a gracious God who is capable of beckoning us from our self-fascination.

By suggesting that this book aspires to be entertainment, I do not mean it is not "serious." When you are discussing matters of life and death, to say nothing of war, you had better be serious. Yet part of the fun of doing theology is the way in which such matters are reframed once theological discourse is used in an unapologetic manner. If readers sometimes find themselves surprised by some of these chapters, they should know that I remain equally surprised, and thus entertained, by what happens when everyday Christian speech and practices are allowed to do their imaginative work.

With this book I should like to attract some readers who are not accustomed to reading Christian theology. Even though many of the current debates surrounding multiculturalism—which specific texts are to be read and interpreted, the moral status of liberalism—are conducted in secular terms, they are the result of past religious conflict, and ironically they continue to mimic theological disputes. For example, the debate over the status of texts is but the secular analogue of debates occasioned by the Reformation concerning the status of Scripture. I am not suggesting such analogies sufficient to rekindle interest in theology by those who believe Christianity has been rightly left well behind; instead, I am only suggesting that they may be surprised to discover that Christian theological reflection still has descriptive power.

One of the difficulties faced by the theologian in our time is the decline of religious knowledge. However, as I argue in this book, knowing about Christianity, and/or Judaism, does one little good, but certainly a great deal of harm. Far too often, people, whether they are Christian or not, "know" just enough to prevent any serious use, either positively or negatively, of Christian language. In the following pages I try to suggest some of the exercises necessary if Christians are to learn to speak truthfully. I hope some readers, who have largely given up on "religion," may at least find this discussion a challenge.

I confess that part of the fun of being a theologian is locating the incoherences built into the secular. For example, the current fashion to identify with the "oppressed," admirable though it may be, lacks moral intelligibility. We end up in the shabby game of trying to figure out who is the most oppressed. New readers may find my up-yours attitude about such cultural sentimentalities a bit off-putting, but I hope it is clear that I take no comfort in the moral confusion of our lives. Nor do I assume that Christians have any magic solutions to make our lives coherent. What I offer is not resolution, but a challenge that can only make our lives more difficult and interesting.

I hope readers of my past work also will find this book to be of interest. Those who have attended to my more abstract accounts of character and virtue should find here a thicker display of those themes. In particular, I think I have done a better job of showing, rather than simply saying, how theological convictions must be practically embodied. I have now been writing more than twenty-five years, and, while I certainly have changed my mind along the way, I also like to think that my work has continued to develop in some interesting ways. I hope that those who have been good enough to read what I have done in the past will find that these chapters add some interesting twists.

This book would not exist if Rachel Toor was not persistent. As a good editor, she made me imagine what a book with Duke University Press might look like. Then she, along with Paula Gilbert, convinced me that I ought to take the time to do it right. I do not know if it is "right," but I know it would not have been nearly as good without Rachel's good criticism. She was aided in that endeavor by two wonderful readers' reports on the first draft by Robert Bellah and Scott Davis. They read the book in confidence, but confidently revealed themselves. Only they know how deeply I am in their debt for suggesting how the text should be reorganized as well as rewritten.

I have dedicated this book to four people, all of whom now work at the University of Notre Dame. Jim Langford is Director of University of Notre Dame Press. He not only has supported my work from the beginning, but he has been a good friend. He also quoted me (November 28) in the 1993 *Cub Calendar,* thereby making me as close as I will ever come to being immortal. Ann Rice was my original editor at the University of Notre Dame Press. She had to work over my prose when I did not even know how to write well enough to know I did not write well. To the extent that I write better than I did, I am in her debt.

The debt I owe Alasdair MacIntyre is obvious to anyone who knows

3

his work. His early work on the philosophy of mind and action was important for my dissertation. His ongoing project in moral philosophy not only is crucial for my own work but for many who attempt to do theology without apology. Alasdair is a good friend, even though we disagree about Trollope.

Thomas Shaffer teaches law at the University of Notre Dame Law School. He likes to style himself as a student of "my" theology, but if that is true, I learn more from how he uses me than I do from my own work. Simply knowing that a person like Tom is there makes it all worthwhile. He, and Professor David Solomon, also of Notre Dame, were the first to tell me I should read Trollope.

The many graduate students who have worked with me over the last years have immeasurably made me—and hopefully the way I think and live—better. For me, they constitute a community even though they do not always know one another, coming as they did at different times to study at Duke. They are Greg Jones, Michael Cartwright, Steve Long, Paul Lewis, Pat Browder, Jeff Powell, Reinhard Hutter, Steven Hoogerwerf, Therese Lysaught, David Matzko, Kathy Rudy, Mike Broadway, Carol Stoneking, Jim Lewis, Chuck Campbell, Phil Kenneson, Michael Baxter, Fritz Bauerschmidt, Michael Battle, Bill Cavanaugh, Dan Bell, John Berkman, David Jenkins, Gail Hamner, and David Toole. I am particularly grateful to Jeff Powell who is coauthor of the tribute to William Stringfellow. Dr. Jim Fodor, a Canadian postdoctoral student, has been kind enough to read, edit, and help me think through many of these essays. I owe Mr. Mark Baker much for the index.

I have been fortunate to be at Duke in a time of wonderful intellectual ferment. I have been taught much by my colleagues throughout this university. Ms. Wanda Dunn has typed and retyped this book. She combines skill and humor in a remarkable fashion. I completed the manuscript while on sabbatical at the National Humanities Center. It is an academic heaven, and I am deeply grateful for the support I received there as well as for the many colleagues who provided such stimulating conversation. In particular, it was a joy to learn from Professor John Wilson of Princeton University.

Finally, I thank God for Paula and for her willingness to share her life, and in particular her love of God, with me.

4

IN THE CHURCH AND UNIVERSITY

BUT NOT OF EITHER

Theology as Soul-Craft

Stanley Fish, my friend and next-door neighbor, likes to remind students who express admiration for Milton's poetry that Milton does not want their admiration, he wants their souls.[1] I lack Milton's art, but my ambition can be no less than Milton's. I must try, like Milton, to change lives, my own included, through the transformation of our imaginations. I must do that using the leaden skills of the theologian, which at their best are meant to help us feel the oddness and beauty of language hewn from the worship of God. Theology is a minor practice in the total life of the church, but in times as strange as ours even theologians must try, through our awkward art, to change lives by forming the imagination by faithful speech.[2] Thus, I tell my students that I do not want them to learn "to make up their own minds," since most of them do not have minds worth making up until I have trained them. Rather, by the time I am finished with them, I want them to think just like me.

The strangeness of our times for Christians is apparent in the kind of response a paragraph like the one above elicits. "Who do you think you are to tell anyone else how to live? What gives you that right? You must be some kind of fundamentalist or a fanatic." I am, of course, a fanatic. I want, for example, to convince everyone who calls himself or herself a Christian that being Christian means that one must be nonviolent. In the process I hope to convince many who currently are not Christians to place themselves under the discipline of Christians who are trying to learn how to live peaceably.[3] I find it odd that in our time many people believe we can or should avoid telling one another how to live. From my perspective, that is but a sign of the corruption of our age and why we are in such desperate need of conversion.[4]

A more interesting challenge to my desire to change my readers' lives is that my focus on the imagination and language is insufficient to the task. Surely, being a Christian involves more than learning a language. But what could be more important than learning a language and in particular one that, if I am to become a competent speaker, forces me to acknowledge my existence as a creature of a gracious God. That is why one must begin to learn to pray if one is to be a Christian.

Descriptions are everything.[5] The kind of descriptions Christians use are not easily learned, since those among us called saints tell that a lifetime is too short to begin to get it right. That saints, even in a lifetime, cannot get it right is a reminder that Christians do not believe they exist as individuals, but rather they are members of a community called church that makes them skilled speakers.

Such a view, of course, challenges the deepest conceits of what it means to be "modern"—that is, that we all live in the same world, we all want the same thing, we all see the same things. Accordingly, conflict is thought to be irrational—"a failure to communicate." This view has had disastrous results for those who would have their speech and lives determined by Christian discourses and practices. For Christian and non-Christian alike assume that Christians are pretty much like everybody else. Thus, the power of the Christian imagination is stilled, and our language does no work.

This book comprises essays that I hope exhibit the difference which Christian discourse can make for the shaping of lives and the world. It is not my intention to emphasize the difference that being Christian makes, because I think difference a good in and of itself. Yet anyone who believes, as Christians must, that salvation comes from the Jews is surely going to appear a bit odd. At the very least, they will appear as odd as the Jews.

That Christians are odd, of course, will not be good news for most American Christians, including the smart ones who may be theologians. To suggest, as I do, that Christians should be suspicious of the moral presuppositions as well as the practices that sustain liberal democracy cannot but appear as rank heresy to most American Christians.[6] Most Christians in America are willing to allow fellow Christians doubt that God is Trinity, but they would excommunicate anyone who does not believe, as I do not believe, in "human rights."[7] Not surprising, since most Christian theologians spend most of their time trying to show that Christians believe pretty much what anyone believes.

As a result, Christian linguistic practices cannot help but appear epiphenomenal. Why should one worry about Trinity when such language seems to be doing no discernible work? Thus, the agony of liberal Christianity, whose advocates seek to show that Christianity can be made reasonable within the epistic presuppositions of modernity, only to discover, to the extent they are successful, that the very people they were trying to convince could care less. Why should anyone be interested in Christianity if Christians were simply telling them what they already knew on less obscurantist grounds? Robbed of any power by the politics of liberalism, what remains for Christianity is to become another "meaning system." Accordingly, theology is seldom read by Christians and non-Christians alike because it is so damned dull.

By suggesting, therefore, that my task is to change lives, I am attempting to make what Wittgensteinians call a "grammatical point." Christian discourse is not a set of beliefs aimed at making our lives more coherent; rather, it is a constitutive set of skills that requires the transformation of the self to rightly see the world. By suggesting that this transformation involves a battle for the imagination, I mean that it is more than simply a matter of "ideas." The Christian imagination resides not in the mind, but rather in the fleshy existence of a body of people who have learned to be with someone as fleshy as those called "mentally handicapped." Such a people have the resources to refuse to accept reality devoid of miracles.

It is a pretentious comparison, but the kind of imaginative transformation I am trying to effect is similar to the way Foucault tried to force new disciplines on his readers. I lack Foucault's intellectual power, but I have an advantage he did not have: I am part of a tradition that does not require the kind of self-generation in which Foucault excelled. Yet to enter the world envisioned in Christian discourse means we will be forced to see that those habits we have learned to call "freedom" may contain more violence than even Foucault saw.

That I do Christian theology in such an unapologetic, radical manner will seem particularly offensive to those with liberal sensibilities.[8] Nonetheless, I hope that these exercises for the imagination may attract some to live as Christians. Living in a morally incoherent culture is a resource for such a task, since many continue, for example, to think that they ought to live honorably or at least strive to live lives of integrity.[9]

They have little idea why honor or integrity is a good—or even what each might entail—but they still seem like "good ideas." I am willing, and I hope not dishonestly, to make use of these lingering ideals to suggest how some accounts of honor and integrity draw on Christian practices for their intelligibility. By doing so, I am not suggesting that non-Christians cannot lead lives of honor, but rather I hope to show the difference that Christian practice can make for how honor is understood. Equally, if not more important, is how the virtues of constancy and honor as practiced by Christians are integral to other matters we care about, such as love and politics.

Accounts of the moral life associated with honor, of course, are hierarchical and elitist. I have no wish to deny either characterization. I have little use for the democratization of our moral existence so characteristic of egalitarianism. Indeed, I regard egalitarianism as the opiate of the masses and the source of the politics of envy and influence so characteristic of our lives.[10] The interesting question is not whether hierarchies or elites should exist, but what goods they serve. A skilled sculptor or poet is rightly privileged in good communities because of his or her ability to help us be more than we could otherwise be.

The heart of this book is constituted by two essays built around the work of Anthony Trollope. Trollope, of course, seems an odd choice since he appeared to have little use for the kind of Christianity I defend—enthusiasts for fox hunting are seldom pacifists. Moreover, the "ethic of the gentleman" not only seems unredeemably sexist, but it implies a social conservatism that is at odds with my determinative anti-Constantinian stance.[11] I hope to show, however, that Trollope's account of the kind of constancy required of those who would live honorably implies a more radical stance than is apparent—particularly when juxtaposed with our social options.

I use Trollope because I love to read Trollope.[12] Yet Trollope also helps me display Christian convictions at work. Through the thickness of his narratives we can begin to see why constancy cannot be sustained without forgiveness. That Trollope gained his understanding of forgiveness from the most conventional forms of Anglicanism is but a reminder of the radical possibilities that lay in the conventional. It is part of my strategy to help us discover moral commitments that have implications we hardly imagine in such practices as caring for the sick, keeping our promises, being people who want to hear the truth as well as tell it.

Trollope-like novels are my best allies and resource for the display of the kind of redescriptions required to live as a Christian, particularly in a liberal society. In this respect I like to think of what I am trying to do as a form of gossip. I realize that gossip is not a particularly happy way to characterize my work, since it generally is thought to be a bad thing. We all love to talk about other people, but few of us like to think we are gossips. Yet the novel is in many ways but a highly refined form of gossip; through the novel we are entertained by other lives in a manner that helps us discover ourselves or at least who we would like to be. Gossip is the casuistry of everyday life.

We are, after all, opaque beings. It is our very opaqueness that draws us into endless investigations to discover who other people "really are." In the process of exchanging information about one another, we hope to discover who we may be, since our privileged relationship to our own history does not mean we are any less opaque to ourselves.[13] Interesting to note that a gossip was the name of the person spiritually related to another through sponsorship at baptism—that is, the gossips were those charged with the task of telling the stories necessary for the baptized to know what kind of people they had been made part. In liberal cultures gossip becomes the insufficient way to supply the stories we need to live well—in spite of our allegiance to the private/public distinction. That gossip is open to terrible abuse does not count against its importance for helping us live better.

The "method" of these essays is probably best characterized as that form of gossip generally known as journalism. I work as a Christian reporter renarrating widely shared stories by suggesting how Christian practices provide compelling redescriptions of our engagements. What I do is not quite theology, not quite ethics, not quite cultural criticism. Yet in the spaces created by the "not quite," I hope to entice the reader to enter a world that will change his or her life.

Which, of course, raises the question of what people I assume my "readers" to be and why they need to have their lives changed—journalists, after all, allegedly are supposed to write in a manner accessible to anyone. They are able to do so, particularly in the English-speaking world, given the pretension that English is a universal language that anyone can learn and/or translate. As Alasdair MacIntyre has pointed out, however, such a view of English and translation is produced by the practices of the cosmopolitan cultures of modernity that I wish to challenge.[14] By providing some attractive examples of Christian speech, I hope to change some who are captured by the English correlative to those practices that can be broadly labeled liberal. I am, therefore, attempting to entice readers to read a foreign-language newspaper called Christian.

On the Politics of Liberalism and the University

One of my friends, a prominent neoconservative, tells me I am the most apolitical person he knows. He does not mean it as a compliment. I frustrate him because I often refuse to take sides in the current cultural and political wars. From his perspective, my refusal is at best politically naive and at worst politically irresponsible. It seems I fail to appreciate that politics is finally an arena of limited options in which ideas must be wedded to the power of self-interest for the realization of relative goods. I have to confess I am inclined to agree with his analysis, as I often find myself outmaneuvered, even within the restricted politics of the university, by those more astute.

I like to think—and it may be self-deception—that my seeming apolitical stance has to do with a commitment to the practice of a different kind of politics. I refuse to believe that politics does not have to do with truthfulness, which is first of all made possible by the presence of truthful people. I believe that any politics capable of discovering goods in common requires friendship among good people. Friendship involves shared judgments about matters that matter. Politics names those practices necessary over time for a community of friends to exist. Accordingly, I believe that nonviolence is not only the necessary prerequisite for such politics, but that the creation of nonviolent community is the means and end of all politics.

I am well-aware that this account of politics will appear terribly naive if not anarchistic.[15] I am not particularly troubled by either characterization. As for the practice associated with the nation-state and studied in most political science departments, I see no good reason to call that behavior "politics," except in the most degraded sense. Such a politics unfortunately has come to characterize the life of most universities, which understandably mirror the character of the society they serve. At the very least, it is increasingly the case that university administrators have the same managerial facelessness as American politicians.[16]

That my politics is so anarchistic helps explain why I am seen as an untrusty ally by both the left and the right. In truth, I do not admire the kind of issue-politics created by liberal political theory and practice. I am convinced by critics of classical liberalism who argue that the left and the right in America are really brothers and sisters in spite of all their seeming disagreements. Both believe that good societies are characterized by freedom and equality of individuals, which then require trying to achieve as much cooperation as possible between those individuals in spite of the fact that they share nothing in common other than their commitment to the abstractions "freedom and equality." As a result, I often refuse to choose sides on the "issues," since I resist the presuppositions that make this or that an "issue"—that is, a matter over which different interest groups must have their interest balanced.

For example, I have found it hard to know how to enter the debate about abortion since I do not believe the issue for Christians can be framed in "pro-life" or "pro-choice" terms. Such descriptions are attempts to win the political battle on the most minimum set of agreements—that is, that abortion is primarily about the sanctity of life or freedom of women. As a result, abortion is abstracted from those practices through which our lives are ordered that we might as a community be in a position to welcome children. It is a political necessity to make our moral discourse, and our lives, as thin as possible in the hopes of securing political agreement. As a result, the debate is but a shouting match between two interest groups.[17]

My relation to liberal politics is complicated, as should be clear by now, because I try to think and write as a Christian. Christian ethics, as a field, began as part of the American progressivist movement which assumed that the subject of Christian ethics in America is America.[18] I do not begin with that assumption, but with the claim that the most determinative political loyalty for Christians is the church. That claim, of course, creates the political problem of how the church is to negotiate the manifold we call the United States of America. I am not particularly interested in the compromised character of most American politicians; I assume the genius of American politics is to produce just such people. The more interesting political question for me is what is required of the church in such a society to produce congregations who require that a ministry exists which has the courage to preach truthfully.[19]

This understanding of the significance of virtue also creates my difficulty in relating to current politics. Aristotle rightly argued that descriptions of our activities are correlative to the kind of person we are. It is not enough that we do the right thing rightly, but we must do it for the right reason, with the right feeling, and at the right time. Good politics are about the production and enablement of people being what they appear to be. Yet liberalism produces characters who believe what they do is not who they are as well as moral theories, deontic and utilitarian alike, that are designed to underwrite the lack of connection between our being and our doing. It should not be surprising that the "ethical theory" produced in such social orders is not about what is necessary for people to be virtuous, but rather becomes just one or another kind of decision theory.

The American left and the American right provide interesting exhibits of the incoherence of liberal political and ethical theories. For example, neoconservatives celebrate the "free market," but they insist that we must distinguish between the economic, political, and cultural realms since they do not want the habits acquired in the market to invade other aspects of our lives. Accordingly, they endlessly celebrate the importance of the family for developing people of virtue. Yet they fail to tell us how the family can be maintained culturally in an economy in which we are taught to regard our lives as self-interested units of desire. In like manner, the left's support of the distinction between the public and the private in matters such as free speech and censorship robs the left of the resources to make questions of economic distribution or the quality of our environment morally intelligible.

The current politics of the university associated with questions of political correctness and multiculturalism merely mirror the incoherence of our wider politics. Multiculturalism can be seen as the continuing outworking of interest group politics in the realm of "ideas." Those who rebel against political correctness in the name of "objectivity" of the "scholarly enterprise" represent established disciplines whose politics have long been hidden exactly to the extent that they support the status quo.[20] In short, what we are currently experiencing in the university is the playing out of the game of liberal politics by which groups, who have lacked "voice," become part of the "pluralist" world.

It is interesting to observe that many of those who currently protest the development of multiculturalism were civil rights liberals deeply committed to free speech and academic freedom. From their perspective, current demands for black cultural centers, courses taught from a feminist perspective, or gay studies seem to appear as "resegregation" or as a failure to meet "academic standards" so important for the maintenance of "civilized discourse."[21] Yet such identity-politics is what liberalism at once was designed to create and then domesticate through the politics of pluralism.

In an odd way, what is being played out in the current cultural politics is the failure of the success of the civil rights movement. That movement, which was made possible because of the religious substance of the black church, was narrated in terms of the liberal principles of freedom and equality. Yet those principles are too thin to express the thick history of African Americans or, I suspect, of anyone else who has a history of significant suffering. The problem is the lack of any substantive political practices for the expression of such histories.[22]

Most universities find themselves peculiarly ill-prepared to entertain such challenges since the university serves the wider liberal polity through the suppression of conflict. Universities, of course, pride themselves on "freedom of speech," as well as providing a "safe" place for "radical opinions," but that is exactly how conflict is domesticated. Namely, you can think and say anything you wish as long as you accept the presumption that you do not expect anyone to take you seriously.[23] Thus, the presumption that students ought to be educated to "make up their own minds" since indoctrination is antithetical to "education." Of course, teaching students to "make up their own minds" is a form of indoctrination, but since it underwrites the hegemonic character of liberalism, few notice it as such.

Students, as a consequence, approach curricula not primarily as students but as consumers. Teachers are expected to present in class in an objective fashion various alternatives. If asked, "Which one do you think is true?" the teacher is expected to say, "That is not my task. I am trying to help us understand the best options so that you can come to a reasonable judgment on your own." Students are thus further inscribed into capitalist practices in which they are taught to think that choosing between "ideas" is like choosing between a Sony or a Panasonic. It never occurs to them that the very idea they should "choose" is imposed.

One of the ironies created by the ethos of liberalism is the increased concern for "ethics" as part of university curricula. The "ethics" taught in such courses usually exemplifies the very practices that make people think they now need a theory to provide reasons to be honest or truthful. If anyone needs a course or theory for that, then no course or theory will be capable of doing them any good. Indeed, such a course will more likely create further ambiguities about what it means to be honest or truthful. It is difficult to sustain an honor code in the university since the very practices necessary to make honor intrinsic to the universities' task has been lost for teacher and student alike.[24]

The deepest problem for most of us associated with the university is that we have no idea who our constituency is or might be. We lack any sense of what or why we should teach. As a result, academics end up writing primarily to one another about matters that matter only for those associated with our academic guilds. At their best, professors seek to instill in a few students their passion for Dante or Aquinas in the hope that the student will go on to study what the professors study—thus becoming a university professor who lacks any sense of how what they do might help better anyone's life except her or his own. From this perspective, the controversies surrounding multiculturalism and/or political correctness are distractions from the main challenges confronting the university.

As a Christian theologian and academic, I find the current situation amusing and challenging as well as a wonderful opportunity. The kind of attacks made by feminists, African Americans, and postmodernists against the alleged political neutrality of the knowledges currently enshrined as university subjects have ironically created a space for a new theological engagement with the university as well as within it. Of course, the university exists only in the minds of liberal intellectuals, so the possibility of theological discourse will differ from place to place.

Indeed, I suspect the kind of engagement for which I hope is a greater possibility in those institutions that do not have the burden of a religious past. Universities sponsored in the past by the Protestant establishment remain too embarrassed by that past to enjoy the recovery of nonapologetic theological discourse. Religious representatives in such institutions usually end up making sure that everyone understands that they are not "fundamentalist" or that they are defending academic freedom in the interest of "fostering discussion" in the hopes of "better understanding" between peoples.[25]

Religion departments, of course, are more likely to be made up of people who most fear being caught with a religious conviction. Religion professors usually are willing to study a religion if it is dead or they can kill it. They may be "personally" religious, but they think it would be "unprofessional" for their students to get a hint that they may actually believe what they teach. We live in an academic world where some professors can enthusiastically promote capitalism between consenting adults, but the same professors would be outraged if they heard that Christian theology was being taught, as if what Christians believe and practice might be true.

As a result, we have developed conventions in the contemporary university that enable the teaching of religion without offense. For example, students are offered courses in "Hebrew Bible" to avoid the Christian designation Old Testament. The problem with such a strategy is that courses in Hebrew Bible usually consist of the reconstruction of the history of the text created by Protestant liberalism.[26] As a result, Jewish, Christian, and secular students are robbed of the opportunity to see why Torah and the Old Testament are not the same book. These efforts not to give offense I take to be but a small instance of the general strategy of the university to reduce all significant disagreements between communities to differences in opinion in the interest of producing the kind of bland souls necessary to sustain the "peace" of liberal social orders.

By suggesting that I am not interested in helping students make up their minds, I am trying to challenge the hegemony of liberal discourse so pervasive in university cultures. I am aware that teaching young people who are not well-formed, pedagogical questions cannot and should not be avoided. Yet if the task of the university is remotely about the formation of people to want to know their world more truthfully—even if that knowledge means the possibility of conflict—then I do not see how any course that matters can avoid trying to change students' lives.

The reason most teachers shy away from the responsibility to change our students' lives, I suspect, is the absence of any sense of legitimacy or authority for that task. Who gives us the right to want to change our students' lives? The answer is obvious—no one. Liberals celebrate this answer, teaching us to call the absence of authority—and the hierarchy on which any account of authority depends—freedom. The irony is how much time people, in the name of being free, spend supervising their lives to make sure that they do not appear authoritarian or intolerant (since you can be anyone you want as long as you do not think that what you want ought to be what anyone else should want). Moreover, with no acknowledged hierarchies, we end up being ruled by the bureaucrats whose power is absolute exactly because they allegedly do not rule but only "administer."

To provide what I hope will be an imaginative contrast, I have included in this book a commencement address I gave at Goshen College in Goshen, Indiana, on April 18, 1992. Goshen is a college sponsored and supported by the Mennonite church, though non-Mennonites are among the faculty and students. While I have no illusions about the eloquence of the address, I think it obviously will appear "completely different" (in the Monty Python sense) from most commencement speeches. That difference comes not from my peculiar idiosyncracies, but because I could draw on the continuing practice of Christian non-violence by Mennonites that made it possible for me to address them with authority.

I should report that many of the faculty and friends of Goshen College responded to the address confessing that I idealized them, that they are not "that good." I told them I know they are not that good, but it is nonetheless a remarkable thing that they have a memory of what they ought to be as a community of reconciliation that makes it possible for them to have a commencement speaker who could suggest the intellectual significance of forgiveness. I suspect they have a better chance of avoiding the cant concerning the "classics" of Western civilization than the faculty at universities like Duke.

I rejoice that schools like Goshen College still exist. I wish them well, but I fear for their future. They represent cultural lags made possible as much by ethnic identity as by theological convictions and practice. Which is only a reminder that ethnic identity, which in one context is a form of Constantinianism, in another context can be a resource for Christian resistance to the powers that would subvert the Gospel. Roman Catholics are a fascinating example of such a process in America.

I obviously do not teach at a school like Goshen, but I see no reason why I should be any less aggressively Christian at a school like Duke. I recognize that the disestablishment of Protestantism is not culturally complete, especially in the South, but fortunately Christianity is discredited sufficiently on most campuses to give Christians freedom to make their convictions work intellectually. Not to do so is simply a betrayal of their non-Christian colleagues and students.

George Bush was right to suggest that we—that is, people in America—confront a "new world order." He is no doubt also right to think that the trick will be to convince the rest of the world to call American imperialism "peace." There is another aspect of the new order that is apparent but cannot be acknowledged by George Bush or Bill

Clinton. What I suspect the West confronts today is the flailings of a dying Christian civilization confronting a regnant Islam. Our difficulty is that we—that is, most secular intellectuals—cannot name that conflict as religious, since most of us have been trained to believe that religion is a thing of the past or a matter of one's "private" beliefs.[27] Liberalism emasculated Christianity in the name of societal peace, but the kind of societies thus created lack the moral resources to face those who would rather die, and kill, than live religiously unworthy lives.

That the Christian tradition is intellectually and morally discredited for most people in universities robs Christian and non-Christian alike of resources for understanding our world. One of the difficulties we now confront in the university is the lack of any significant understanding of Christian discourse and practice by many secular intellectuals, some of whom may be Christian. Christianity for too many people simply appears as twenty impossible things to believe before breakfast. They are not to be blamed for such a perception, since intellectually powerful accounts of Christian convictions have not played any significant role in the culture of the university. Indeed, insofar as Christianity, or Judaism, has any compelling presentation, it is usually through the work of novelists and poets who do not bear the burden of "academic respectability." Given what I take to be the character of Christian convictions, I suspect that is the way it should be.

I do not expect any reappreciation of the work of Christian theology in the university in the foreseeable future. The disciplinary character of the knowledges that so dominates the university impedes any serious theological engagement. The loss of social power by Christians means fewer will be attracted to the ministry and/or the even less enticing work of theology. But what a wonderful time to be a Christian and theologian. Since no one expects Christians to make the world safe, since Christians are no longer required to supply the ideologies necessary "to govern," since Christians are not expected to be able to provide philosophical justifications to insure the way things are or the way things should be, we are free to be Christians. If we make moral and intellectual use—which are of course closely interrelated—of the freedom that God has given us, we may find that we have some interesting things to say because we find our living such a joy.

"But You Are So Violent to Be
a Pacifist—Just Who in the Hell Are You?"

The military imagery contained in this book's title is meant to challenge the widespread assumption that pacifists are passive. The kind of Christian pacifism I have learned from John Howard Yoder is but part of the practices of the church that gain their intelligibility from the truthful worship of God. Nonviolence is not an end in itself but is intrinsic to the Christian practice of reconciliation that requires the exposure of falsehood in the hopes of our becoming a people capable of worshiping God faithfully. Those committed to Christian nonviolence do not seek conflict, but in a world that has learned to call violence order, they know they cannot avoid confrontation.[28]

I cannot deny, however, that the title also derives from my sense of being embattled. I want to be liked but cannot seem to make anyone happy. My theological colleagues in mainstream Protestant seminaries describe me as "sectarian, fideistic, tribalist."[29] They do so because I (allegedly) defend a theology and ethic that requires Christians to withdraw from the responsibility to create more nearly just societies. While I do not share their general enthusiasm for liberal democratic practices defended in the name of being "responsible," that does not mean I am calling for Christians to withdraw from social engagements. I just want them to be engaged as Christians.

The image of withdrawal or retreat is all wrong. The problem is not that Christians, to be faithful, must withdraw. The problem is that Christians, particularly in liberal social orders like that of the United States, have so identified with those orders that they no longer are able to see what difference being Christian makes. I am not trying to force Christians to withdraw but to recognize that they are surrounded. There is no question of withdrawing, as all lines of retreat have been cut off. The interesting questions now are what skills do we as Christians need to learn to survive when surrounded by a culture we helped create but which now threatens to destroy us.

Of course, the image of being surrounded may be far too coherent to describe the situation of Christians. When surrounded, you know who the enemy is and where the battle lines are drawn. Most Christians, especially in America, do not even know they are in a war. The "secular" I engage is not "out there" in a world that no longer identifies itself as religious, but it is in the souls of most people, including myself, who continue to identify themselves as Christian.[30]

Much of the battle engaged in this book is with my own troops. In effect, I try to help Christians see the radical challenges they present to a liberal culture, challenges that are intrinsic to their common practices and convictions—for example, that they can pledge fidelity to another person for a lifetime, bring children into a inhospitable world, pray for reconciliation with enemies, live lives of truthfulness and honesty. These dispatches are not being sent to a people safely back behind the lines, but to combatants who have not recognized they are in fact in a war.

When I began my "career" as a theologian I had no idea I would be led to the kind of position I now represent. As a working-class kid from Texas who wandered into Yale Divinity School, I thought nothing could be more wonderful than to get a Ph.D. in theology in order to teach in a university.[31] I was trained to be a theologian, but one who was acceptable in the contemporary university. Somehow along the way I have managed to find myself caught in a position that offends most Christians, as well as fitting uneasily into the culture of the university.

I did not go to Yale Divinity School to prepare for the ministry, but to explore further whether all of this Christian "stuff" made sense. I did not know that it was possible to pursue a Ph.D. in theology without going to a divinity school, so I found myself surrounded by people preparing for the ministry and taking courses that at least had some relation to that project. I was sure if I was to be a Christian, I would be a politically "liberal" Christian as well as a liberal theologian. Yet I was equally sure that for Christian convictions to have any claim on one's life, the challenge of Christian complicity with the destruction of the Jews had to be met. Much to my surprise I discovered that it was Karl Barth, not the Protestant liberals, who had the theological resources to stand against that terrible reality.

From Barth I learned that theology is not just another "discipline" in the university. To be a theologian is to occupy an office, admittedly a lesser office, in the church of Jesus Christ. Accordingly, I am not in service to a state, or a university, but rather I am called to be faithful to a church that is present across time and space. To be in such service is a wonderful and frightening gift, since only God knows how one can be faithful to this most ambiguous calling. At least as a theologian I do not have the burden of being "a thinker"—that is, someone who, philosopher-like, comes up with strong positions that bear the stamp of individual genius.[32] Rather, it is my task to take what I have been given by friends, living and dead, some Christians and some not, to help the church be faithful to the adventure called God's Kingdom.

Yet for me to claim to be a theologian is not unlike my claiming to be a pacifist. I often make the claim to be a pacifist, even though I dislike the term; it seems to suggest a position that is intelligible apart from the cross and resurrection of Christ. Yet I claim the position even at the risk of being misunderstood. To be so identified not only is necessary to begin, but it creates expectations in others whom I trust to help me live nonviolently. I know myself to be filled with violence; by creating expectations in others, I hope they will love me well enough to help me live faithful to the way of life I know to be true. In like manner, I find that to the extent I am a theologian, it is because I have Christian friends whose lives make no sense if the God we worship in Jesus Christ is not God—they force me to try to think faithfully.

Yet even the claim that I am a theologian, or even more strongly that I have been called to service to the church through the activity of theology, may be self-deceptive. Thus comes the challenge: "show us the church that has commissioned you, that you actually serve. In particular show us the church that looks like the church you assume exists or should exist. In fact, you are not a church theologian, but yet another academic theologian who continues to draw off the residual resources of Constantinian Christianity to fantasize about a church that does not and probably cannot or should not exist, given the political and economic realities of our times."[33]

Since I think that the most important arguments are ad hominem, I find this kind of challenge particularly interesting.[34] Moreover, in no way can I in principle defeat such a response. My own theological convictions will not let me escape by distinguishing between visible or invisible churches, or by suggesting that I am recommending ideals to be realized, or by claiming that the theologian's task is to say what the church ought to be, not what it is. If Christian convictions have any claim to being considered truthful, then my church has to exist as surely as the Jews have to be God's promised people. That, of course, is why I cannot do without friends who live lives more faithful than I write.

Friends are not a church, of course, but many who have claimed me as friend are churched. It is strange but wonderful to have liberal and conservative Roman Catholics, some Southern Baptists, some evangelicals, some Presbyterians (very few), some Mennonites, some Calvinists, some Episcopalians, some Lutherans (not many), some from the Church of the Servant King (Gardenia, California), some liberal Protestants, some feminists, some liberationists, and even some Methodists tell me that, while disagreeing with this or that, generally they find what I am doing helpful. But how can that be? Paul may have thought he should be all things to all people, but that is probably not good advice for theologians. I suspect that one of the reasons the kind of position I represent cuts across divisions from the past is that the basis for those divisions simply no longer matters.

Of course, part of the explanation may be, as I indicated, that I am a Texas Methodist who went to Yale, came under the influence of Barth and Wittgenstein, taught two years with the Lutherans at Augustana College (Rock Island, Illinois), fourteen with the Catholics at Notre Dame, and finally have ended up with the Methodists at Duke. To have had the opportunity to be part of so many different communities is a wonderful gift, but it often makes me wonder who I am. At one of our departmental retreats at Notre Dame we were discussing, one more time, what it meant to be a theology department in a Catholic context; the Missouri Synod Lutheran said what it meant to be part of such a department as a Lutheran, as did the Dutch Calvinists, the Mennonites, and even the Jesuits. I sat in uncharacteristic silence trying to figure out what it meant for me to be there as a Methodist. Suddenly, I thought, "Hell, I am not a Methodist. I went to Yale."[35]

That thought, of course, embodies the melancholy truth that for most of us who were trained to be theologians, where we went to graduate school is more important for our self-understanding than our church identification. Theologians now are identified by positions, Bultmannians, Barthians, Process, Liberal, Post-liberal—that help us forget we serve no recognizable Christian community. Yet it is probably because I was trained in theology at Yale that I feel uncomfortable to be in such a position. At Yale, at least during the years I was there, I was taught to engage in the activity of theology as a tradition-determined activity without ever being determined by any one tradition—other than Yale. No wonder I have come to care so deeply for the church; it is the only protection I had against Yale.

I suppose my Yale breeding is one of the reasons I find the charge that I am "fideistic, sectarian, tribalistic" so puzzling. Admittedly, I have been, and continue to be, strongly influenced by John Howard

Yoder. I like to think of myself as a Mennonite camp follower—an odd image but one I like since I think Mennonites need camp followers as otherwise they might forget they are an army in one hell of a fight. Nevertheless, that I have been influenced by Yoder is not sufficient to identify me as a sectarian, for as Yoder eloquently argues in *The Priestly Kingdom,* he is not a Mennonite theologian, but a theologian of the church catholic [36]—an ambition I also share. It was Yoder who taught me to be suspicious of mainstream Christian theologians' celebration of pluralism, as that is the way the mainstream underwrites its presumption of superiority. Thus, "we" understand, and appreciate, the "sect" better than its members can appreciate themselves. The way the game works is that the one with the most inclusive typology at the end wins.

That I have become so deeply identified with the kind of Christological nonviolence defended by Yoder, I regard as one of God's little jokes. I began by trying to recapture the significance of the virtues for the display of Christian convictions. I am better acquainted with the text of the *Nicomachean Ethics* than I am of the New Testament. I am often more interested in issues in epistemology and philosophical ethics than I am in most of the work done as "systematic theology." Yet in an odd way it was my increasing appreciation of the importance of Aristotle's understanding of *phronesis,* the kind of politics necessary to sustain an ethic of virtue, and the corresponding historicist perspective required by each that led me to appreciate Yoder's significance.

Of course, one of the reasons that Yoder has been so unfairly ignored or put in the box of "Christ Against Culture" by theologians in the Protestant mainstream is because he is so free of the kind of theory that led me to him. For example, he notes in *The Priestly Kingdom* that while he is not disrespectful of the ministry of self-critical conceptual analysis, he is skeptical about the possibility that such exercises can come logically, chronologically, or developmentally first. You cannot start trying to establish the conditions of meaningful discourse if such discourse is not already in good working order. There is simply no place to start thinking prior to being engaged in a tradition. As Yoder says: "What must replace the prolegominal search for 'scratch' is the confession of rootedness in historical community. Then one directs one's critical acuity toward making clear the distance between that community's charter or covenant and its present faithfulness." [37]

Yoder did not need to be schooled by antifoundationalist epistemologies to know that foundationalism was a mistake. In like manner, he does not spend all of his time in methodological considerations about how theology ought to be done if anyone ever gets around to doing any. Rather, Barth-like, he simply begins in *The Politics of Jesus* to train us to read the New Testament with eyes not clouded with the presumption that Jesus cannot be relevant for matters dealing with what we now call social and political ethics.[38] In the process he helps us see that salvation, at least the salvation brought through God's promise to Israel and in Jesus' cross and resurrection, *is* a politics. As he says: "The cross of Calvary was not a difficult family situation, not a frustration of visions of personal fulfillment, a crushing debt or a nagging in-law; it was the political, legally to be expected result of a moral clash with the powers ruling his society."[39]

In this respect, Yoder presents a decisive challenge to the dominance of Reinhold Niebuhr's understanding of the Christian's relation to liberal democracies. The irony of Niebuhr's account of Christian social theory is that in the interest of justifying a "realist" perspective in the name of the Christian understanding of the sinful character of the "human condition," he depoliticized salvation. Because he was intent on justifying the Christian use of violence in the name of politics, Niebuhr, like so many Protestants, provided what is essentially a gnostic account of Christianity.[40] Thus, the cross, for Niebuhr, is a symbol of the tragic character of the human condition and that *knowledge* "saves" us by keeping us "humble."[41]

As one long schooled in a Niebuhrian perspective, I was helped by Yoder to see that the politics accepted in the name of being "responsible" gave lie to the most fundamental Christian convictions. In effect, he forced me to see that the most orthodox Christological or Trinitarian affirmations are essentially false when they are embedded in lives and social practices which make it clear that it makes no difference whether Jesus lived, died, or was resurrected.

That Yoder continues to be dismissed by those in the Christian mainstream as "sectarian" appears a bit odd in light of the celebration of Yoder as a "post-modern theologian" by Fredric Jameson in his *Post-Modernism, or, the Cultural Logic of Late Capitalism.* Jameson notes that the central hermeneutic of theological modernism was posed by the anthropomorphism of the narrative character of the historical Jesus. Modern theologians assumed that

> only intense philosophical effort is capable of turning this character into this or that christological abstraction. As for the commandments and the

ethical doctrine, casuistry has long since settled the matter; they also need no longer be taken literally, and confronted with properly modern forms of injustice, bureaucratic warfare, systemic or economic inequality, and so forth, modern theologians and churchmen can work up persuasive accommodations to the constraints of complex modern societies, and provide excellent reasons for bombing civilian populations or executing criminals which do not disqualify the executors from Christian status.[42]

It is Yoder who challenges such an accommodation by reminding us that Jesus is a politics.

From the perspective of Protestant liberalism, the kind of Christianity represented by Yoder ought to be unintelligible to the kind of intellectual Jameson represents. That Yoder can be appreciated by a thinker like Jameson indicates, I think, profound changes for the context of theology that I hope is embodied in my own work and in particular in this book. I am not suggesting that Yoder (or myself) should try to write for someone like Jameson (Yoder will not be impressed to know that Jameson admires his work); rather, I should like to point out that the cultural contradictions characteristic of liberal societies so acutely analyzed by Jameson provide an opportunity for Christians to rediscover that Christianity is more than a set of beliefs.

It is not accidental that I set out to say a bit about myself, but ended up talking about Yoder. I should like to think I have made some contributions to the theological enterprise, but I have increasingly become suspicious of being an "author" doing "original work." Thus, when I was asked to contribute to the *Christian Century* series "How My Mind Has Changed," I began with the story of the Mennonite in Shipshewana, Indiana, who was confronted with the question, "Brother are you saved?" Nothing in all his years as a Mennonite had prepared him to answer a question so posed. After a long pause, he asked for a pencil and paper, wrote a list of names on it, and handed it back to his interrogator. He explained that the list was made up of names of people, most of whom he thought to be his friends and some who might be less than friendly toward him. But he suggested that the evangelical go ask them whether they thought him saved or not, since he certainly would not presume to answer the question on his own behalf.

I do not know if this story is true or not, but it exemplifies my growing sense of who I am—that is, I am best-known through my friends. This is not a confession of humility, but rather it denotes my increasing theological, epistemological, and moral conviction that theology is done in service to the church and accordingly cannot be the product of the individual mind—that is why any theology that does not aspire to be catholic cannot help but be distorted. By trying to submit my life and work to the imaginative demands of the practices and discourse of the church through time, I hope to serve my friends and even more hopefully make some new friends.[43]

Yet such an endeavor seems antithetical to the polemical, if not violent, character of my essays. I will not apologize for being at war with war. I will not apologize for exposing the sentimentalities of liberal culture that suppress all strong positions in the name of pluralism. I am angry as hell, but it is not an anger directed at the secular or even at liberalism. Rather, I am angry at Christians, including myself, for allowing ourselves to be so compromised that the world can no longer tell what difference it makes to worship the Trinity.

The Politics of Forgiveness, Medicine, and War

Some readers no doubt will be puzzled by a book that begins with essays on Trollope, a critique of the theological justification of democracy, challenges the use of just war theory to legitimate war, and then considers issues in medicine and medical ethics. What could possibly be the interconnection between these diverse subjects, and why should this compendium be called theology? It would be foolish to claim any strong interrelation, but I believe the patient reader will find surprising interconnections. All of the essays, of course, hopefully display my determined attempt to write as a theologian. More important for me, however, are the actual theological practices of forgiveness and reconciliation and how and why they require a community that is eschatologically shaped.

Forgiveness and reconciliation name the politics of that community called church that makes possible a different way of being in, as well as seeing, the world. There is a danger in focusing on such themes, as generally forgiveness is seen as a "good thing" by most people. Yet I am not interested in forgiveness and reconciliation in general, but in that which is unintelligible if Jesus was not raised from the dead.

One danger of what I have attempted in this book is that it may appear I am simply trying to present in a new guise what Christians have always thought. While I would like to think I represent the great tradition of Catholic Christianity, the position I develop will appear unusual for Christian and non-Christian alike. Many current Christians,

25

for example, do not think there is any relation between worshiping God and the practice of forgiveness and nonviolence. My purpose is to show that they are closely interrelated.

The theologically informed reader of these essays will no doubt find me insufficiently "theological." The nontheologian may find these essays far too theological—for example, why begin the essay "Can a Pacifist Think About War?" with the long quotation from Yoder which asserts that the cross and not the sword determines the meaning of history?[44] What does that have to do with a people constituted by the practice of forgiveness and reconciliation? I hope these essays show that the re-descriptions of war offered by a community constituted by the practice of forgiveness are compelling and that you cannot have the one without the other.

I argue that those who think about the ethics of war often fail to ask, "Why do I call this 'war'?" What are the practices that produce as well as sustain that description so that people are led to believe they can do things in war that they could never do in 'normal' life?" What we often fail to notice are that the questions asked concerning the justifiability of a war are morally incidental, as the decisive moral decision has been made by calling it a war.[45] I suggest that at the heart of the Christian account of just war was an attempt not to simply test if Christians could participate in this or that war, but rather to see if this particular combat deserved the description "war." Therefore, the Christian description of war was generated from a community whose speech and practices were nonviolent. Yet that carefully disciplined use of the grammar of war became the property of anyone through the development of Christendom and, as a result, Christians lost their hesitancy to kill in the name of war.

I am aware that these matters involve not only conceptual issues but the way in which historical evidence is read. My aim is to engage the reader in the questions in a way that the practical and theological issues are inseparable. Reinhold Niebuhr was the great master of theological redescription, but many thought that they could have his insights about the human condition and realist politics without his theology. They liked to identify themselves as "atheists for Niebuhr." Whether Niebuhr desired such a following I do not know, but, given the thinness of his theology, I think they were not wrong to believe they could have Niebuhr's politics without his Christianity. I desire no such following. If you want to be for peace—and most will not—you will need the God Christians worship. That many will not want the peace of God is understandable, but then at least some will have learned why they do not want to have anything to do with being Christian.

I have followed the chapter on the democratic policing of Christianity in which I treat Rauschenbusch and Niebuhr with an essay that is a tribute to William Stringfellow. Stringfellow never had or aspired to have the influence of Reinhold Niebuhr. He was not an academic or professional theologian. He was an attorney who worked in Harlem after he graduated from Harvard Law School. An Episcopalian layman, he was a friend of the Berrigans and defended them at Harrisburg. His theology was "conservative" and "radical." That, of course, is why I find him so interesting, for, unlike Niebuhr, his Christian speech was never policed in the interest of being "socially responsible." Rather, he opposed the "republic of death" by reminding Christians that we are meant to be God's apocalyptic people.

The essays on medicine are designed to help illumine how the republic that war serves and embodies also resides in the very practices designed to "help" people. I hope it is clear that I have no particular animus against health care professionals. Yet it is almost impossible to avoid medicine as a moral topic since health care has become the primary institution of salvation in liberal societies.[46] I often suggest to people that if you want to have a sense of what medieval Catholicism felt like, become part of a major medical center. You will discover there an exemplification of the Byzantine politics often associated with the papacy in its heyday. For example, tourists marvel at medieval cathedrals and wonder who could have built them. They seem to have served so little purpose. Moreover, most of the people who worked on them would never see them completed. Indeed, it is not clear they even knew what it meant for them to be completed. Yet I suspect someday people will look in equal puzzlement at our hospitals. Such buildings wonderfully embody different accounts of salvation—Christians sought through the worship of God to avoid the wrath to come, and we—that is, those of us schooled by the politics of liberalism—seek to avoid death. As is often observed by sociologists of medicine, few come closer to being priests in our society than those who bear the burden of being physicians.

War and medicine deal with matters of life and death. Accordingly, war and medicine are unavoidable subjects for Christian reflection; Christian discourse and practices are designed to teach a community how to live and die. I often think that my best conversation partners are in the military, since military people know that any serious moral position requires sacrifice. The conflict between us, of course, comes from our different accounts of what makes such a sacrifice worthy. Many in the armies that serve liberal societies are caught in the terrible irony of asking people to kill and die for social orders that do not believe there is anything worthy of such sacrifice. That is why the most serious moral training anyone can receive in societies like ours comes through the military or medical schools.

The difficulty with the virtue taught by the military and medicine, however, is that such a morality must be restricted to those contexts. The ethics of liberal societies by design are meant to be disconnected.[47] The concentration on decisions and quandaries so characteristic of the ethical theories produced by liberalism is but the other side of issue-politics. Issue-politics and quandary ethics are designed to make it impossible for us to think a relationship might exist between how we conduct our private lives and what we do in our public ones. We are thus taught to become consumers of our own lives, and in the process we are consumed.

Which, of course, brings me back to Trollope. For through Trollope we can begin to imagine why moral practices such as keeping our promises, acquiring the skills necessary for truthful speech, loyalty to friends are as necessary for us to live as to sustain nonviolent communities. The kind of falsehood characteristic of democratic politics, as well as the character types produced to serve in such polities, is a source of the violence that grips our lives. If Christians are to survive as well as serve such social orders, we will do so first by our willingness to speak and live truthfully.

PART I ▼ BEHIND THE LINES

CHAPTER 1 ▼ CONSTANCY AND FORGIVENESS

THE NOVEL AS A SCHOOL FOR VIRTUE

"Character is not cut in marble; it is not something solid and unalterable. It is something living and changing, and may become diseased as our bodies do," said Mr. Farbrother.

"Then it may be rescued and healed," said Dorothea.

—George Eliot, *Middlemarch*

MacIntyre on Constancy

Alasdair MacIntyre makes Jane Austen the heroine of his *After Virtue* because she is "the last great effective imaginative voice of the tradition of thought about, and practice of, the virtues."[1] According to MacIntyre, Austen's greatness was her uniting of Christian and Aristotelian themes in a determinative social context—the genteel household—that required as well as nourished recognition of the central importance of the virtue of constancy. For constancy, like Aristotle's *phronesis,* is a prerequisite for the possession of all of the other virtues.

I am sure that MacIntyre is right to call our attention to the importance of constancy, and in particular to Austen's development of it, yet I hope to show that his basic insight can be developed further by attending to Anthony Trollope's sense of constancy, at least as it is reflected through Trollope's understanding of the ethics of a gentleman. Trollope saw a necessary relation between forgiveness and constancy, a relation that suggests why constancy is as conceptually elusive as it is important for a well-lived life. Through such an analysis, moreover, I intend to show why novels, or at least novels like Austen's and Trollope's, are an irreplaceable resource for training in moral virtue. However, before I can turn to Trollope I must give an account of MacIntyre's understanding of constancy and why the virtue is so difficult to characterize.

In spite of his argument for the centrality of constancy, MacIntyre is singularly unable to provide us with concrete images and/or depictions of it. That such is the case, however, denotes its special character. For unlike all of the other virtues, which can be spelled out in reference to concrete practices, integrity or constancy cannot be specified "at all except with reference to the wholeness of a human life."[2] So unless there is "a *telos* which transcends limited goods or practices by constituting the good of a whole human life, the good of a human life conceived as a unity, it will both be the case that a certain subversive arbitrariness will invade the moral life and that we shall be unable to specify the context of certain virtues adequately."[3] In particular, we will not be able to distinguish counterfeit virtue from true virtue.

Through her novels, Jane Austen explored the demanding and difficult task, both for the observer and for the agent, of distinguishing true from false virtue. She knew well that the distinction is as much a problem for the agent as for the observer, since there seems to be no end to our capacity for self-deception. Living at a time when the outward appearance of morality might always disguise "uneducated passions," she knew only a relentless honesty could assure true virtue. It may thus seem surprising that Austen places such emphasis on amiability, which Aristotle called agreeableness, since no virtue seems more open to pretense. Indeed, for Aristotle pretense is required for amiability, since as a virtue amiability is formed by our quest for honor and expediency. For Austen, however, the possessor of amiability must have a genuine loving regard for other people and not only the impression or regard too often disguised by perfect manners.[4] For amiability to be a virtue, therefore, a rigorous form of self-knowledge sustained by constancy is required.

MacIntyre observes that the identification of constancy as a virtue is relatively recent. Kierkegaard simply assumed constancy as a crucial characteristic of the moral life when in *Enten-Eller* he contrasted the ethical and aesthetic ways of life. The ethical life was portrayed as one of commitments and obligations that unite past with future so that life is given a unity. In Austen's world, however, "that unity can no longer be treated as a mere presupposition or context for a virtuous life. It has itself to be continually reaffirmed and its reaffirmation in deed rather than in word."[5] It is this reaffirmation that is called constancy.

Beyond this account, MacIntyre (and Austen) primarily tells us what constancy is by suggesting in what ways it is similar to but unlike other virtues:

> Constancy is reinforced by and reinforces the Christian virtue of patience, but it is not the same as patience, just as patience which is reinforced by

and reinforces the Aristotelian virtue of courage, is not the same as courage. For just as patience necessarily involves a recognition of the character of the world, of a kind which courage does not necessarily require, so constancy requires a recognition of a particular kind of threat to the integrity of the personality in the peculiarly modern social world, a recognition which patience does not necessarily require.[6]

MacIntyre suggests it is particularly telling that the Austen heroines who most exhibit constancy, that is, Fanny Price of *Mansfield Park* and Anne Elliot of *Persuasion,* are also the less charming than Austen's other heroines. For charm is the quality used by those who simulate the virtues to get by:

> Fanny is charmless; she has only the virtues, the genuine virtues to protect her, and when she disobeys her guardian, Sir Thomas Bertram, and refuses marriage to Henry Crawford it can only be because of what constancy requires. In so refusing she places the danger of losing her soul before the reward of gaining what for her would be a whole world. She pursues virtue for the sake of a certain kind of happiness and not for its utility.[7]

Like all of Austen's heroines, these two must seek the good "through seeking their own good in marriage. The restricted households of Highbury and Mansfield Park have to serve as surrogates for the Greek city-state and the medieval kingdom."[8]

Without question MacIntyre has rightly directed our attention to constancy as a significant virtue not only for Jane Austen but for ourselves. In a fragmented world that can only encourage our bent toward mendacity and self-deception, surely constancy is required. Yet it remains unclear what constancy is and how it may be best characterized. The sense of unity that constancy entails involves a sense of self-possession and self-mastery, but it is equally clear that constancy cannot be explained solely in those terms.

Moreover, constancy seems to suggest a sense of being set, of being a person who can be trusted not to change. Yet Austen (and, we will see, Trollope) depicts the person of constancy not only as one who is able but who is required to change. If, as MacIntyre (with Austen) suggests, constancy names the quality that allows us to reaffirm the unity of our projects, it seems plausible to suggest that we may have to change, since there are aspects of our selves, past commitments we have made, that ought not to be honored. How, if at all, can constancy be adequately characterized to account both for our need for unity, on which our claims to be responsible seem to lie, and for the equally strong demand that we be ready to change?

I think there is no "solution" to the problem of characterizing constancy in a formal mode. MacIntyre wisely does not attempt such an analysis in *After Virtue* because he rightly senses that constancy is of a different order than courage, temperance, kindness, and similar virtues. Moreover, that it is so helps explain why novelists such as Austen and Trollope are crucial for our better understanding of the nature of constancy. Because of its teleological and temporal character, constancy cannot be formally defined; it can be displayed only through the unfolding of a character's life. The telos of a human life, which MacIntyre rightly argues makes possible as well as requires constancy, is not an end that can be known in and of itself, but rather it can be enacted only through the telling of a story. Thus, in a decisive sense we cannot know what constancy involves apart from tales like Austen's of Fanny Price or Trollope's of Plantagenet Palliser.

Individuality, Constancy, and the Bearing of a Gentleman

The problem of characterizing constancy is similar to the difficulty of describing what it means, or meant, to be a gentleman. Indeed, as Shirley Letwin makes clear in *The Gentleman in Trollope: Individuality and Moral Conduct,* almost all attempts to characterize formally what it meant to be a gentleman proved to be insufficient, and worse, contradictory.[9] Though a gentleman might be a person of ancestry, wealth, power, or fashion, none of these conditions in themselves were sufficient or even necessary for someone to be a gentleman. The gentleman often is described as having a talent for being agreeable in a variety of circumstances and with different people, but how he is to do that, and at the same time maintain the integrity or honesty that seems to exist at the heart of being a gentleman, is not easily explained. Again, a gentleman is expected to preserve a certain mildness, no doubt deriving from inner calm and self-possession based on a sense of his worth, but how such a demeanor is to be maintained while defending the helpless, fighting for the right, or maintaining lasting indignation is left unclear.[10]

Letwin further suggests that there is great confusion about the relation between having manners and being a gentleman. Manners count, everyone agrees, but the idea that a gentleman can be made through "conformity to a 'code' of behaviour, to the 'convenances' of society, of etiquette, or the rules of fashion is steadily denounced as a sign of vulgarity. The stickler for the proprieties of the dinner table or the correctness of his pronunciation is definitely held not to be a gentleman but a gentel parvenu." [11] Letwin thus concludes an examination of books and articles from the sixteenth to eighteenth centuries on what it meant to be a gentleman with the observation that it is "impossible to doubt that a gentleman is a character whose native habitat is England. But a coherent explanation of what identifies him is not to be found among either the Englishmen or the foreigners who have written so much in praise of the gentleman." [12]

That such is the case, however, is not accidental. For what it means to be a gentleman offers

> no ideal to realize, no goal to achieve, no pattern to fulfill, no absolute targets, indisputable commands, inevitabilities, or final solutions. Nor is anything given in the form of drives or structures from within, or forces from without, pushing men to do this or that. In this picture, the only thing given to a human being is the power to choose what to see, feel, think, and do, which constitutes his rationality and humanity. In other words, rationality has a totally different character. It is not a link to something outside the human world, neither to Nature or Spirit; nor is it a power of discovering any other non-human source of eternal truth such as natural "processes" or "structures." Though called reason, it must not be confused with a cosmic principle of "Reason." It is a purely human property which enables men to make of themselves what they will. [13]

Thus, what defeats all attempts to characterize what it means to be a gentleman, and, I think, the virtue of constancy as well, is the inextricable individual stamp that constancy and being a gentleman entail. Such individuality has nothing to do with the doctrine of individualism with which the world of Austen and Trollope was just beginning to suffer and which has become our fate. Rather, constancy is a correlative of a character that allows our lives to be narrated in an ever-changing but still steady manner. "Seeing human beings as 'characters' means recognizing that they make their individuality for themselves by how they choose to understand and respond to what they encounter, and that this individuality is the essence of their humanity." [14]

The world of the gentleman is therefore not one in which we are but manifestations of the more real or but parts of a whole. "Each is in himself a whole." [15] We are what we learn to be, and we learn by submitting ourselves to the authority of a master. Our individuality emerges, therefore, from society with other selves and can be expressed only by the means provided by that society. Yet virtue does not consist in conformity with societal expectations, since by definition the morality of a gentleman must be personal. The gentleman does not seek to be free from all restraints in order to discover "his true self," because he knows his self is made from the materials provided by his communal life. "The richer the materials, the more subtle and various can be the product." [16]

A gentleman does not seek, therefore, to find certainty amid a world that offers none. Rather, the fixity, or constancy, of the gentleman is of a different sort:

> It is a conquest of mutability not by renouncing or trying to overcome or stifle it, but by developing a steady way of dealing with it. This manner of conducting himself constitutes the moral excellence that defines a gentleman and is called "integrity." The quality of integrity may or may not be present in a character because the connections constituting a character may be more or less jumbled. Just as a picture may be nothing more than the shapes and colours contained within a finite frame, or may be a self-contained unity without the frame, so may the connections that constitute a man's character be unified only by being attached to the same person or by such a profound coherence that everything about him seems to be a necessary part of a whole. Such coherence constitutes the integrity of a gentleman. It might be said to make a gentleman self-possessed, self-determined, self-contained, well-regulated, or collected. But each of these words carries distracting connotations. It is perhaps less misleading to see a gentleman as the opposite of someone whose steadiness depends on conformity to something outside himself, and where such a support is missing, contradicts himself and fragments his life. When a man contradicts himself, he becomes an adversary of himself, and when he divides his life into separate compartments, he hides himself from himself and is only partly alive, like someone who walks in his sleep. Because a gentleman is aware of himself as engaged in shaping a coherent self, he would not do either. [17]

But the language of self-awareness, of shaping a coherent self, is far too strong. For as Letwin observes, self-awareness in a gentleman need not be self-conscious, especially if self-consciousness is understood in the sense of "being aware." Such awareness can indicate a sense of "effort" that is inconsistent with the ease that characterizes a gentleman as a gentleman. To be a gentleman requires skills that include those of self-examination, of course, but such skills do not involve our modern preoccupation with our psyches.

That being a gentleman requires or assumes certain skills is perhaps why being a gentleman has so often been associated with certain familial connections or with the owning of an estate. Aspirants at least hope that the habits and responsibilities which go with such inheritance "naturally" put one on the way to being a gentleman. It by no means follows that such possession will insure one's becoming a gentleman.

It is impossible to reduce what it means to be a gentleman to a set of rules or characteristics. To be a gentleman is to be a person of judgment. What is right or wrong is not determined by generally agreed-upon rules, though such rules may certainly be helpful. Instead, deeply held convictions give him a sense of what he must do to be true to himself. That is why a gentleman, though holding profound convictions about what is appropriate and inappropriate behavior, often tolerates the behavior of others. Other judgments and behavior count if they are the judgments and behavior of gentlemen. That is why it is so often crucial in Austen's and Trollope's novels for their characters to know if they are or are not dealing with a "gentleman." [18]

Thus, to be a gentleman is impossible without integrity or constancy. As Letwin observes:

> An antipathy to self-contradiction is at the heart of integrity, and a gentleman understands himself as one among others like himself, his respect for his own integrity entails respecting the integrity of others. He will think of others in the same way as he thinks of himself. He will recognize them as personalities, as characters, whose distinctiveness he is obliged to respect, and whom he must treat as he wishes himself to be treated. He is not thereby bound to regard all men as equally good, any more than he is obliged to deny his own failings; the ability to respect others, like the ability to respect oneself, requires taking accurate note of the different qualities of different characters. [19]

But what makes such respect possible is the conviction that another's difference springs from the same constancy as one's own.

Letwin is suggesting that the virtues which sustain a gentleman's constancy, his integrity, differ from those that would arise from a vision of morality as conformity to a previously determined code or pattern. A gentleman is thus characterized by discrimination, which is the recognition

> that the same sort of action may have been inspired by different motives, by an ability to acknowledge ideas and purposes alien to oneself, by care to distinguish between malice and error, disagreement and depravity. It does not prevent a gentleman from making moral judgments. On the contrary, it keeps him from evading an obligation to judge through confusing prudence with weakness. Discrimination enables a gentleman to recognize that though charity is admirable, charity to a murderer may imply indifference to the fate of victims; that if he rejects a friend's criticism of someone else, he is criticizing his friend; that whereas even unjustified censure may have been preceded by a serious effort to understand and excuse, tolerance may be inspired by nothing more generous than a servile desire to please; that although being suspicious is ugly, unseemly conjecture should be distinguished from reasonable doubt and that squeamishness about suspecting conspiracy may hand over its country to enemies.[20]

Discrimination is thus a virtue that names the gentleman's ability to command a rich vocabulary of responses that to an observer may appear inconsistent, but for the gentleman it is the resource necessary to remain constant. Of course, the gentleman possibly can become oversubtle, but if he does so it is only an indication that he has failed to learn adequately how to be discriminating.

Second, the gentleman is sustained by the virtue of diffidence. Rather than a sense of unworthiness, gentlemanly diffidence is profound recognition of his limits and the limits of the human condition. For a gentleman does not assume that everything is or ought to be subject to his control, or, more importantly, that he is indispensable to the future of the world. Thus, when Mr. Harding in *Barchester Towers* refuses to accept his appointment as dean, his refusal is based not on false humility, but on an accurate reading of the facts. As he tells his daughter, Mrs. Grantly:

> The truth is, I want the force of character which might enable me to stand against the spirit of the times. The call on all sides now is for young men, and I have not the nerve to put myself in opposition to the demand. Were the *Jupiter,* when it hears of my appointment, to write article after article, setting forth my incompetency, I am sure it would cost me my reason, I

ought to be able to bear with such things, you will say. Well, my dear, I own that I ought. But I feel my weakness, and I know that I can't. And, to tell you the truth, I know no more than a child what the dean has to do.[21]

Such diffidence, moreover, is based on a profound sense of how much of our lives depends on luck, on *fortunata*. That some have been born to money, or to nobility, is a matter of luck. That it is so means that the gentleman attributes to himself no special virtue for having been so born, but rather he accepts the duty that goes with such birth. That is why it is so hard, perhaps, for those who must struggle to better their condition to remain or become gentlemen.[22] The struggle invites us too easily to believe the false assumption that luck or the good favor of others has played no part in our rise and thus gives us false illusions of control and power. Mr. Harding would never have been offered the deanship if Mr. Slope had not arranged the appointment of Mr. Quiverful (rather than Mr. Harding) to become warden of Hiram's hospital. And that would not have happened if Mr. Slope had been able to see more clearly what kind of marriage might best serve his own ambitions. But that is why Mr. Harding is a gentleman and Mr. Slope is not. Mr. Harding would never think of trying to live his life by attempting to calculate what a vain and ambitious man like Mr. Slope might or might not do.[23]

Third, courage is required to sustain the kind of constancy characteristic of a gentleman. His courage means not simply that he faces what he would rather avoid, but that he stands firm while recognizing that what he is doing may be problematic. The gentleman sees "that while it is impossible to live without constantly making judgments, nothing can guarantee the correctness of a judgment or render it immune to criticism, and yet a man swayed by every hostile voice will soon reduce his life to an absurdity."[24]

The final virtue necessary to sustain constancy is honesty. This virtue is so central that it comes close to being constancy itself. A gentleman's

honesty, rests on recognizing his own integrity as an objectivity. To do so, he must know what belongs to himself, and instinctively connect every utterance and action with that selfhood. What matters is that his words should be consistent with a steady understanding. A man who lacks integrity cannot speak honestly because what he thinks now has only a fortuitous connexion with what he thought yesterday and may think tomorrow. A man of integrity, on the other hand, though he may and probably will change, either deliberately or unselfconsciously, will always feel obliged to recognize that he has done so by connecting what is new with what has gone before, even if only by acknowledging a change. And therefore everything he says has a reliable connexion with the coherent consciousness that constitutes his personality.[25]

Letwin's account of the gentleman and the virtues that characterize a gentleman is important for no other reason than that depiction, just as MacIntyre's account of constancy in Austen, represents a moral tradition that has not found expression in recent moral theory. Yet Letwin, I suspect, would be the first to admit that the analysis of a gentleman provided is still insufficient because the enumerated virtues are not equivalent to what it means to be a gentleman or to be constant. To flesh out Letwin's account, an analysis of the person whom she takes to be the most perfect "gentleman" in Trollope's novels—Madame Max Goesler—is required.

Though I am sure Letwin is right about the significance of Madame Max, I will try to broaden her account by directing attention to a theme Letwin does not develop as crucial for the life of the gentleman and for constancy—the centrality of forgiveness as a virtue in Trollope. In the process I hope not only to confirm much of what MacIntyre has said about constancy, but to show why constancy (and the ethics of forgiveness) found its natural, if not necessary, home in the novel.

On Constancy and Forgiveness in Trollope

It is not hard to document the central place of constancy and forgiveness throughout Trollope's work. That he saw these themes as central no doubt has much to do with his sense that the England he loved and cherished, the England of the gentry and the honest workman, was in danger of being lost under the onslaught of the new commercial culture. Thus, in his *Autobiography* he says: "A certain class of dishonesty, dishonesty magnificent in its proportions, and climbing into high places, has become at the same time so rampant and so splendid that there seems to be reason for fearing that men and women will be taught to feel that dishonesty, if it can become splendid, will cease to be abominable."[26] The threat of such people, vividly portrayed in Lopez (*The*

Prime Minister) and in Melmotte (*The Way We Live Now*), was not that they were unambiguously evil, but that they could so easily be mistaken for gentlemen. Even though Trollope was no doubt concerned with the passing of a certain social class, he was yet more deeply concerned with the accompanying threat to moral order. It is that concern which shapes his entire literary enterprise.

The problem of distinguishing counterfeit from true morality was as central to Trollope's artistic endeavor as it was to Jane Austen's. The crucial test was again that of constancy, which was more often than not tested by a demand for unwavering loyalty to a promise of love, even though marriage was often impossible because of insufficient financial resources. Lily Dale, whom Trollope thought to be something of a "female prig" but who was and is one of his most popular characters, is a model of constancy.[27] Even though she has been jilted by the scoundrel Crosbie, she remains true to her pledge of love despite recognizing that it has been misplaced. Her loyalty extends even to preventing her uncle from speaking evil of Crosbie, though she has no illusions of his worth. Being reprimanded, her uncle "did not answer her, but took her hand and pressed it, and then she left him. 'The Dales were very constant!' he said to himself, as he walked up and down the terrace before his house. 'Ever constant!' "[28] Moreover, such constancy cannot insure happiness, for that same constancy also prevents Lily's marriage to her early lover, the equally constant Johnny Eames. As she turns Johnny down for the last time, her concern for her own constancy is evident:

> "I cannot be your wife because of the love I bear for another man."
> "And that man is he,—he who came here?"
> "Of course it is he. I think, Johnny, you and I are alike in this, that when we have loved we cannot bring ourselves to change. You will not change, though it would be so much better you should do so."
> "No: I will never change."[29]

Thus, Trollope leaves his popular lovers, lovers that his readers were begging to have married, forever apart. That he does so makes clear that for him constancy, while often tested by love, is hardly determined by love. Indeed, for Trollope nothing could be more disastrous and a greater threat to constancy than romantic love. Thus, he has Lily try to explain, and her explanation witnesses a growth we hardly thought possible from her first infatuation with Crosbie:

"I cannot define what it is to love him. I want nothing from him,—nothing, nothing. But I move about through my little world thinking of him, and I shall do so to the end. I used to feel proud of my love, though it made me so wretched that I thought it would kill me. I am not proud of it any longer. It is a foolish poor-spirited weakness—as though my heart has been only half formed in the making. Do you be stronger, John. A man should be stronger than a woman. I have none of that sort of strength. Nor have you. What can we do but pity each other, and swear we will be friends." [30]

We do not find how to be constant by being in love, but we had better be constant if we are to play the game of love and marriage in Trollope's world—a lesson that Phineas Finn learns with great difficulty. [31] Lily is right that her love is a poor-spirited weakness, but recognizing it to be so does not change her need to stay true to it. Not to stay true would be to lose the character that has allowed her to discover how "poor-spirited" it was. That is also why Lily must never return to the now somewhat chastened Crosbie, even though he renews his quest when he realizes that he does love Lily. Lily's very forgiveness of Crosbie makes such a reunion impossible, as she says to her mother:

"He would condemn me because I had forgiven him. He would condemn me because I had borne what he had done to me, and had still loved him—loved him through it all. He would feel and know the weakness;—and there is weakness. I have been weak in not being able to rid myself of him altogether. He would recognize this after awhile, and would despise me for it. But he would not see what there is of devotion to him in my being able to bear the taunts of the world in going back to him, and your taunts, and my own taunts. I should have to bear his also—not spoken aloud, but to be seen in his face and heard in his voice,—and that I could not endure. If he despised me, and he would, that would make us both unhappy. Therefore, mamma, tell him not to come; tell him that he can never come; but, if it be possible, tell him tenderly." [32]

That constancy is a theme present throughout Trollope is evident; equally evident is the complexity of that theme. For Trollope was acutely aware of the deep difficulty of explaining constancy and at the same time accounting for the fact of change. At times, for example, it is not only appropriate but morally necessary to forget a mistaken love in order to be faithful to a new lover. Alice Vavasour learns to love John Grey after she finally faces the truth of her first love's baseness in *Can You Forgive Her?* In *The Prime Minister* Emily Wharton Lopez's refusal to accept Arthur Fletcher, whose own constancy has never wavered despite her marriage to Lopez, is condemned as weakness rather than strength.[33] Speaking for Trollope, Fletcher tells Emily: "There are passages in our life which we cannot forget, though we bury them in the deepest silence. All this can never be driven out of your memory,—nor from mine. But it need not therefore blacken all our lives. In such a condition we should not be ruled by what the world thinks."[34]

Change is as much necessary for constancy as loyalty is to past decisions. That such is the case presented Trollope not only with a moral issue but with an aesthetic problem. Commenting on the development of the characters that make up his semi-political series, he says:

> In conducting these characters from one story to another I realized the necessity, not only of consistency,—which, had it been maintained by a hard exactitude, would have been untrue to nature,—but also of those changes which time always produces. There are, perhaps, but few of us who, after the lapse of ten years, will be found to have changed our chief characteristics. The selfish man will still be selfish, and the false man false. But our manner of showing or of hiding these characteristics will be changed,—as also our power of adding to or diminishing their intensity. It was my study that these people, as they grew in years, should encounter the changes which come upon us all; and I think that I have succeeded. The Duchess of Omnium, when she is playing the part of Prime Minister's wife, is the same woman as that Lady Glencora who almost longs to go off with Burgo Fitzgerald, but yet knows that she will never do so; and the Prime Minister Duke, with his wounded pride and sore spirit, is he who, for his wife's sake, left power and place when they were first offered to him;—but they have undergone the changes which a life so stirring as theirs would naturally produce.[35]

The theme, or problem, of the relation between constancy and change is a familiar one for those who have attempted to analyze Trollope's art. Yet it is surprising that another major theme in Trollope's work has not been stressed equally—namely, that of forgiveness. Forgiveness is a subject close to the surface in any of Trollope's novels. The fact that he wrote a novel with the title *Can You Forgive Her?* does not mean that he limited his interest in forgiveness to that work. It is a constant theme through the semipolitical novels. In *The Duke's Children* we see Palliser wrestling again with the problem of forgiving Glencora's love of Burgo Fitzgerald as he tries to come to terms with his daughter's love of Tregear. To accept Tregear, the Duke must finally accept his own reconciliation with Lady Glencora and their subsequent life together. To love Glencora he must accept her as a woman who was infatuated with Burgo Fitzgerald, for that infatuation is but one form of a liveliness that he had learned was indispensable for his own happiness. Thus, forgiveness is crucial if Palliser is to be reconciled to his love for Glencora, indeed to his own life, as well as to Mary's love of Tregear.[36] Perhaps not as demanding, but no less important, is the Duke's having to ask for and accept the forgiveness of Mrs. Finn (Madame Max) for having accused her wrongly of aiding the alliance between Mary and Tregear. The Duke, if he is to be constant, must be as ready to be forgiven as to forgive.

Indeed, the quality that most nearly makes a gentleman a gentleman for Trollope is exactly the capacity for forgiveness. In describing Sir Joseph Mason in *Orley Farm,* Trollope says:

> He himself was a big, broad, heavy-browed man, in whose composition there was nothing of tenderness, nothing of taste; but I cannot say that he was on the whole a bad man. He was just in his dealing, or at any rate endeavoured to be so. He strove hard to do his duty as a country magistrate against very adverse circumstances. He endeavoured to enable his tenants and labourers to live. He was severe to his children, and was not loved by them; but nevertheless they were dear to him, and he endeavoured to do his duty by them.[37]

Not a remarkable man, perhaps, Sir Joseph still has many marks of a gentleman. Nonetheless, Trollope's judgment is firm against him as he says, in a most uncharacteristic summary judgment:

> But yet he was a bad man in that he could never forget and never forgive. His mind and heart were equally harsh and hard and inflexible. He was a man who considered that it behooved him as a man to resent all injuries, and to have his pound of flesh in all cases. In his inner thoughts he had ever boasted to himself that he had paid all men that he owed. He had, so he thought, injured no one in any of the relations of life. His tradesmen got their money regularly. He answered every man's letter. He exacted nothing from any man for which he did not pay. He never amused himself, but devoted his whole time to duties. He would fain even have been hospitable, could he have gotten his neighbors to come to him and have induced his wife to put upon the table sufficient for them to eat.[38]

He was a bad man because he could not forgive. It is crucial, moreover, to see that Trollope's emphasis on the importance of forgiveness is not simply another theme running through his novels alongside that of constancy. Rather, forgiveness is as crucial to constancy as constancy is the necessary basis of forgiveness. It is only by forgiveness that a gentleman can remain constant and yet undergo those changes that cannot be avoided if we are to live life truthfully. Forgiveness is not simply an ideal with which Trollope happens to be impressed; it is at the very heart of his moral vision.

Only a person of moral substance has the status capable to forgive. There is no possibility of Lizzie Eustace being able to forgive, because she simply lacked the "steady connections" necessary for her to have feelings sufficient to know if she had wronged or been wronged.[39] Lacking such connection, Lizzie cannot feel deeply enough to have anything to forgive or for which to repent.

Moreover, it is the quality of forgiveness that determines whether a rejected lover is ultimately a gentleman. Mr. Gilmore in *The Vicar of Bullhampton* is inconsolable at the loss of Mary Fenwick. He is unable to respond to the Vicar's plea that he do his duty by continuing to live as a squire in the country.[40] In contrast, Roger Carbury in *The Way We Live Now*, "though he was a religious man, and one anxious to conform to the spirit of Christianity, would not at first allow himself to think that an injury should be forgiven unless the man who did the injury repented of his own injustice." He finally learned to acknowledge that Hetta did not love him and to forgive both Hetta and her lover, his own friend, Paul Montague.[41] Roger refused to play the tragic lover but instead realized:

> I ought not to have allowed myself to get into such a frame of mind. I should have been more manly and stronger. After all, though love is a wonderful incident in a man's life, it is not that only that he is here for. I have duties plainly marked out for me; and as I should have never allowed myself to be withdrawn from them by pleasure, so neither should I by sorrow. But it is done now. I have conquered my regrets.[42]

Carbury accomplishes his duty by adopting Paul and thus insuring that his estate will stay in the family.

Such examples could be multiplied throughout Trollope's work, but perhaps it is wise to show how the themes of constancy and forgiveness are developed in one of Trollope's less-known but most interesting novels, *The Vicar of Bullhampton*. Since the central theme of that novel is forgiveness, it provides a test case for Trollope's understanding of the relation between constancy and forgiveness.

In his *Autobiography* Trollope says that *The Vicar of Bullhampton* "is not very bad, and it certainly is not very good."[43] Indeed, he says he cannot remember what the heroine does and says, except that he has her fall into a ditch. Trollope's attitude is not surprising since Mary Fenwick, the heroine of the book, is one of his least likable women. She is hopelessly romantic and certainly deserves her fate of falling in love and marrying the irresolute Captain Marrable rather than the much more admirable Mr. Gilmore. The love triangle among these three is, however, only background for the real story of the book. Trollope with his usual craft manages to intertwine his characters' lives in a manner that illumines both their strengths and their weaknesses.

The primary story in *The Vicar of Bullhampton* centers on Carry Brattle, a miller's daughter, who had been misused by men and set on a life of prostitution. Trollope says that the novel was written chiefly

> with the object of exciting not only pity but sympathy for a fallen woman, and of raising a feeling of forgiveness for such in the minds of other women. I could not venture to make this female the heroine of my story. To have made her a heroine at all would have been directly opposed to my purpose. It was necessary therefore that she should be a second-rate personage in the tale;—but it was with reference to her life that the tale was written, and the hero and heroine with their belongings are all subordinate.[44]

To deflect some of the criticism that might be forthcoming because he sought to deal with such a theme, Trollope took the extraordinary step of beginning the novel with a preface in which he denies any attempt to make her situation attractive or a temptation to other young women. Rather, he says, he writes to suggest that perhaps other women can do something to "mitigate and shorten" situations like Carry's without themselves being contaminated with vice. In particular, Trollope condemns the double standard:

> In regard to a sin common to the two sexes, almost all the punishment and all the disgrace is heaped upon the one who in nine cases out of ten has been the least sinful. And the punishment inflicted is of such a nature that it hardly allows room for repentance. How is the woman to return to decency to whom no decent door is opened? Then comes the answer: It is to the severity of the punishment alone that we can trust to keep women from falling. Such is the argument in favour of the existing practice, and such the excuse given for their severity by women who will relax nothing of their harshness. But in truth the severity of the punishment is not known

beforehand; it is not in the least understood by women in general, except by those who suffer it. The gaudy dirt, the squalid plenty, the contumely of familiarity, the absence of all good words and all good things . . .—and then the quick depreciation of that one ware of beauty, the substituted paint, garments bright without but foul within like painted sepulchres, life without a hope . . . , utterly friendless, disease, starvation, and a quivering fear of that coming hell which still can hardly be worse than all that is suffered here! This is the life to which we doom our erring daughters, when because of their error we close our door upon them! But for our erring sons we find pardon easily enough.[45]

Trollope wrote to elicit the possibility of repentance and forgiveness for one so fallen. In the process he certainly gives himself no easy task, for Carry Brattle's father, Jacob, was a man of extraordinary sternness. For sixty-five years he had known no other occupation than running a mill, and he had always been hardworking, sober, and honest. But he was also cross-grained, litigious, moody, and tyrannical. As Trollope says:

He was a man with unlimited love of justice; but the justice which he loved best was justice to himself. He brooded over injuries done to him,—injuries real or fancied,—till he taught himself to wish that all who hurt him might be crucified for the hurt they did to him. He never forgot, and never wished to forgive. . . . In matters of religion he was an old Pagan, going to no place of worship, saying no prayer, believing in no creed,—with some vague idea that a supreme power would bring him right at last, if he worked hard, robbed no one, fed his wife and children, and paid his way. To pay his way was the pride of his heart; to be paid on his way was its joy.[46]

Carry was his favorite daughter, and she had shamed and dishonored him. In Jacob there seemed little of the forgiveness Trollope sought to elicit from his readers. Nor, as long as that forgiveness was withheld, could the proffered goodwill of Carry's mother, sister, and brother be effective, because Carry could not share their roof.

Yet there is an agent of hope who takes as his task not only to save Carry from the life into which she has fallen, but to reconcile her to her father—that agent is the Vicar of Bullhampton, Mr. Frank Fenwick. Trollope leaves no doubt that Mr. Fenwick is a gentleman. A friend of the area's squire, Mr. Gilmore, it turns out Fenwick displays even more breeding than the squire. "Though he esteemed both his churchwardens and his bishop, [he] was afraid of neither." [47]

Mr. Fenwick is a man of great constancy who respects the same in others. He greatly admires the miller, for example, in spite of the latter's refusal to come to church, because he thinks the man possessed "a stubborn constancy which almost amounted to heroism." [48] Nor is the Vicar a man to be put off his project simply because he displeases someone. Thus, he refuses to abandon his support for Carry, even though the Marquis of Trowbridge has decided on hearsay that she is worthless and should be driven from the parish.

Nor will Fenwick desert Carry's brother, Sam, who has become associated with suspected robbers and murderers as he tries to aid his sister. The Marquis makes it clear to Mr. Fenwick that he thinks it unseemly for the Vicar to continue association with such people. But the Vicar of Bullhampton rejects the Marquis' judgments by asserting that Mr. Brattle should no more turn out his accused but unconvicted son than the Marquis would be expected to turn out his daughters in such circumstances.

Mr. Fenwick's gift of using analogies and stories to help others appreciate their position, however, is too much for the Marquis. [49] To have his daughters compared to the Brattles is more than he can take. In an attempt to punish Mr. Fenwick, therefore, the Marquis not only writes a letter to the Bishop implying the Vicar's gross immorality, but he gives permission for the Methodist pastor, Mr. Puddleham, to build an extraordinarily unsightly chapel directly across from Mr. Fenwick's church.

Though Mr. Fenwick is a fighter, he does not try to have the building stopped. He assumes that the chapel is being built on the Marquis' land and that the Marquis has the right to do as he wishes with the land. The Vicar even asks his wife to stop complaining about the matter. Even though he dislikes the chapel as much if not more than she, it is their duty to show no sign of anger that might disturb the peace of the community. He thus continues to act graciously toward Mr. Puddleham, even though Puddleham never misses an opportunity to criticize and slight him. Trollope tells us that, though outwardly calm:

> In his heart of hearts he hated the chapel, and in spite of all his endeavors to the contrary, his feelings towards Mr. Puddleman were not those which the Christian religion requires one neighbor to bear to another. But he made the struggle, and for some weeks past had not said a word against Mr. Puddleham. In regard to the Marquis the thing was different. The

Marquis should have known better, and against the Marquis he did say a great many words.[50]

Trollope makes it clear that Mr. Fenwick is, as the miller puts it, a "meddler with folk." [51] His meddling derives from a charity alloyed with very strong steel. Pressured by his wife, who does not understand why he persists in trying to help Carry Brattle, Mr. Fenwick responds:

> "For her and not for others, because she is an old friend, a neighbor's child, and one of the parish." That question was easily answered.
> "But how is it possible, Frank? Of course one would do anything that is possible to save her. What I mean is, that one would do it for all of them, if only it were possible.
> "If you can do it for one, will not even that be much?"
> "But it is permitted to them not to forgive that sin."
> "By what law?"
> "By the law of custom. It is all very well, Frank, but you can't fight against it. At any rate, you can't ignore it till it has been fought against and conquered. And it is useful. It keeps women from going astray." [52]

But the Vicar refuses to accept the common wisdom that though it is "difficult to make crooked things straight," it is not impossible. Moreover, he refuses to accept the proposition advanced by his wife and many others in the novel that the only thing keeping other young women from falling into Carry's trap is the harshness of the punishment. In the presence of the Marquis he corrects Mr. Puddleham for alleging that Carry is a prostitute and thus a "lost soul":

> "What you said about poor Carry Brattle. You don't know it as a fact."
> "Everybody says so."
> "How do you know she has not married, and become an honest woman?"
> "It is possible, of course. Though as for that,—when a young woman has once gone astray—"
> "As did Mary Magdalene, for instance!"
> "Mr. Fenwick, it was a very bad case."
> "And isn't my case very bad—and yours? Are we not in a bad way,— unless we believe and repent? Have we not all so sinned as to deserve eternal punishment?"
> "Certainly, Mr. Fenwick."
> "Then there can't be much difference between her and us. She can't deserve more than eternal punishment. If she believes and repents, all her sins will be white as snow."

"Certainly, Mr. Fenwick."

"Then speak of her as you would of any other sister or brother,—not as a thing that must be always vile because she has fallen once. Women will so speak,—and other men. One sees something of a reason for it. But you and I, as Christian ministers, should never allow ourselves to speak so thoughtlessly of sinners. Good morning, Mr. Puddleham." [53]

The Vicar is determined to show that a crooked thing can be made straight. He finds Carry through the aid of her brother, sees that she is boarded at least for a while in a good home, and seeks to persuade Mr. Brattle to forgive his daughter. But the final task proves too much even for the Vicar, as Mr. Brattle will not even permit his daughter's name to be mentioned, feeling she has brought shame and ruin on the family. Nor can Mr. Fenwick get Carry's married sister, Mrs. Jay, to offer her a home. Mr. Jay tells the Vicar, "I don't know whether almost the best thing for 'em isn't to die,—of course after they have repented, Mr. Fenwick. You see, sir, it is so very low, and so shameful, and they do bring such disgrace on their poor families." [54] Indeed, Trollope tells us that the Vicar was not in a good humor after confronting such an attitude:

> He was becoming almost tired of his efforts to set other people straight, so great were the difficulties that came in his way. As he had driven into his own gate he had met Mr. Puddleham, standing in the road just in front of the new chapel. He had made up his mind to accept the chapel, and now he said a pleasant word to the minister. Mr. Puddleham turned up his eyes and his nose, bowed very stiffly, and then twisted himself round, without answering a word. How was it possible for a man to live among such people in good humour and Christian charity?" [55]

I think Trollope believes good humor and Christian charity are possible, even for a busybody such as Mr. Fenwick, because, finally, forgiveness is made possible by the force of events.[56] Carry, unable to stay away any longer, makes the terrifying journey to rejoin her family on her own. She is received by her mother and sister. Her father is eventually told of her presence. He is unable to turn her from his home, allows her to stay, but refuses to forgive her, or even to remain under the same roof with her. He retreats to the mill. That he has allowed her to come back means, he says, that "I shall never be able to show my face again about the parish." [57] Yet, finally, Carry, summoning every bit of courage she can muster, confronts her father early one morning with the simple words:

> "Father," she said, following him, "if you could forgive me! I know I have been bad, but if you could forgive me!"
>
> He went to the very door of the mill before he turned; and she, when she saw that he did not come back to her, paused upon the bridge. She had used all her eloquence. She knew no other words with which to move him. She felt that she had failed, but she could do no more. But he stopped again without entering the mill.
>
> "Child," he said at last, "come here, then." She ran at once to meet him. "I will forgive thee. There. I will forgive thee, and trust thou mayest be a better girl than thou has been." [58]

There is no sentimentality to Brattle's forgiveness, because it has not come cheaply. Indeed, as he tells Carry's sister, Fanny, " 'I will bring myself to forgive her. That it won't stick here,' and the miller struck her heart violently with his open palm. 'I won't be such a liar as to say. For there ain't no good in a lie. But there shall be never a word about it more out o'my mouth,—and she may come to me again as a child.' " [59] Not only has he forgiven her, but he is willing to accompany her to testify at the murder trial in which the man who had wronged her is being tried. Brattle has found that his willingness to forgive does not make it impossible for him to act as a man or to show his face about the parish— indeed, the exact opposite is the case.

Trollope has a comedic plot running alongside the relationship between Carry and Brattle in which the Vicar learns that he also had some forgiving to do. By accident it was discovered that the ground the Marquis had given to the Methodists for their chapel was in fact glebe land that did not belong to the Marquis. At first, the Vicar resolves to do nothing about it, saying that the chapel "shall be my hair shirt, my fast day, my sacrifice of a broken heart, my little pet good work. It will enable me to take all the good things of the world that come in my way, and flatter myself that I am not self-indulgent. There is not a dissenter in Bullhampton who will get so much out of the chapel as I will." [60] Such a position, of course, also gives him unending power over the Marquis.

But through the agency of the Marquis' son, Lord St. George, and after an apology from the Marquis himself, who was foolish but not a bad man, the Vicar is made to forgive and make peace with the Marquis.

As Trollope tells us: "It may be a doubt whether it should be ascribed to Mr. Fenwick as a weakness or a strength that, though he was very susceptible of anger, and though he could maintain his anger at glowing heat as long as fighting continued, it would all evaporate and leave him harmless as a dove at the first glimpse of an olive branch."[61] "Though he was fond of a fight himself, he had taught himself to know that in no way could he do the business of his life more highly or more usefully than as a peacemaker; and as a peacemaker he had done it."[62] Thus, he accepts the Marquis' apology, not only for the chapel, but also for those allegations of immorality the Marquis had made to the bishop, because more important than his power over the Marquis is the peace of the parish for which he is responsible. The chapel is torn down to be built elsewhere.

Though I have been unable to capture the complex texture of *The Vicar of Bullhampton,* particularly as it weaves the triangular love affair among Miss Fenwick, Captain Marrable, and Mr. Gilmore into the theme of forgiveness, perhaps enough has been said to suggest how central forgiveness is to this novel. That effort also may illumine the theme in other Trollope stories. For forgiveness is the substance that makes possible the life of constancy as well as the society that sustains it. Through forgiveness a gentleman sustains the standard necessary to remain constant in his loyalty to others; yet at the same time forgiveness allows him not to remain indifferent to conduct that is clearly immoral. Moreover, it is through forgiveness that gentlemen can live together without violence. Their differences cannot help but entail conflict, but conflict is controllable because gentlemen are as ready to accept forgiveness as to give it.[63] It is such a world that Trollope creates for us time and time again by inviting us to live with him among his characters and thus to learn the nature as well as the skill of constancy.

In attending to Trollope's richly textured account of constancy and forgiveness, however, we must be careful not to overlook the obvious. As it turns out, forgiveness is no more easily defined than constancy. Like constancy, forgiveness requires display through the temporal narration of lives. Insofar as novels provide such display, they help us imaginatively to capture the complex character of forgiveness. Such complexity, as MacIntyre suggests, results from a kind of self-knowledge that comes from those who have learned the skills of repentance. Those skills are honed by the kinds of experience that it is the peculiar virtue of the novel to display. Repentance is not so much a matter of awareness, though it may involve that, as it is a set of skills formed by a life open to others. Such life is the novel's natural subject and form.

The Novel as a School of Virtue

We learn to understand and appreciate the moral significance of constancy and forgiveness only when they are depicted through a narrative. This I think provides an essential insight about the moral significance of novels like Trollope's and Austen's. Their novels are not important morally just because, as Trollope suggests in the preface to *The Vicar of Bullhampton,* they have the power to elicit our sympathy and thus change our attitudes. That is certainly no small matter, but these works are still more fundamentally important. Whatever their effect may be, the novels remain epistemologically crucial, for without them we lack the means to understand a morality that makes constancy its primary virtue.

It has become the fashion to deny the novel any direct moral import. Novels allegedly should be ends in themselves rather than attempts to help us be good. When literature is subjected to moralistic purposes, the results are almost always bad, with the resulting art mediocre or sentimental. Indeed, the realistic novel, the kind of novel that Trollope helped develop, is portrayed as an enemy of morality because it must depict life as it is, not as our moral fantasies would have it.

No attitude could be more foreign to Trollope. Certainly he understood himself to be a realistic novelist, though he by no means thought realism excluded what he called the sensational. Stories, he says, ought to

> charm us not simply because they are tragic, but because we feel that men and women with flesh and blood, creatures with whom we can sympathise, are struggling amidst their woes. It all lies in that. No novel is anything, for the purposes of either comedy or tragedy, unless the reader can sympathise with the characters whose names he finds upon the pages. Let an author so tell his tale as to touch his reader's heart and draw his tears, and he has, so far, done his work well. Truth let there be,—truth of description, truth of character, human truth as to men and women. If there be such truth, I do not know that a novel can be too sensational.[64]

It is generally acknowledged, moreover, that no writer is Trollope's equal when it comes to characterization. For him it was the writer's task to make the reader so acquainted with his characters that they

> should be to them speaking, moving, living human creatures. This he can never do unless he know those fictitious personages himself, and he can never know them unless he can live with them in the full reality of established intimacy. They must be with him as he lies down to sleep, and as he wakes from his dreams. He must learn to hate them and to love them. He must argue with them, quarrel with them, forgive them, and even submit to them. He must know of them whether they be cold-blooded or passionate, whether true or false, and how far true, and how far false. And as here, in our outer world, we know that men and women change,— become worse or better as temptation or conscience may guide them,— so should these creations of his change, and every change should be noted by him.[65]

The heroines and the heroes, the weak and the villains, are never one-dimensional figures in Trollope's world. We sense that Lily Dale's constancy to her love for Crosbie is mixed with a stubborn pride that is not admirable. We learn never quite to trust Phineas Finn as we watch his ambition lead him from one promising love affair to another. The Reverend Septimus Harding's humility and lack of ambition are at least partly the result of his inability to endure conflict in pursuit of the good. Lopez and Melmotte, villains to be sure, elicit from us sympathy as we sense the thousand small slights they have received as lowborn—slights that fuel their resentment and ambition. We know that Mrs. Proudie, whom Trollope calls his "old friend," tyrant though she is, lives and cares deeply for the church she rules in the name of her husband, the Bishop. We cannot help but admire the strange combination of pride, manliness, resentment, weakness, and madness that forms that most foreboding of characters, Mr. Crawley. We even come to appreciate the aged Duke of Omnium, who could or wished to do nothing other than to be the Duke of Omnium, because he did that so well.[66] Even beyond these, of course, is the complex character of Palliser, whom Trollope regarded as his greatest achievement.

The drawing of such characters with their good and their bad, Trollope thought in no way contradicted the moral purpose of his art. As he tells us:

I have always desired to "hew out some lump of the earth," and to make men and women walk upon it just as they do walk here among us, — with not more of excellence, nor with exaggerated baseness, — so that my readers might recognise human beings like to themselves, and not feel themselves to be carried away among gods or demons. If I could do this, then I thought I might succeed in impregnating the mind of the novel-reader with a feeling that honesty is the best policy; that truth prevails while falsehood fails; that a girl will be loved as she is pure, and sweet, and unselfish; that a man will be honoured as he is true, and honest, and brave of heart; that things meanly done are ugly and odious, and things nobly done beautiful and gracious.[67]

Some ridicule the idea that the novelist can be a teacher of virtue, Trollope says, because they assume the novel to be simply an idle pastime, at best. In contrast, he has always thought of himself

as a preacher of sermons, and my pulpit as one which I could make both salutary and agreeable to my audience. I do believe that no girl has risen from the reading of my pages less modest than she was before, and that some may have learned from them that modesty is a charm well worth preserving. I think that no youth has been taught that in falseness and flashiness is to be found the road to manliness; but some may perhaps have learned from me that it is to be found in truth and a high and gentle spirit. Such are the lessons I have striven to teach; and I have thought that it might best be done by representing to my readers characters like themselves, — or to which they might liken themselves.[68]

These outright declarations of his moral purpose, however, can mislead us in understanding the complex manner that Trollope's art works morally. His novels instruct us morally not simply because we identify with the characters he draws and thus learn some of our own proclivities, but because their very form exhibits the virtue he commends. Novels such as Trollope's are possible only when they manifest the forgiveness which he commends through their pages. His ability to depict characters "realistically" entails a spirit that has the power to form an art sufficient to shape our response to forgive in a similar fashion. We are able to do so because we have learned literally to see another sympathetically rather than sentimentally or with resentment.

Thus, the very reading of the novel is a moral training. By forcing our eyes from one word to the next, one sentence to the next, one paragraph to the next, we are stretched through a narrative world that gives us the skills to make something of our own lives. To make something of our own lives requires our being able to locate our story in an unfolding narrative so that we can go on. Without such a story, we lack the means of constancy, and without forgiveness we lack the means of making our lives our own. For a truthful story cannot avoid the bad we have done or allowed any more than it can fail to record that the good we have done has been the result of mixed motives. Novels are the means, though not the only means, to be sure, that we have to attain the skills of locating and telling our individual stories, not as instances of some grand schemes, but as uniquely ours. Just to the extent they are ours, they make constancy possible.

Constancy, Forgiveness, and Conventional Religion

Some may find it surprising that I have written much of forgiveness but have made little of explicit Christian teaching and practice of forgiveness. However, I thought it inappropriate to attribute to Trollope a sense of forgiveness that required theological backing. No doubt, as some of the quotations suggest, Trollope assumed that forgiveness was at the heart of the Christian religion, but his Christianity so pervaded countrysides such as that of Bullhampton that it did not need to be made explicit.

Indeed, Trollope seems not to have thought very much about religion one way or the other.[69] No doubt, as with most issues in his life, he simply accepted the conventions of his day as normative. He was a member in good standing in the Church of England. I do not mean that he did not take the beliefs and practices of the church seriously, because I have no doubt he did. But we never see him wrestling with the basic challenges to the Christian faith in a manner like George Eliot. He was a conventional Christian holding the beliefs of the church in a conventional manner.

That he did so only shows the power of convention. There can be no doubt that Trollope understood profoundly that at the heart of the Christian faith is the demand to forgive. But in this understanding he merely assumed he was believing what any good Anglican should believe—the only question was how to put beliefs into practice. In this respect he stands as a challenge to our modern sense that one can believe seriously only by having gone through a religious crisis of belief and unbelief—that we can know true belief only when we have struggled to free ourselves from conventional religion. That we think this way is a sad commentary on our times, for we fail to see that the real issue is whether our conventions are truthful. As a result, we hover close to cynicism, captives of our morbid self-awareness.

In contrast, Trollope would never assume that our task is to reject convention, but rather the task is to live out the substance of our conventions. The significance of religion for Trollope is, therefore, not that it recommends forgiveness as a norm, but that Christianity, at least as Trollope found it in the prayer book of the Church of England, provided exactly that sense of the "wholeness of a human life" which MacIntyre thinks necessary for the virtue of constancy. If we lack a narrative that makes it intelligible to think of each human life as a unity, then in fact we lack the means to make intelligible our confidence that our lives can acquire a story.

I am not suggesting that Trollope explicitly held such a view. It was simply the presupposition that went with how he worked. Trollope is certainly not satisfying as an explicitly religious novelist, but then few writers are. He is certainly one of the more interesting novelists for Christians, however, because the world he created helps us see the imaginative power of our beliefs.[70]

BY WAY OF A COMPARISON OF KARL BARTH

AND TROLLOPE

On Trying to Justify Comparing Barth and Trollope

My aim is to show that Karl Barth's main problem is that he did not read enough Trollope. Indeed, I can find no evidence that Barth ever read Trollope. I am aware that this thesis may well strike many readers as a bit odd. How can I possibly think that any juxtaposing of two people as different as Barth and Trollope makes sense? After all, theologians and novelists generally do not mix. Moreover, they come from completely different times and seem to have strongly different sensibilities about human existence—somehow I do not think Mozart was Trollope's favorite composer. Barth was formed personally and intellectually by confronting Hitler. Trollope faced the English postal service. In spite of such obvious obstacles, I am determined to bring Barth and Trollope into conversation for no other reason than that I have learned much from each, and, therefore, I cannot help but believe that there must be some sense in which they are complementary.

Such a comparison, of course, is fraught with difficulties, not the least of which is that neither Barth nor Trollope is easily summarized. Indeed, one of the things I most like about Barth is that his position defies summary because he was so determinedly unsystematic, making it almost impossible to know what it would mean to be a "Barthian." Gerhard Sauter reports that he jokingly tells his students "You cannot quote Barth," because a countercitation can always be found from Barth himself. Sauter observes that this does not mean that Barth failed to think consistently, but rather it indicates that Barth's trend of thought is not a one-dimensional movement nor a clear progression. Barth saw that theology is incapable of saying everything at one time. So any attempt to wrap everything up in one concept that is continually unfolded simply will not work. Thus, Sauter quotes Barth as describing his theology as trying "to trace the bird's flight."[1]

In that respect I think it is not so odd to compare Barth's work with that of a novelist. For just as any good novel cannot be captured by a summary of its plot, by a description of the characters, or by trying to say what it is about, so Barth's theology cannot be summarized. There is no substitute for reading *Church Dogmatics,* just as *Church Dogmatics* tries to remind us that nothing can substitute for reading the Bible.[2] As Hans Frei puts it, Barth was in the business of

> conceptual description: he took the classical themes of communal Christian language moulded by the Bible, tradition and constant usage in worship, practice, instruction and controversy, and he restated or redescribed them rather than evolving arguments on their behalf. It was of the utmost importance to him that this communal language, especially its biblical *fons et origo,* which he saw as indirectly one with the Word of God, has an integrity of its own: it was irreducible. But in that case its lengthy, even leisurely unfolding was equally indispensable.[3]

If this is true, and I certainly think it is, then the procedure adopted in this chapter is even more doubtful. For by concentrating on one aspect of Barth's ethics, and what appears to be a decidedly minor theme, it risks distorting his overall perspective. In no way, of course, can we avoid the possibility of such misrepresentation. Rather, all that can be done is to ask the reader's patience to see whether a comparison of Barth with Trollope does not in fact illumine Barth's method and help to locate some of the difficulties with his ethics.

The method used is straightforward. Barth's discussion of the concept of honor at the end of *Church Dogmatics* (III/4 (56.3)) will be briefly presented. Then an attempt will be made to exhibit Trollope's understanding of honor by discussing one of his late novels, *Dr. Wortle's School.* The second task is in many ways more difficult, as care will have to be taken not to turn Trollope's novel into a "position" in the interest of schematic comparison. For it is exactly the strength of Trollope's and Barth's understandings of honor to resist reducing honor to a formula or principle.

But why honor, of all things? Honor is usually associated with what is owed to grandmothers in the South or what is still talked about but not embodied in military academies. It is my conviction, however, that any people who seek to live worthy lives require an account of honor. Moreover, if we live in an age when honor is no longer a working moral notion, we are the poorer for it. By analyzing Barth and Trollope on honor, I therefore hope to develop some rather broad themes about why Christians have a stake in the notion of honor, as well as how that stake may help us understand better our relation to a world that no longer honors honor.[4]

There are, however, certain methodological reasons for focusing on the notion of honor. In a fine article, "Command and History in the Ethics of Karl Barth," William Werpehowski has challenged my criticism of Barth's alleged inability to provide a morally compelling account of the moral continuity of the self, or better, moral character.[5] As Werpehowski notes, underlying my criticism was a suspicion that the "Barthian self is unable to express itself as shaped through history."[6] My worry in this respect was and is very similar to Richard Roberts's analysis of Barth's account of time. As Roberts observes, for Barth "human existence, and thus time which is 'real so far as He wills and posits it a real existence' raises a difficulty inherent in the *Church Dogmatics* as a whole: How does this 'real existence' relate to that existence experienced by the human subject as a mere percipient being?"[7] Or as Roberts puts it later, Barth's account of time—and with it, I think, his correlative sense of personal continuity—risks Docetism insofar as it is determined by an account of revelation whose temporality is not to be confused in any way with the time we experience as humans.

Werpehowski, drawing on Hans Frei's insistence on Barth's program of "conceptual description," argues that my criticism fails to appreciate how Barth's account of continuity is congruent with our everyday sense of self. Barth's method is to locate the everyday within the Christian world through his description of our sense of ourselves. For Barth

the concrete invitation is freely and actively to conform one's personal history or "narrative" to the "narratives" of the creatures portrayed in Scripture, who themselves are depicted as constituted by a history of relationship with God. One is not only to ally oneself with them formally, in the awareness of having been given a commission, but one must also, in one's different time and situation, make the command of the mission given to them one's own, "not as something new and special, but as the renewal and confirmation of the task laid upon them." (*CD* II/2:706)[8]

Werpehowski substantiates his defense of Barth by noting that Barth extends the logic of the divine command in his account of vocation, which includes the "givens" of life—our age, our special situation, our personal aptitudes, and our specific "field of ordinary everyday activity."[9]

Summarizing his criticism of Barth's critics, Werpehowski argues:

> Barth incorporates a conception of "history" which grounds reasons for action, character, and growth-in-continuity in his category of "history of relationship with God." The everyday conception of history, remember, explains the changes through self-expressing actions of a continuous subject. As *continuous*, Barth's Christian person stands loyal to the cause of Jesus Christ. As *changed* through his or her actions, he or she comes to a deeper self-understanding through a deeper understanding of God's plans for him or her. And as *changing*, he or she approaches concrete ethical events armed with a range of theonomous reasons which help to frame and limit the possibilities of obedient action. All the conditions are met for characterizing the Christian as one who does indeed express oneself through one's history. This history has an incarnational quality, in that the extraordinary history of relationship with God is manifested in and through the everyday history of self-expression, rather than having it manifested at the "limit" or "boundary" of the everyday.[10]

Now I must admit that Werpehowski almost convinces me. I am sure he is right that the way Barth uses the language of command and/or act does not in itself entail a discontinuous account of the self nor a denial of moral rationality. Moreover, he is certainly right to direct attention to Barth's account of vocation at the end of *Church Dogmatics* (III/4), and I am sure in my presentation of Barth's ethics that I failed to appreciate the significance of that aspect of Barth's ethics. Yet I remain bothered by a peculiar "abstractness" to Barth's ethics that gives his account of the moral life an aura of unreality.[11] I hope to exhibit this unease by turning to Barth's account of honor, which is an extension of his account of vocation, and in particular, by contrasting Barth's abstractness with the concreteness of Trollope's *Dr. Wortle's School*. By doing so, I hope to test Werpehowski's defense of Barth on its strongest grounds, since any account of honor seems to entail a self capable of constancy.

Barth on Honor (*CD* III/4, 56.3)

It is a testimony to Barth's extraordinary imagination that he treats the question of honor. For as Peter Berger has suggested, the "obsolescence" of the concept of honor is a correlate of the rise of a new humanism concerned with the dignity and rights of the individual. As Berger points out, the "same modern men who fail to understand an issue of honour are immediately disposed to concede the demands for dignity and for equal rights by almost every new group that makes them—racial or religious minorities, exploited classes, the poor, the deviant, and so on." [12] This new egalitarian emphasis has therefore tended to undermine the significance of institutional roles and inequalities of service that are crucial to sustain an ethos of honor.

Barth, however, maintains that while the forms of honor will change from time to time and society to society, no collective can exist without concepts of honor—that is, "with their various standards, with their internal nuances and external frontiers, according to which the life of society and nations in their various groups, strata and classes, and also the personal life of the individual both in isolation and in relation to his fellows, usually tries to some extent to direct and regulate itself" (*CD* III/4:669). Indeed, Barth argues that without a tacit or open acceptance of the concept of honor, man could not be man, whether we be isolated or in the company of others (*CD* III/4:669). In even stronger language, Barth says: "We may call honour the supreme earthly good. It may well be true that to lose honour is to lose everything" (*CD* III/4:663).

Moreover, Barth suggests there is no reason for Christians to object to such concepts of honor.

> On the contrary, if the fact that there are, and that man, even as a transgressor, does not seem able to avoid forming and maintaining such concepts (however curious), we have to recognize the *character indelebilis* of the honour which God gives man by the mere fact that he is his Creator and Lord and man his creature. Even the oddest man attests this, whatever his intention or self-understanding, and however curious his concept of honour. So, too, does the most singular and questionable tradition or new invention in this sphere. All honour to it alongside the views and opinions which seem more illuminating and authoritative and normative to us! There is basically no objection to the existence and validity of such

collective and individual concepts of honour. Indeed, there is much to be said for them. (*CD* III/4:669)

Barth's positive view of honor is correlative to his understanding of human existence in limitation. For honor is distinction—that is, honor is a claim to special, particular, and specific recognition of a concrete and individual man. It cannot be a characteristic that can be attributed to the human race collectively. "If the term is not to be empty, it must mean the honour of the concrete and therefore always the individual man, the dignity and estimation due to every man, but due to each as this particular man, not merely as a specimen of the race, but directly, personally and exclusively" (*CD* III/4:655). Of course, any honor that is true or real can only be a reflection of the honor that God has done us by giving us our time and our vocation. In a typical Barthian mode we are told:

> If we are to be accurate from the outset, we must say that first and finally it (the honour of man) can be understood only as the reflection of the honour of God falling on every man as such, and especially of the fact that God is not arbitrary or false, but true to Himself as God, when He does man this great honour in His command. God finds and sees in every man as such something which certainly cannot be classified with the honour which He does him when He calls him to his service, which in comparison with this can be only an improper honour, but which is still an honour granted to man by God and therefore a true honour as such. It is the honour which God has done and still does every man in the fact that He was and is invested in virtue of the fact that he may have his existence as the creature of God and may be under His rule. (*CD* III/4:651) [13]

"All honour of man is always God's honour" (*CD* III/4:654), but God allows us to participate in His honor. For God does not will to be God without man. Yet God's honoring of man has a twofold sense. There is the honor that comes to us as creatures of God, and an honor that comes to us by our calling to the service of God. These two have been treated on the same plane by theologians, with the result being an over-emphasis on the distinctively soteriological and ecclesiastical element and a hesitation to take seriously the general honor of man as such, or an overemphasis on the latter element and a hesitation to speak of the special honor of the divine calling except as a form of the general human concept of honor. In contrast, Barth argues that "theological ethics has to take seriously in their different ways both the honour of man as created by God and the honour of man as called by God. It has thus to understand the two as both unmixed in their distinction and yet inseparable in their interrelationship" (CD III/4:653).[14]

Therefore any honor that comes to us from others, if it is to be the honor based on a call from God, must be that which comes from the service assigned by God. Any human action that lacks the character of service is either not yet or no longer honorable (CD III/4:659). Of course, such honor may be misunderstood by others since there are a very large number of possibilities of lack of appreciation and misunderstanding. It is only in service that two men

> learn to know and respect one another, not by simply observing or think-ing about one another, or even by living with one another, however great their concord or even friendship, in indolence or caprice, self-will or arro-gance. Mere companions and comrades cannot appreciate either their own honour or that of the other. The honour of two men is disclosed and will be apparent to both when they meet each other in the knowledge that they are both claimed, not by and for something of their own and therefore incidental and non-essential, but for and by the service God has laid on them. (CD III/4:659)

It follows, therefore, that man can be honorable only in pure thankful-ness, deepest humility, and in free humor (CD III/4:664). Because we know our honor does not belong to us, we can only respond in thank-fulness, manifesting the deep quiet and assurance that derives from the knowledge of our inadequacy yet the faithfulness of God. That is why humor, the opposite of all self-admiration and self-praise, is so impor-tant. Humor is the profound recognition that all honor comes from God. The honorable man cannot help but be modest as

> only in the sincere and complete withdrawal of the recipient before the Giver and His gift, only in the relaxation in which he wills to be only what he may become and to have only what he may receive, and all in the course and event of the divine action which his own action only follows, which it only serves, to which it only adapts itself, from which it cannot therefore loose itself, in the face of which it cannot want to play its own game. (CD III/4:666)

Such modesty is completely compatible with healthy pride, for such modesty is but the positive recognition of God's honoring us by claiming us for service.

The fact that all worldly concepts of honor must be tested by the honor of God does not mean that the honor of service ascribed to man may not in large measure correspond to what is called honor by the world. It is not necessary, therefore, that the honor which comes to us from God must contradict worldly honor. As Barth points out, did not Joseph and Moses in Egypt, and David, Solomon, and Job receive superabundantly that which the world also regards as honor? And certainly Jesus as a child is said to have increased "in wisdom and stature, and in favour with God and man" as well as in the exercise of his ministry Jesus received all kinds of worldly honor (*CD* III/4:671).

But just as God is free to make worldly honor correspond to his honor, and therefore to our expectations and hopes, God is also free to have it otherwise. If there is no law "in virtue of which man's honour before God must be continually and necessarily in contradiction and conflict with what he would like to regard as his honour from the human and worldly standpoint, there is also no law in virtue of which the two must normally agree" (*CD* III/4:672). We must recognize that God may force us to see that we have fashioned a small and limited idea of honor and that more is demanded of us than we or our environment has provided. In such a case we cannot be satisfied with personal or collective concepts of honor, as they are all inadequate. We do not owe humility to such concepts; we owe it to God. God, moreover, may make higher claims for himself and therefore for others so that in the deepest humility we will have to have great courage. For God may well call us, like the disciples, to be raised higher than our society's concept of honor, or we may be called, like Job, to an obedience that seems lower than the existing standards of honor (*CD* III/4:673).

More likely than the conflict envisaged by the call to a higher or lower sense of honor is that most of us will find the

> form of divinely willed and allotted honour in which there will be little or no evidence either to ourselves or others of either exaltation or abasement. The actual life of most men, and the main span even of those distinguished on the one side or the other, is passed at a mid-point, where the chief problem is not to persevere as consistently as possible, whether exalted or abased, in a clear conflict between the esteem intended for them by God and their own concepts of honour, but quite placidly, i.e., without such conflict, to be content actually to be honoured by God. (*CD* III/4:676)

As Barth reminds us, those without problems are just as much needed in the service of God as genuine heroes and sufferers.

Since our honor is that bestowed by God, does that mean that Christians are prevented from defending their honor against words and acts of others? Certainly it means that Christians may accept, if not everything, at least a great deal. Barth observes that experience shows that most lies are short-lived and what is written in the press is particularly short-lived. He reports that in recent

> theological history there is at least one instance of a man who is supposed to have died of a review written against him. But he had no business to do this. If he did, it is more to his own shame than that of the reviewer. Above all, it should always be regarded only as *ultima ratio* to allow ourselves to become entangled in judicial proceedings in respect of the so-called wounding of honour. (*CD* III/4:679)

Nonetheless, we may be commanded to take legitimate steps in confirmation or defense of our honor. For to fail to defend ourselves might prejudice our honor in the eyes and judgments of others and therefore in our own eyes. As a result, the service laid on us might be called into question. Since I am responsible for the discharge of my calling and vocation, I may be called on to defend my honor to protect them. But the way in which our honor is defended requires careful attention to what might entail at least an apparent compromising of our honor in our own behavior. I must uphold it before myself before I can expect to be able to do so before others. In every way that we seek to rehabilitate our honor, we must appeal to something known to our detractors aiming in our action to restore fellowship on the basis of what is well-known to both of us.

> If others have no honour, what is the use of defending mine against them and before them? . . . He who seeks to secure his self-respect is thus asked: Do you respect yourself? Even more: Have you first respected before you wish to procure respect for yourself? And more again: Is it more important, more urgent and more necessary for you to respect or procure respect for yourself? (*CD* III/4:684)

Such is honor according to Barth. I have tried to present his account fairly and without commentary, hoping to avoid distortions resulting from summary. I shall, moreover, withhold any critical commentary until I have discussed Trollope. At this point I am content with the observation that Barth's account of honor is characteristic of his ethics in general, as it is at once a mixture of extraordinary insights about human behavior and theological claims that make one unsure about the status of such behavior. By discussing honor at such a general level, while noting it must take concrete form in this or that time or society, Barth is able to have his theological cake and eat it. It seems to make sense, but I suspect it does so because we fill up the formal analysis with our own categories without knowing how those categories are to be theologically controlled. What we need to know is how honor in this or that context may or may not be appropriate to the service to which we are called as Christians. Such concreteness is exactly what I hope to show Trollope offers.

Dr. Wortle's Honor

Summarizing Barth is difficult, but summarizing Trollope's novel— even one as spare as *Dr. Wortle's School*—is impossible. Still, I think it is worth the effort, for this is a novel about honor, or at least about acting as a gentleman (which for Trollope was the same as acting honorably), in which Trollope explores why honor may require us to act against our society's moral conventions. That theme makes the novel particularly interesting for our purposes, since normally to act honorably is to act in accordance with the ideals of one's society. By placing Dr. Wortle in a position that forced him to act contrary to societal convention, Trollope explores how honorable people extend their society's morality through being who they are.

The novel is primarily about two people—Dr. Wortle and the Reverend Mr. Peacocke. Dr. Wortle, we are told in the book's first sentence, is a man much esteemed by others as well as himself. He combines two professions: Rector of Bowick and proprietor and headmaster of a school at Bowick established as a preparatory to Eton. His school is highly successful, attracting students of the best families as well as providing Dr. Wortle with an extremely good income. Dr. Wortle is a man who will not bear censure from any human being, though he does not look for controversy.[15] Thus, he remains on good terms with his bishop, so long as in all things the bishop allows him to be his own master. In short, Dr. Wortle is successful and well-established, a man with impeccable reputation, with a wife and daughter who adore and honor him in every regard.

Dr. Wortle's comfortable world is upset by his hiring Mr. Peacocke, a former fellow of Trinity College, Oxford, to be an usher at the school as well as serving as curate. Mr. Peacocke, though a well-respected classics scholar, had left Oxford to be vice president of a classical college in St. Louis, Missouri. Five years later, with a beautiful American wife, he returned to Oxford, looking for employment. Given Dr. Wortle's convictions, it is surprising that he hired Mr. Peacocke, since being a Tory the Doctor hated all things associated with the republic as well as distrusting anyone who seemed to be a rolling stone. But Mr. Peacocke's scholarship and teaching were excellent, he could at once be an usher and curate, and his wife could serve as a matron. So, after many inquiries, Dr. Wortle, as "one who thought that there should be a place of penitence allowed to those who had clearly repented of their errors" (p. 13), employed Mr. Peacocke and his wife.

Dr. Wortle soon comes to value Mr. Peacocke's contribution at the school. Aware that Mr. Peacocke's scholarship is "deeper" than his own, Dr. Wortle even allows certain changes to be made in the curriculum, which everyone assumes is done at the advice of Mr. Peacocke. It is apparent, however, that the relationship between Dr. Wortle and Mr. Peacocke goes beyond their professional relation as the personal respect with which Dr. Wortle treats Mr. Peacocke seems to imply that the two are equal—that is, they are both gentlemen. Mrs. Peacocke is no less valuable since, being every inch a lady, she performs her duties in an exemplary manner, even nursing a young lord when it is not among her duties.

Only two matters bother Dr. Wortle: Mr. Peacocke begins to preach only after being pressured to do so, and the Peacockes refuse to be entertained in Dr. Wortle's home. While they are exemplary in every way, a mystery surrounds the Peacockes that is sufficient for Mrs. Stantiloup, an enemy of Dr. Wortle because he had sued her for her refusal to pay the full costs of her son's education, to create rumors about the Peacockes' five years in America. These rumors finally reach the ears of the Bishop, so that the Bishop, in the kindest manner, finally asks Dr. Wortle to inquire about Mr. Peacocke's lost years in America. These reports are based on nothing more than a lack of information, but as Trollope notes, "so much in this world depends upon character that attention has to be paid to bad character even when it is not deserved. In dealing with men and women, we have to consider what they believe, as well as what we believe ourselves" (p. 26).

Though thinking such suspicions are monstrous, unreasonable, and uncharitable, Dr. Wortle agrees to make inquiry of Mr. Peacocke; yet he continually puts it off because he finds the task so disagreeable. Finally, bringing himself to arrange an interview with Mr. Peacocke, he discovers that Mr. Peacocke does have a story to tell; and in fact Mr. Peacocke confesses he had been considering asking Dr. Wortle if he would do him the "favor to listen to the story of my life" (p. 39). Before doing so, however, Mr. Peacocke asks for a week to think the matter through. Dr. Wortle grants his request, noting that

> of course I cannot in the least guess what all this is about. For myself I hate secrets. I haven't a secret in the world. I know nothing of myself which you mightn't know too for all that I cared. But that is my good fortune rather than my merit. It might well have been with me as it is with you; but, as a rule, I think that where there is a secret it had better be kept. No one, at any rate, should allow it to be wormed out of him by the impertinent assiduity of others. If there be anything affecting your wife which you do not wish all the world of this side of the water to know, do not tell it to anyone on this side of the water." (pp. 40–41)

The story that Mr. Peacocke resolves to tell Dr. Wortle is, in brief, that he and Mrs. Peacocke are not in fact man and wife. Mr. Peacocke had become acquainted with Mrs. Peacocke in St. Louis as the wife of a Colonel Lefroy, who with his brother were southerners who had been ruined both financially and morally by the War between the States. Mrs. Lefroy had been married to Colonel Lefroy when she was only seventeen because her father (also a ruined southern planter) had died leaving her no way of supporting herself.

When Mr. Peacocke became acquainted with Mrs. Lefroy and the two brothers, there was a great scandal in St. Louis about the cruel treatment the wife had received from her husband. Lefroy was going to Texas to pursue his fortune with a band of desperadoes and he was violently trying to force her to accompany him. Certain persons in St. Louis intervened to prevent this from happening, Mr. Peacocke being among them, so the brothers went alone to Texas. Mrs. Lefroy was left to provide for herself and Mr. Peacocke was among those who aided her. In the process, we are told, a certain intimacy was created, but not of the sort that would be injurious to the fame of the lady.

Things continued in this way for two years until news came that Colonel Lefroy had been killed by a party of American soldiers. It was not clear from the news, however, which Colonel Lefroy had perished, since both brothers bore that title. Seeing the distress of Mrs. Lefroy in the face of such inexact news, Mr. Peacocke went to the Mexican border to discover the truth. Mr. Peacocke learned from the younger brother, Robert Lefroy, that the husband had in fact been killed. On returning, he proposed marriage, after which they enjoyed six months of married happiness.

Then Ferdinand Lefroy, the husband, suddenly appeared in St. Louis, confronting the Peacockes, and making himself known more generally. But just as suddenly as he appeared, he was gone again. The Peacockes' consternation can be imagined. She immediately said she must go, but Mr. Peacocke refused, bringing her back to England as his wife and subsequently finding a position with Dr. Wortle's school at Bowick. This is the story Mr. Peacocke resolves to tell Dr. Wortle, realizing that in the telling he must leave the school.

Before he is able to relate the story, however, Robert Lefroy arrives in England, presenting himself to Mr. Peacocke and threatening to tell all unless compensated. At being refused by Mr. Peacocke, he recounts the story to Dr. Wortle, thinking Dr. Wortle might be willing to pay to preserve his school from scandal. Mr. Peacocke then asks for an interview with Dr. Wortle, during which the following exchange takes place:

> "Colonel Lefroy has been with you, I take it."
>
> "A man calling himself by that name has been here. Will you not take a chair?"
>
> "I do not know that it will be necessary. What he has told you—what I suppose he has told you—is true."
>
> "You had better at any rate take a chair. I do not believe that what he has told me is true."
>
> "But it is."
>
> "I do not believe that what he has told me is true. Some of it cannot, I think, be true. Much of it not so—unless I am more deceived in you than I ever was in any man. At any rate, sit down." Then the schoolmaster did sit down. "He has made you out to be a perjured, willful, cruel bigamist."
>
> "I have not been such," said Peacocke, rising from his chair.
>
> "One who has been willing to sacrifice a woman to his passion."
>
> "No, no."
>
> "Who deceived her by false witnesses."
>
> "Never."
>
> "And who has now refused to allow her to see her own husband's brother, lest she should learn the truth."
>
> "She is there—at any rate for you to see."

"Therefore the man is a liar. A long story has to be told, as to which at present I can only guess what may be the nature. I presume the story will be the same as that you would have told had the man never come here."

"Exactly the same, Dr. Wortle."

"Therefore you will own that I am right in asking you to sit down. The story may be very long—that is, if you mean to tell it."

"I do—and did. I was wrong from the first in supposing that the nature of my marriage need be of no concern to others, but to herself and me."

"Yes—Mr. Peacocke; yes. We are, all of us joined together too closely to admit of isolation such as that." There was something in this which grated against the schoolmaster's pride, though nothing had been said as to which he did not know that much harder things must meet his ears before the matter could be brought to an end between him and the Doctor. The "Mister" had been prefixed to his name, which had been omitted for the last three or four months in the friendly intercourse which had taken place between them; and then, though it had been done in the form of agreeing with what he himself had said, the Doctor had made his first complaint by declaring that no man had a right to regard his own moral life as isolated from the lives of others around him. It was as much as to declare at once that he had been wrong in bringing this woman to Bowick, and calling her Mrs. Peacocke. He had said as much himself, but that did not make the censure lighter when it came to him from the Doctor, getting up from his seat at the table, and throwing himself into an easy-chair, so as to mitigate the austerity of the position; "Let us hear the true story. So big a liar as that American gentleman probably never put his foot in this room before." Then Mr. Peacocke told the story. (pp. 83–85)

After questioning Mr. Peacocke, there is no doubt in Dr. Wortle's mind that the Peacockes are unfortunate victims of scoundrels and circumstance. Indeed, Dr. Wortle goes so far as to tell Mr. Peacocke: "I would have clung to her, let the law say what it might—and I think that I could have reconciled it to my God. But I might have been wrong, I might have been wrong. I only say what I should have done" (p. 88). Dr. Wortle assures Mr. Peacocke of his friendship, but he asks for time to consider what he should do, since it is unclear whether the Peacockes can remain at Bowick.

As he tells Mrs. Peacocke of his interview, Mr. Peacocke assumes that they must leave. He says they must go since "a man cannot isolate the morals, the manners, the ways of his life from the morals of others. Men, if they live together must live together by certain laws"

(p. 90). But Dr. Wortle is no ordinary man, and though his "first con-science" told him he owed his primary duty to his parish, his second duty to his school, and his third duty to his wife and daughter; his "other conscience" told him that Mr. Peacocke was more sinned against than sinning, "that common humanity required him to stand by a man who had suffered so much, and had suffered so unworthily" (p. 92). More-over, he is reminded that this is a man preeminently fit for his duties and that, if he is to lose him, he cannot hope to find a replacement his equal.[16]

Yet he does not make the decision without consultation. Mrs. Wortle is certain that they should be turned out, fearing what Mrs. Stantiloup and the Bishop will say. Dr. Wortle remains convinced, so he seeks counsel from Revd. Mr. Puddicombe, "a clergyman without a flaw who did his duty excellently in every station in life . . . one who would preach a sermon or take a whole service for a brother parson in distress, and never think of reckoning up that return sermons or return service were due to him" (p. 54); but whom Dr. Wortle does not quite like as he is a little too pious and given to asking troubling questions—e.g., "So Mr. Peacocke isn't going to take the curacy?" (p. 54).

Yet Dr. Wortle knows he can trust Mr. Puddicombe, for though he is apparently an unsympathetic man, he is not given to harshness. So with Mr. Peacocke's permission, Dr. Wortle tells Mr. Puddicombe the story. Mr. Puddicombe's response is that Mr. Peacocke has harmed Dr. Wortle by not telling him from the first all the facts and suggesting that they should have separated. As a result, Mr. Puddicombe main-tains that Dr. Wortle has no choice but to send them away. At the end of their conversation the Doctor thinks the man "a strait-laced, fanati-cal, hard-hearted bigot. But though he said so to himself, he hardly thought so; and was aware that the man's words had had effect upon him" (p. 100).

Troubled as he is about what he should do, a plan begins to unfold in the Doctor's mind. During his interview with Lefroy, Dr. Wortle has got the impression that though the brother had not been dead when the marriage between the Peacockes took place, he might now be so. If that is the case, then things may yet be put straight. So Dr. Wortle suggests to Mr. Peacocke that he should return to America with Lefroy to discover if in fact the brother is dead. Lefroy is willing to do so on the promise of a thousand dollars if he helps to document the truth of his brother's death. In the meantime, Mrs. Peacocke will continue to live at the school. The Doctor, of course, will have to bear all expenses of the expedition, but he is determined to have the matter resolved. Mr. Peacocke naturally accepts and leaves immediately with Lefroy for America.

Of course, this "solution" is no solution as far as the Doctor's reputation is concerned. The story will surely be told, and "all the world" will know that he has been protecting at his school a couple who lived together but were not man and wife. This occurs, and Dr. Wortle soon finds himself admonished by the Bishop, who feels "that the Doctor was the bigger man; and . . . , without active malignity, he would take advantage of any chance which might lower the Doctor a little, and bring him more within episcopal power. In some degree he begrudged the Doctor his manliness" (p. 114). Nor does Dr. Wortle receive support from Mr. Puddicombe, who sympathizes with his "generosity and kindness of heart," but not with "his prudence." He has even more difficulty with Mrs. Wortle, though he finally convinces her that she should periodically visit Mrs. Peacocke, since otherwise Mrs. Peacocke is completely isolated.

For my purpose I need not detail the plot further. Any reader of Trollope knows he wrote comedies and would expect all to be resolved happily. Mr. Peacocke's trip to America proved to be a trying adventure, though in the process we come to see Mr. Peacocke as a man of considerable courage and resourcefulness. For example, holding only an unloaded gun, he coolly blocks the attempt of a drunken Lefroy to rob and kill him. He does discover that the other Lefroy did die in San Francisco of delirium tremens. Moreover, from the still-living brother he learns that the husband returned to St. Louis and left again because the marriage was a "lark."

Back in England, however, things were not going nearly so smoothly for Dr. Wortle. As he anticipated, the news of the Peacockes is all that Mrs. Stantiloup needed to stir up a scandal about the school. Soon Dr. Wortle begins receiving cancellation notices from important families for the next term. Indeed, it begins to look as if he might have to consider closing the school.

Even worse, the affair soon gets in the local *Broughton Gazette*. Dr. Wortle again seeks the advice of Mr. Puddicombe as to how he should respond, but he receives no comfort, being told that everything the *Gazette* says is true, since the Doctor had in fact fallen into a "misfortune." He adds that Dr. Wortle should have expected the adverse reaction since in fact he has "countenanced immorality and deceit in a fellow clergyman in his diocese" (p. 142). Though denying such a charge and affirming that he has never come "across a better man than Mr. Peacocke," Dr. Wortle nevertheless comes to understand that he must hold his peace no matter how much he may be attacked.

This resolve is soon tested to the limit, however, as the London weekly, *Everybody's Business,* runs the story insinuating by a choice phrase that Dr. Wortle's behavior might be explained by his own attraction to the very handsome Mrs. Peacocke. This again brings the Bishop into action, writing to Dr. Wortle to suggest that he pay no more visits to Mrs. Peacocke until the matter is settled. The Doctor responds by admonishing the Bishop for paying attention to allegations made in such a paper. So furious is he with the Bishop that he even begins a lawsuit against the paper, which would mean dragging the Bishop into court to prove that Dr. Wortle has been injured. The Doctor knows that the Bishop has made a terrible mistake in writing to him and alluding to the article that he can use to "crush" the Bishop. At first he is inclined to do so, since his lawyer assures him that he certainly will win a settlement.

Yet "in the cool of the evening" our good Doctor, "combative but yet soft of heart," changes his mind. As he thought to himself, such a paper "is beneath my notice. What is it to me what such a publication, or even the readers of it, may think of me? As for damages, I would rather starve than soil my hands with their money. Though it should succeed in ruining me, I could not accept redress in that shape" (p. 168). Therefore, he refuses even the offer of the editor of *Everybody's Business* to print an apology, knowing that he is letting the Bishop escape by so doing.

So the Doctor is left with the possibility of losing everything, yet realizing he can do nothing else. In the meantime, Mrs. Peacocke has finally told her story to Mrs. Wortle, entirely winning her sympathy. Mrs. Wortle confesses to her husband that she now does not see how Mr. Peacocke could have acted other than he did in remaining with Mrs. Peacocke. To which Dr. Wortle responds:

> "It would have been very hard to go away if he had told her to do so. Where was she to go? What was she to do? They had been brought together by circumstances, in such a manner that it was, so to say, impossible that they should part. It is not often that one comes across events like these, so altogether out of the ordinary course that the common rules of life seem to be insufficient for guidance. To most of us it never happens; and it is

better for us that it should not happen. But when it does, one is forced to go beyond the common rules. It is that feeling which has made me give them my protection. It has been a great misfortune; but placed as I was I could not help myself. I could not turn them out. It was clearly his duty to go, and almost as clearly mine to give her shelter till he should come back." (p. 213)

Then the word comes by mail of Mr. Peacocke's success, and it is arranged for Mrs. Peacocke to meet him as soon as he returns and for Dr. Wortle to marry them. In the meantime, however, Dr. Wortle thinks that something must be done to make those who have been his enemies understand how the matter now stands—that is, as he has felt unjustly treated. He therefore drafts a letter to be sent after the wedding explaining that matters have now been put right and that he has no hesitation in reemploying the Peacockes.

Before sending the letter, however, he thinks to show it to Mr. Puddicombe. He does not intend to send him the letter since he has not interfered in the school and has on the whole acted as a friend. Moreover, the Doctor hopes he might finally gain some praise from Mr. Puddicombe, but is disappointed that Mr. Puddicombe dislikes the letter because "It does not tell the truth." For the truth is that Dr. Wortle condoned the Peacockes' living together when they were not man and wife. Mr. Puddicombe says, "I am not condemning you. You condoned it, and now you defend yourself in this letter. But in your defence you do not really touch the offence as to which you are, according to your own showing, accused. In telling the whole story, you should say: 'They did live together though they were not married;—and, under all circumstances, I did not think that they were on that account unfit to be left in charge of my boys' " (p. 257).[17]

So Mr. Puddicombe recommends the Doctor to say, "Nothing, not a word. Live it down in silence. There will be those, like myself, who, though they could not dare to say that in morals you were strictly correct, will love you the better for what you did." The Doctor turns "his face toward the dry, hard-looking man and showed that there was a tear in each of his eyes" (p. 258). Noting that "a man should never defend himself," Dr. Puddicombe then offers, if it would suit Dr. Wortle's plans, to go to London with him to assist at the marriage. Dr. Wortle agrees, goes home, and burns the letters. Soon, his school again enjoys the support of the noble families in England, and Dr. Wortle once again is honored as a man of courage and learning.

Why Barth Needs a Puddicombe

I am sure that Dr. Wortle would never be tempted to read Barth, and that if he had, he probably would have found him unintelligible. I suspect that Trollope, however, would have been much more sympathetic, and that Barth would well have liked *Dr. Wortle's School*. At least, I hope that Barth has read it by now, for what good is heaven if it does not give us the time to read all of Trollope's novels? In terms of this essay, however, it is interesting that many of Barth's suggestions about the nature of honor are confirmed in Trollope's novel.

Barth and Trollope alike see honor, finally, more as a quality of person, of character, than social recognition. Honor denotes that sense of self which is willing to risk social standing rather than abandon what is seen to be our duty. That is why Dr. Wortle cannot abandon Mr. Peacocke. It is a matter of honor since honorable people support one another, for without such support the risk is loss of honor. Therefore, Dr. Wortle, as he tells Mrs. Wortle, must do what he thinks he must, not only because he cannot do otherwise, but because it is his duty— that is, it is what he owes himself, society, and God. He acts honorably, combining humility with pride, just as Barth suggests is required of a person of honor.

Moreover, Barth and Trollope are acutely aware that most of the time we are not and should not be called to act in an extraordinary way to preserve our honor. Yet there is a sense in which both of them know that our ordinary lives, in order to be sustained as ordinary, require people who are capable of acting in an extraordinary way when they find it necessary. No doubt the recognition of such "necessity" depends greatly on the development of relationships and friendships based on respect such as that between Dr. Wortle and Mr. Peacocke.[18] For Trollope leaves no doubt that Dr. Wortle acts as he does because of his genuine admiration for Mr. Peacocke.

Trollope's novel also illumines Barth's contention that acting honorably may sometimes require us to appear to act against societal standards. Even though being honorable depends greatly on embodying the highest ideals of our society as well as having them mirrored in our friends, it is still the case, as we saw with Dr. Wortle, that we may have to act in a way that seems to be against the best wisdom of our society and friends. To do so is but to remind us, as Barth argues, that it is finally the honor of God that matters.[19] That such is the case does nothing to lessen the terror and loneliness occasioned by acting against the stream. Yet such loneliness can be confident, at least if we believe people like Dr. Wortle, who says that he thinks Mr. Peacocke's support of Mrs. Peacocke, as well as his own support of them, can be reconciled with God.

Barth and Trollope even seem to agree about how honor is to be defended. For the temptation is to try to relieve our loneliness by attacking those we believe are slandering us. Barth and Trollope obviously give little weight to the world of print, thinking that those whose judgments are formed there lack the means to be honorable, for they are not their own people. The only matters that matter are those determined by honorable people. That is why Dr. Wortle is so concerned with the Bishop, whose occupancy of that office means that he must be a gentleman. Dr. Wortle thinks that the Bishop should support him as he has supported the Peacockes, since that is the way gentlemen should act toward one another. Yet even Dr. Wortle comes to see that, finally, the only defense is to live confident that God will honor our actions if they deserve such honor.

So it seems that, rather than using Trollope as a foil to Barth, I have succeeded only in supporting Barth's account of honor. While I have no reason to be unhappy with that result, I think it is not the whole story. For while it is no doubt true that at one level Trollope's novel confirms Barth's analysis of honor, I think that in another way Trollope offers the kind of concrete account of honor that Barth's method seems to prevent. For example, ask yourself the question, "If you had to choose between recommending Barth or *Dr. Wortle's School* to a young person beginning to think about honor, which would you recommend?" I think that most of us would recommend Trollope for the very good reason that Trollope's people are real.

Put more directly, Barth simply fails to provide an account from where Wortles, Peacockes, and, most important, Puddicombes come. Missing from Barth's account of honor is the kind of societal ethos, the concrete community, that is capable of producing a Wortle. For example, we have no idea on the basis of Barth's account of how Wortle's natural aggressiveness, ambition, and passion result in a person capable of such loyalty and passion. Trollope makes no attempt to hide Wortle's high estimation of his own abilities and importance, exactly because Wortle finally does not hide them from himself. Wortle is honorable, not in spite of but because he would like to defend himself. Wortle is honorable because he is a man capable of recognizing that in many ways Mr. Peacocke is his superior, and yet he is wise enough to use those talents for service to himself and his school. What Barth fails to help us see is where such honesty comes from and how it is sustained. And note that this is not a "psychological or biographical" question, but rather a question of how Christian moral formation takes place.

Werpehowski is no doubt right to remind us that Barth was engaged in a project of conceptual description through which honor—as well as other moral qualities such as humility, justice, prudence—are theologically disciplined by the imagination. In his discussion of honor, Barth certainly denotes the sense of constancy necessary to have a character capable of being honorable. Yet he seems to negate his own insight by insisting that God can and does command us to act "out of character," insuring that our lives never exhibit God's honor. Barth is right to insist that an honorable person may be called by God to act against his or her society's sense of honor, but Barth uses that point to suggest that he or she in so acting may act against any and all human sense of honor. That seems to me an unintelligible claim.

Another way to put my criticism is to note that what is missing in Barth is Puddicombe. Puddicombe is the embodiment of Trollope's contention that honor is only possible in a society in which secrets are abhorrent. For only if we are able to live our lives openly can we avoid the manipulative and intrusive existence of *Everybody's Business*. By confessing that he hated secrets, Dr. Wortle, of course, was not suggesting that anyone had a right to know how often he and Mrs. Wortle had sex. Rather, he was suggesting that the health of a society depends on people who are unashamed of the way they live. Modern moral philosophy tries to underwrite such a commitment by its insistence that moral actions can be justified only when reasons can be given that are anyone's. But, ironically, that results in the creation of the kind of moral anonymity that destroys a society capable of sustaining Puddicombes. For impersonal principles, or even commands of God, are not sufficient to replace the flesh and blood of Puddicombes.

But flesh-and-blood Puddicombes are possible only because they draw on the flesh and blood of the church. The church is surely made up of sinners, but that is why the church appreciates the importance of the Wortles, Peacockes, and Puddicombes to help us through our muddles. Barth simply fails to provide any conceptual or empirical account of how honor requires the existence of such a community.[20] As a result, his account of honor is susceptible to an individualistic interpretation that his theological program is meant to counter.

Why Barth overlooked or failed to emphasize the importance of the kind of community that makes honor possible, I do not know. I do find it odd, however, given his struggle against totalitarianism. For no breeding ground is more rich for the development of totalitarians than that prepared by a society that encourages individuals to live lives of secrecy. Of course, it can be suggested that Barth was simply acknowledging the fact that we no longer live in societies in which honor is valued. But if that is the case, then I only can wonder why Barth failed in his discussion of honor to indicate the challenge confronting Christians—and even more the church—to be people of honor in such societies and times.

CHAPTER 3 ▼ WHY TRUTHFULNESS

REQUIRES FORGIVENESS

A COMMENCEMENT

ADDRESS FOR GRADUATES OF A COLLEGE OF

THE CHURCH OF THE SECOND CHANCE

Ian Bedloe, the hero of Anne Tyler's novel *Saint Maybe,* had not meant to say anything. He only had gone into the storefront church, whose plate-glass window bore the name The Church of the Second Chance, because he had been attracted by the hymns sung by the fifteen or so people he found inside. Yet he felt he just had to say something after he had uncontrollably laughed when a "sister," Lula, had asked the church to pray for her. It seems that Chuckie, her paratrooper son, had just died in Vietnam because he forgot to put on his parachute before he jumped. Ian had done shameless things before, but to laugh out loud at a mother's bereavement was perhaps one of the most shameless. Tyler continues her narrative:

> He wished he could disappear. He wanted to perform some violent and decisive act, like leaping into space himself.
> "No prayer is unworthy in the eyes of our Creator."
> He stood up.
> Heads swiveled once again.
> "I used to be—" he said.
> Frog in his throat. He gave a dry, fake-sounding cough.
> "I used to be good," he said. "Or I used to be not bad, at least. Not evil. I just *assumed* I wasn't evil, but lately, I don't know what's happened. Everything I touch goes wrong. I didn't mean to laugh just now. I'm sorry I laughed, Mrs. . . . ."
> He looked over at the woman. Her face was lowered and she seemed unaware of him. But the others were watching closely. He had the sense they were weighing his words; they were taking him seriously.

Ian's confession of sin, or at least of "wrong," derived from the recent death, a possible suicide, of his brother. His brother had married a young woman who had two children from a previous marriage. Ian often baby-sat for her and had come to suspect, even though she was pregnant, that she might be unfaithful to his brother. One night when Ian was sitting, she failed to return at the appointed time. As a result, Ian was unable to keep a date with his girlfriend, which meant he probably missed his first sexual opportunity. Asked by the awkward but intense Reverend Emmett if he had gotten a response to his prayer, Ian confesses:

> "Response."
> "Did you get a reply?"
> "Well, not exactly."
> "I see," Reverend Emmett said. He watched an aged couple assist each other through the door—the very last to leave. Then he said, "What was it that you needed forgiven?"
> Ian couldn't believe his ears. Was this even legal, inquiring into a person's private prayers? He ought to spin on his heel and walk out. But instead his heart began hammering as if he were about to do something brave. In a voice not quite his own, he said, "I caused my brother to, um, kill himself."
> Reverend Emmett gazed at him thoughtfully.
> "I told him his wife was cheating on him," Ian said in a rush, "and now I'm not even sure she was. I mean I'm pretty sure she did in the past, I know I wasn't *totally* wrong, but . . . So he drove into a wall. And then his wife died of sleeping pills and I guess you could say I caused that too, more or less . . ."
> He paused, because Reverend Emmett might want to disagree here. (Really Lucy's death was just indirectly caused by Ian, and maybe not even that. It might have been accidental.) But Reverend Emmett only rocked from heel to toe.
> "So it looks as if my parents are going to have to raise the children," Ian said. Had he mentioned there were children? "Everything's been dumped on my mom and I don't think she's up to it—her or my dad, either one. I don't think they'll ever be the same, after this. And my sister's busy with her own kids and I'm away at college most of the time . . ."
> In the light of Reverend Emmett's blue eyes—which had the clean transparency of those marbles that Ian used to call gingerales—he began to relax. "So anyhow," he said, "that's why I asked for that prayer. And I

honestly believe it might have worked. Oh, it's not like I got an answer in plain English, of course, but . . . don't you think? Don't you think I'm forgiven?"

"Goodness, no," Reverend Emmett said briskly.

Ian could not believe his ears. To be told he was not forgiven seemed to contradict everything he assumed about Christianity—"I thought God forgives everything." Reverend Emmett, agreeing, pointed out, "you can't just say, 'I'm sorry, God.' Why anyone could do that much! You have to offer reparation—concrete, practical reparation, according to the rules of our church." "Rules of our church," of course, was just the problem, for it was clear that this was no ordinary church, filled as it seemed to be with outcasts and misfits. For example, its members used only first names in church because, as Reverend Emmett told him: "Last names remind us of the superficial—the world of wealth and connections and who came over on the Mayflower."

Ian reasonably countered the suggestion that he had not been forgiven by observing, "but what if there isn't any reparation? What if it's something nothing will fix?" Reverend Emmett responded, using that "itchy" word, Jesus. Jesus "helps us do what you can't undo. But only after you've tried to undo it." Ian could not imagine what such an undoing would take. Reverend Emmett, however, was more than ready to tell him what he must do—he would have to begin by "seeing to the children."

"Okay. But . . . see to them in what way, exactly?"

"Why, raise them, I suppose."

"Huh?" Ian said. "But I'm only a freshman!"

Reverend Emmett turned to face him, hugging the stack of hymnals against his concave shirt front.

"I'm away in Pennsylvania most of the time!" Ian told him.

"Then maybe you should drop out."

"Drop out?"

"Right."

"Drop out of college?"

"Right."

Ian stared at him.

"This is some kind of test, isn't it?" he said finally.

Reverend Emmett nodded, smiling. Ian sagged with relief.

"It's God's test," Reverend Emmett told him.

"So . . ."

"God wants to know how far you'll go to undo the harm you've done."

"But He wouldn't really make me follow through with it," Ian said.

"How else would He know, then?"

"Wait," Ian said. "You're saying God would want me to give up my education. Change all my parents' plans for me and give up my education?"

"Yes, if that's what's required," Reverend Emmett said.

"But that's crazy! I'd have to be crazy!"

" 'Let us not love in word, neither in tongue,' " Reverend Emmett said, " 'but in deed and in truth.' First John three, eighteen."

"I can't take on a bunch of kids! Who do you think I am? I'm nineteen years old!" Ian said. "What kind of a cockeyed religion is this?"

"It's the religion of atonement and complete forgiveness," Reverend Emmett said. "It's the religion of the Second Chance."

Then he set the hymnals on the counter and turned to offer Ian a beatific smile. Ian thought he had never seen anyone so absolutely at peace.

This scene from Tyler's novel should help you capture what it means to graduate from Goshen College, a school of the Mennonite church. For graduations can be and often are a symbol of legitimation. You have finally made it. You have gotten your college degree, and now you are on the path to success in America.

You just have one big problem—you are graduating from Goshen College, a college sponsored by the Mennonite church. That means to the world you are about as odd as the Church of the Second Chance. From the world's perspective, it is something of a disability that your degree is from a strange little college in Goshen, Indiana, sponsored by the Mennonite church. If you want to make it in the world, you made a big mistake when you applied to Goshen College, and you may be even making a bigger mistake to graduate here. You are graduating from a storefront college.

Of course, you have earned your reputation for oddness for exactly the same reason that Reverend Emmett told Ian he was not forgiven. For Mennonites, after all, refuse to buy the idea that forgiveness is simply a matter of being told that God has forgiven us. Mennonites have been about reminding other Christians that forgiveness is a community process that makes discipleship possible. Indeed, the nature of discipleship as the hallmark of Mennonite life was determined by people who had learned that forgiveness was a practice of a community committed to the truthful worship of God.[1]

Anne Tyler helps us capture these complex relations between for-

giveness and reconciliation by telling Ian's story. For it is only in doing
what Reverend Emmett said he must do—that is, leave school and raise
those children for the next twenty years—that Ian comes to understand
his "sin." In the process he learns that forgiveness is the gifts that these
children bring to him through making him more than he otherwise
could possibly have been. He learns he must forgive as well as be forgiven, and by so doing he is able to claim the life he has been given as
his own.

Of course, the name you Mennonites have come to give this complex relationship among forgiveness, reconciliation, discipleship, and
truth is peace. For your pacifism is not based on some abstract principle
that all violence, whatever that is, is wrong in and of itself, but rather
peace names those practices and processes of your community necessary
for you to be a people of truth. It seems harsh, and even violent, to be
told that no matter how sorry we are for what we have done, we still
are not forgiven. Yet Mennonites know the truth of that because they
know they are seldom in a position to know the truth about their sin
until they have made their lives available to others in a manner through
which they might be taught the truth about themselves—particularly
in matters where the wrong done cannot be made right—which, in fact,
is the character of most matters that matter. That is why reconciliation
is so painful. It requires us to be ready to confront one another with the
truth so that we will be better able to name and confront those powers
that feed on our inability to make our wrongs right.

As Ian discovers, when you become a member of the Church of
the Second Chance it means that certain options simply are no longer
options for you. He is going to be a cabinetmaker, not a college graduate.[2] He is going to do that because being a cabinetmaker will give him
time to raise the children. When he tells his parents what he intends to
do, they are incredulous. They are not reassured when he reports that
the members of the Church of the Second Chance are going to help raise
the kids.

> "Ian, have you fallen into the hands of some *sect*?" his father asked.
>
> "No, I haven't," Ian said. "I have merely discovered a church that
> makes sense to me, the same as Dober Street Presbyterian makes sense to
> you and Mom."
>
> "Dober Street didn't ask us to abandon our educations," his mother
> told him. "Of course we have nothing against religion; we raised all of you

children to be Christians. But *our* church never asked us to abandon our entire way of life."

"Well, maybe it should have," Ian said.

His parents looked at each other.

His mother said, "I don't believe this. I do not believe it. No matter how long I've been a mother, it seems my children can still come up with something new and unexpected to do to me."

"I'm not doing this to *you*! Why does everything have to relate to *you* all the time? It's for me, can't you get that into your head? It's something I have to do for myself, to be forgiven."

"Forgiven for what, Ian?" his father asked.

Ian swallowed.

"You're nineteen years old, son. You're a fine, considerate, upstanding human being. What sin could you possibly be guilty of that would require you to uproot your whole existence?"

Reverend Emmett had said Ian would have to tell them. He'd said that was the only way. Ian had tried to explain how much it would hurt them, but Reverend Emmett had held firm. Sometimes a wound must be scraped out before it can heal, he had said.

Ian said, "I'm the one who caused Danny to die. He drove into that wall on purpose."

Nobody spoke. His mother's face was white, almost flinty.

"I told him Lucy was, um, not faithful," he said.

He had thought there would be questions. He had assumed they would ask for details, pull the single strand he'd handed them till the whole ugly story came tumbling out. But they just sat silent, staring at him.

"I'm sorry!" he cried. "I'm *really* sorry!"

His mother moved her lips, which seemed unusually wrinkled. No sound emerged.

After a while, he rose awkwardly and left the table. He paused in the dining room doorway, just in case they wanted to call him back. But they didn't. He crossed the hall and started up the stairs.

For the first time it occurred to him that there was something steely and inhuman to this religion business. Had Reverend Emmett taken fully into account the lonely thud of his sneakers on the steps, the shattered, splintered air he left behind him?

Ian had begun the process of being freed from the powers. Those powers often can come in the form of the love of parents who want their children to be successes. Of course, you and your parents already have had that conversation. They wanted you to come, or at least they let you come, to Goshen College. They knew you were going to be odd because they wanted you to be part of that continuing tradition of discipleship as reconciliation so that the world might know that we were intended to live peaceably with one another.

I know it is hard to remember on occasions like this how odd you are. But just think about it. First of all, you have a theologian—who, to put it kindly, has a controversial reputation—giving your commencement address. If Goshen College had any sense, they would have invited, like the University of Notre Dame, George Bush—or at least the governor of Indiana—to give this address. Administrators of Goshen College are obviously not politically savvy. Secondly, just think of what I am talking about. I am talking about forgiveness and reconciliation, and you are graduating from college. What does that have to do with graduating from college? From most colleges, not much, but I hope it has everything to do with your graduating from this college.

I know as an outsider to Mennonite life that I have a tendency to romanticize Mennonites. However, I have too many Mennonite friends to sustain many illusions about what it means to be Mennonite. I know the old joke—the only thing God does not know is how many orders of Catholic sisters there are and how many kinds of Mennonites there are. I even have met Mennonites who are New York Yankee fans. If you are going to be a Mennonite, you might as well join with me and be a Cub fan—Cub fans and Mennonites, after all, know faithfulness does not necessarily mean success.

Yet for all of your faults, I also know that the education you have received at Goshen College has been different. I teach in a university that is at the heart of the so-called PC controversy. Some fear that people will be forced to think what is only politically correct—that is, that they cannot say certain kinds of things about women, blacks, or gays. There is the fear that the curriculum will have introduced into it literature that does not meet the standard of the "classics" of something called "Western culture." The PC debate cannot help but appear in universities like Duke as a clash for power between interest groups. For without the narratives and practices of forgiveness and reconciliation, we are devoid of the resources to tell our diverse histories in a manner that contributes to a common purpose that we Christians call love.

Because you are a college of the Church of the Second Chance, you have such resources. After all, you have never been a college of the "mainstream," so the stories that many people find so oppressive have never been your story. You are descendants of a people who knew that the only thing which Catholics and mainstream Protestants could agree about is that it was a very good thing to kill the Anabaptists. You are a people who have been formed by a strange book called *Martyrs Mirror*.[3] You are a people who knew that (in spite of this country's celebration of something called freedom of religion), as nonviolent followers of Jesus Christ, you were tolerated because at best you were an ethnically quaint people. All of that made a difference for the education you received here. For political science is not taught at Goshen College the way it is taught at Duke, since political science at Goshen College is not at the service of nation-state ideologies. The history you learn is different because you know you are members of a community more determinative than that power called the United States of America. You have learned to distrust abstract claims about objectivity because you are part of the people of the Second Chance who learned long ago that such claims are used to silence the voices of dissent.

I knew, for example, that when I spoke at this assembly there would not be an American flag present.[4] You must remember, however, that this was a hard-won absence. The powers embodied in that flag are hard to resist. That you are able to resist them is the result of the sacrifices made by your mothers and fathers in the faith. But those accomplishments require equal, but perhaps different, sacrifices from you, as you must learn how to live as a people constituted by the practice of forgiveness.

For the power of the flag is, by necessity, violent.[5] It cannot be the nonviolent power of truthfulness that comes from the practice of reconciliation and forgiveness. Because there is no flag here, Goshen College is potentially a more truthful, and thus academically more interesting, educational institution than those that serve such flags. It is so because it is a college made possible and sustained by a people who know that God has made you odd. That is why you know there is no such thing as a "liberal arts education" in which knowledge is an end in itself. Rather, you know that you have been educated in an institution that constantly reminds you that any truth which is neither based on, nor serves, the practice of reconciliation, and thus "peace," cannot be anything other than demonic.

As graduates of the college of the Church of the Second Chance, you must remember, however, that the people who have made you possible do not understand Second Chance to be about only their own lives. For the Church of the Second Chance is the Second Chance for all the world. For the One who has made you a people of the Second Chance has done so that we might be a witness for the Second Chance that God has made possible for all people. As graduates of Goshen College, you have been given skills, cabinetmaking skills, that make you particular kinds of witnesses for the world.

As graduates of Goshen College, the church calls you to be agents of truth in a world of mendacity. Therefore, you must be the most political of people reminding this society of what a politics of truth might look like. For example, when George Bush nominated Justice Clarence Thomas for the Supreme Court, he had to say that Judge Thomas was the most qualified justice he could find. We know that is the politics of the lie. Someone like Justice Thomas should have been nominated for the Supreme Court because the United States is and continues to be a racist society. George Bush could not tell Americans that we need African Americans in such offices so that they might use their power to protect their people in this racist society. He could not say that, because Americans do not want to acknowledge that this is a racist society. We have not the skill to know how to live truthfully with such sin. That is a truth we lack the power to acknowledge because we do not want to pay the price that forgiveness requires, a forgiveness that would make reconciliation possible.

As graduates of the college of the Second Chance, you have been trained to have the power to call those in power to truth. Just to the extent you do that, you make it possible for all of us to be able, as Václav Havel puts it, to live in truth—thus, to live nonviolently. For unless we are able to tell one another the truth through the practice of reconciliation and forgiveness, we are condemned to live in a world of violence and destruction. As people of the Second Chance, we know that we in fact live in a violent world—a world that may be all the more violent when confronted by you who refuse to call that order, built on lies, peace. Yet as people of the Second Chance, we know that we can live with hope, even in that world, because we have been constituted by the practices of reconciliation and forgiveness that have made truth and, thus, peace possible. Go therefore into the world to be disciples of our savior Jesus of Nazareth who has made us Second Chance people. May God bless you as you so live.

PART II ▼ ENGAGEMENTS

CHAPTER 4 ▼ THE DEMOCRATIC

POLICING OF CHRISTIANITY

Democracy and the Death of Protestantism

Protestantism, at least the mainstream variety, is dying in America.[1] I prefer to put the matter more positively, that is—God is killing Protestantism in America, and we deserve it. I am not suggesting that the old-line Protestant denominations will suddenly disappear—people will keep coming to church long after it is clear that God is dead—but rather what survives as well as what replaces the mainstream denomination will have only tangential relationship to Christianity. Of course, such churches will describe themselves as Christian, but the extent to which they honor that description will be and is unclear.

Indeed, I think Harold Bloom is, on the whole, right to suggest:

> [the] American Religion, which is so prevalent among us, masks itself as Protestant Christianity yet has ceased to be Christian. It has kept the figure of Jesus, a very solitary and personal American Jesus, who is also the resurrected Jesus rather than the crucified Jesus or the Jesus who ascended again to the Father. I do not think the Christian God has been retained by us, though he is invoked endlessly by our leaders . . . with especial fervor in the context of war. But this invoked force appears to be the American destiny, the God of our national faith. The most Gnostic element in the American Religion is an astonishing reversal of ancient Gnosticism: we worship the Demiurge as God, more often than not under the name of manifest necessity. As for the alien God of the Gnostics, he has vanished, except for his fragments or sparks scattered among our few elitists of the spirit, or for his shadow in the solitary figure of the American Jesus.[2]

Thus, for most Americans, salvation cannot come through the community or congregation; rather, it is a knowledge that leads to freedom from "nature, time, history, community, and other selves."[3]

Bloom argues, therefore, that gnosticism has always been the hidden religion of the United States. I think, in spite of the counterintuitive aspects of his argument, this suggestion is wonderfully illuminating. It is particularly so just to the extent it helps make sense of the peculiar combination of Americanism and "conservative" forms of American Protestantism. Yet I think his account of the gnostic presuppositions inherent in American religiosity also describes the religious practices, sensibilities, and theological expression of liberal mainstream Protestantism. Indeed, it is my contention that the death of mainstream Protestantism has been self-inflicted, as that form of Christianity had to become "gnostic" in the name of supporting democracy. Bloom, of course, celebrates this transformation exactly because it so subtly kills the great enemy of gnosticism—that is, Christianity.[4]

For example, Leander Keck in *The Church Confident* exhibits a position widely held by American Protestants. As its title suggests, his book is meant to be a clarion call for the church to recover a sense of its own significance.[5] However, he criticizes the title, if not the substance, of the book that Will Willimon and I wrote called *Resident Aliens* because such an accent is not appropriate to the mainline churches.[6] As Keck puts it, "the image of 'resident aliens' is at best ambiguous, for while some resident aliens do participate in public life, many others merely cluster together to perpetuate the ways of 'the old country' " (76). In contrast, he calls for the church to play the role of public theologian—that is, "clarifying, affirming, interpreting, and scrutinizing the deepest impulses of our society, on the assumption that other kinds of Christians, as well as Jews, Muslims, those of other faiths, and those professing no religion, will do the same" (86).

To so participate in society, according to Keck, the churches must renounce the theocratic ideal. We cannot nor should we seek a "Christian America." Instead, our task as Christians is to develop a more secular view of politics. Rather we should come to see that politics is a struggle for power in order to rob politics of all sacralizing temptations. In other words, the great project of Protestant Christianity is to keep politics limited but still subject to moral judgment.

Keck notes that though this account of politics is rooted in specifically Christian convictions, it is expressible in and consistent with elemental moral values that are widely accepted. Cardinal Bernadin once said that "religiously rooted positions must somehow be translated into language, arguments and categories which a religiously pluralistic society can agree on as the moral foundation of key policy positions." If that be granted, then Protestant and Catholic theology should join in the quest for an adequate equivalent of natural law, difficult as this will be. Without something like natural law, the warrants for the moral judgments the churches make about the political process, or any other public matter, will have no influence on the public mind. (87)[7]

I call attention to Keck's account of these matters because he represents, as he acknowledges, what most mainstream Protestant theologians believe. It is, moreover, a belief that has been well worked out over the last century. Crucial to this set of convictions is the assumption that democratic societies and governments are the most natural expression of Christian convictions. The position prides itself on its modesty, but in fact lurking behind Keck's views lies a continuing Constantinian presumption that democratic social processes are the most appropriate expression of Christian convictions.[8]

Accordingly, Christians have learned to police their convictions in the name of sustaining such social orders. They cannot appear in public using explicit Christian language since that would offend other actors in our alleged pluralist polity. But if this is genuinely a pluralist society, why should Christians not be able to express their most cherished convictions in public? If we are in an age of identity-politics, why does the identity of Christians need to be suppressed?[9] Pluralism turns out to be a code word used by mainstream Christians to the effect that everyone gets to participate in the democratic exchange on his or her own terms, except for Christians themselves.[10]

Which is an indication that we have something strange going on in Keck-like justifications of Christian responsibility for the "public."[11] To illuminate at least some of the reasons why Christians take such an odd position, I want to introduce what I take to be the intellectual background of Keck's position—namely, the work of Walter Rauschenbusch and that of Reinhold Niebuhr. That Keck can assume his position is so "self-evident" is the result of a long history of Protestant Christians assuming that Christianity means democracy.

By concentrating on Rauschenbusch and Niebuhr, I do not mean to imply that the concordat established between Protestant Christianity and American democracy was primarily the product of intellectuals. In

his *The Democratization of American Christianity,* Nathan Hatch wonderfully illumines how evangelical Christianity in the process of Christianizing the nation democratized Christianity. As he notes:

> The canon of American religious history grows out of traditions that are
> intellectually respectable and institutionally cohesive. Yet American Prot-
> estantism has been skewed away from central ecclesiastical institutions
> and high culture; it has been pushed and pulled into its present shape by
> a democratic or populist orientation. At the very time that British clergy
> were confounded by their own gentility in trying to influence working class
> culture, American exalted religious leaders short on social graces, family
> connections, and literary education. These religious activists pitched their
> messages to the unschooled and unsophisticated. Their movements offered
> the humble a marvelous sense of individual potential and of collective aspi-
> ration. . . . Religious populism, reflecting the passions of ordinary people
> and the charisma of democratic movement-builders, remains among the
> oldest and deepest impulses in American life.[12]

Hatch notes the irony that these movements in Protestant Christianity toward democratization were usually led by people of profound
authoritarian bent. Thus, "the Methodists under Francis Asbury used
authoritarian means to build a church that would not be a respecter of
persons. This church faced the curious paradox of gaining phenomenal
influence among laypersons with whom it would not share ecclesiastical
authority" (p. 11). This issue is not insignificant for the case I wish to
make against those who would police Christian practices in the name of
democracy. For, ironically, in the process of providing Christian support
of democratic social orders, the church became unable to sustain itself—
in short, it became a "knowledge" rather than a church. By attending to
Rauschenbusch's and Niebuhr's understanding of the relation between
Christianity and democracy, I hope to throw light on why this outcome
was inevitable.

Walter Rauschenbusch on Democracy

The great social gospeler Walter Rauschenbusch was as enthusiastic
about democracy as he was unclear about its nature. Democracy for
Rauschenbusch was not an external social system with which Christianity must come to terms, but a system integral to the very meaning
of the Gospel. As he put it:

The conflict of the religion of Jesus with autocratic conceptions of God is part of the struggle of humanity with autocratic economic and political conditions. Here we see one of the highest redemptive services of Jesus to the human race. When he took God by the hand and called him "our Father," he democratized the conception of God. He disconnected the idea from the coercive and predatory State, and transferred it to the realm of family life, the chief social embodiment of solidarity and love. He not only saved humanity; he saved God. He gave God his first chance of being loved and of escaping from the worst misunderstandings conceivable. The value of Christ's idea of the Fatherhood of God is realized only by contrast to the despotic ideas which it opposed and was meant to displace. We have classified theology as Greek and Latin, as Catholic and Protestant. It is time to classify it as despotic and democratic. From a Christian point of view that is a more decisive distinction.[13]

Like many of the Protestant evangelicals who felt no strain be-tween their authoritarian leadership and their democratic aspirations, Rauschenbusch experienced none of the tension between his under-writing of the Victorian family and his commitment to the democratic ideal.[14] Indeed, he thought them to be closely allied since he assumed that democracy requires the flourishing of morally healthy families and that families flourish under democracy. This assumption continues in Reinhold Niebuhr and Jerry Falwell.[15]

Given his understanding of Jesus' contribution to the doctrine of God, it is not surprising that Rauschenbusch thought the church to be a democratic institution. That it is such is why it is disastrous when the church does not live up to its ideal. In *Theology for the Social Gospel* he argues, "the church, which was founded on democracy and brother-hood, had, in its higher levels, become an organization controlled by the upper classes for parasitic ends, a religious duplicate of the coercive State, and a chief check on the advance of democracy and brotherhood. Its duty was to bring love, unity and freedom to mankind; instead it created division, fermented hatred, and stifled intellectual and social liberty" (pp. 73–74).

The democratic character of Christianity Rauschenbusch thought but a continuation of the essential insight of Israel and, in particu-lar, of the Prophets. In *Christianity and the Social Crisis* he notes that the nomad tribes of Israel settled in Canaan and gradually became an agricultural people.

They set out on their development toward civilization with ancient customs and rooted ideas that long protected primitive democracy and equality. Some tribes and clans claimed an aristocratic superiority of descent over others. Within the tribe there were elders and men of power to whom deference was due as a matter of course, but there was no hereditary social boundary line, no graded aristocracy or caste, no distinction between blue blood and red. The idea of a *mesalliance*, which plays so great a part in the social life of European nations and in the plots of their romantic literature, is wholly wanting in the Old Testament.[16]

Not surprisingly, Rauschenbusch saw a strong similarity between Israel and America. Just as there was an absence of social caste and a fair distribution of the means of production in early Israel, so the same seemed true in the United States. "America too set out with an absence of hereditary aristocracy and with a fair distribution of the land among the farming population. Both the Jewish and the American people were thereby equipped with a kind of ingrained, constitutional taste for democracy that dies hard" (*Christianity*, p. 15).

Rauschenbusch's social and political theory was in like manner uncompromisingly democratic. The essential difference between saved and unsaved organizations is that one is under the law of Christ, the other under the law of Mammon. "The one is democratic and the other autocratic" (*Theology*, pp. 112–13). As is well-known, Rauschenbusch's primary concerns were with the transformation of our economic system. He even could say that the political order had been saved since it is now democratic. The task is now to save the economic realm through the institutionalization of worker cooperatives. "The co-operatives develop men and educate a community in helpful loyalty and comradeship. This is the advent of true democracy in economic life" (*Theology*, p. 112).

Though often accused of naïveté, Rauschenbusch thought he was simply exemplifying the best social science of the day. According to him, the new social sciences have discovered the plasticity of human society as well as the inherent organic character of social relations. For example, through the new biblical sciences and historical method we are being put in the position of the original readers of each book, thus making the Bible more lifelike and social.

We used to see the sacred landscape through allegorical interpretation as through a piece of yellow bottle-glass. It was very golden and wonderful, but very much apart from our everyday modern life. The Bible hereafter will be "the people's book" in a new sense. For the first time in religious history we have the possibility of so directing religious energy by scientific knowledge that a comprehensive and continuous reconstruction of social life in the name of God is within the bounds of human possibility. (*Christianity*, p. 209)

In short, as he says in *Theology for the Social Gospel*: "Where religion and intellect combine, the foundation is laid for political democracy" (p. 165).

One interesting aspect of Rauschenbusch's assumption that Christianity means democracy is his continuing presumption that Christianity is theocratic. Thus, in *The Righteousness of the Kingdom* he says that the Jewish ideal of life is that of "a righteous community ordered by divine laws, governed by God's ministers, having intercourse with the Most High, and being blessed by him with the good things of life" [17] (p. 80). The advent of Christ has not essentially changed this ideal, except now we see that its embodiment is democratic.

Rauschenbusch's account of the relation or, perhaps better, identification of Christianity and democracy appears naive, idealistic, even dangerous to those more attuned to "pluralism." He can write about *Christianizing the Social Order* without embarrassment. That Christianization meant for him democratization does little to assuage our sense that he is just not "secular" enough. He did not understand, as Keck understands, that Christians need to translate their explicit theological convictions into a third language. Rauschenbusch simply had not yet come to terms, as we must, with "pluralism." For that, we must turn to Reinhold Niebuhr.

Yet I suspect there remains more Rauschenbusch in most mainstream Protestants than they are willing to acknowledge. Nowhere is that more apparent than in their often unacknowledged agreement with Rauschenbusch's explicit anti-Semitic and anti-Catholic sentiments. For just to the extent that those traditions represent nondemocratic practices, they are rendered suspect. It is by no means clear that Niebuhr's more "realistic" justification of democracy is any less free of such judgments.

Reinhold Niebuhr on Democracy

Niebuhr's defense of democracy is most famously associated with *The Children of Light and the Children of Darkness*.[18] Though often read as a straightforward justification of democracy, Niebuhr meant his book to discipline what he considered the uncritical celebration of democracy occasioned by World War II. However, as Richard Reinitz observes in *Irony and Consciousness,* one of the ironies of Niebuhr's defense of irony as the interpretative key to American history is Niebuhr's general tendency to be uncritical of America in his *The Irony of American History*.[19] The same tendency, I think, is present in Niebuhr's "realistic" defense of democracy.

"Man's capacity for justice makes democracy possible, but man's inclination to injustice makes democracy necessary" (p. xi) is so familiar that we almost can miss its significance. Not only is it Niebuhr's contention that democracy needs a more realistic vindication, but now that vindication cannot come directly from Christian convictions about God and Christ, as we saw in Rauschenbusch, but rather must be based on a theological anthropology. Niebuhr was so successful in this respect that at least some who read him saw no need to assume the qualifier "theological" was necessary.[20]

Niebuhr, unlike Rauschenbusch, saw that democracy was the result of the bourgeois revolution and as such was an ideology of particular class interest. As he says at the opening of *The Children of Light and the Children of Darkness:*

> most of the democratic ideals, as we know them, were weapons of the commercial classes who engaged in stubborn, and ultimately victorious, conflict with the ecclesiastical and aristocratic rulers of the feudal-medieval world. The ideal of equality, unknown in the democratic life of the Greek city states and derived partly from Christian and partly from Stoic sources, gave the bourgeois classes a sense of self-respect in overcoming the aristocratic pretension and condescension of the feudal overlords of medieval society. The social and historical optimism of democratic life, for instance, represents the typical illusion of an advancing class which mistook its own progress for the progress of the world. (pp. 1–2)

That such is the case sets the problematic of Niebuhr's book. For if democracy is to survive, it requires a more adequate cultural basis that the optimistic philosophical justifications that can be provided by "children of the light." Note that Niebuhr's understanding of the ideological character of democratic presuppositions never makes him question the obvious superiority of democracy as a social system and government. In this respect he stands, in spite of his assumption that Rauschenbusch is a child of the light, in continuity with his Social Gospel forebear.

Niebuhr argues that democracy has profounder roots than those supplied by bourgeois developments. He says:

> Ideally democracy is a permanently valid form of social and political organization which does justice to two dimensions of human existence: to man's spiritual stature and his social character; to the uniqueness and variety of life, as well as to the common necessities of all men. Bourgeois democracy frequently exalted the individual at the expense of the community; but its emphasis upon liberty contained a valid element, which transcended its excessive individualism. The community requires liberty as much as does the individual; and the individual requires community more than bourgeois thought comprehended. Democracy can therefore not be equated with freedom. An ideal democratic order seeks unity within the conditions of freedom; and maintains freedom with the framework of order. (p. 3)

Democracy therefore is that form of society that best serves the vitalities of the human condition without undue constraint. Yet freedom cannot be unlimited, since the very vitalities that are creative can also be destructive. So democracies are justified by the creative balance they are able to maintain between order and justice. Applying these insights to the international arena, Niebuhr notes, "order will have to be purchased at the price of justice; though it is quite obvious that if too much justice is sacrificed to the necessities of order, the order will prove too vexatious to last" (p. 168).

The first task of any community, therefore, is to subdue chaos and create order. But the second task is implicit in the first insofar as the community must also try "to prevent the power, by which the first task is achieved, from becoming tyrannical" (p. 178). Niebuhr accordingly understands democracy primarily in procedural terms, since it would be against the very genius of democracy to be identified with any particular goods or institutions whose purpose it is to secure those goods. Thus, in the second most famous quote of *The Children of Light and the Children of Darkness*—"Democracy is a method of finding proximate solutions for insoluble problems" (p. 118).

Which, of course, sounds wonderful, but in the process one can almost forget that Niebuhr is as vague as Rauschenbusch about what democracy actually looks like. He can be vague about the actual mechanism of democracy because he simply assumed that something like American practice was the norm—for example, democratic voting, freedom of the press, rule of law. More important for Niebuhr than the actual mechanism is the necessity of any democracy to stay open to "the indeterminate possibilities of human vitality" (p. 63).

At the heart of Niebuhr's understanding of democracy, of course, is his insistence that behind every ideal lies self-interest. "There is no level of human moral or social achievement in which there is not some corruption or inordinate self-love" (p. 17). Therefore, democracy is that form of society and government that allows for the constant play between different self-interested groups. As he puts it in *The Self and the Dramas of History*:

> A free society derives general profit from the interested desires of particular groups, each group leaving a deposit of virtue in the community beyond its intentions and interests. The health and justice of the community is preserved, not so much by the discriminate judgment of the whole community, as by the effect of free criticism in moderating the pretensions of every group and by the weight of competing power in balancing power which might become inordinate and oppressive. Democracy in short is not a method which is effective only among virtuous men. It is a method which prevents interested men from following their interests to the detriment of the community—though there must of course be a minimal inclination for justice to furnish a base of community.[21]

Niebuhr's account of democracy as the mechanism for the constant readjustment of the balance of power between interest groups comported well with the developing theories of democracy in social science. In effect, Niebuhr's views could and did serve as a normative justification for what became known as "interest-group liberalism" as well as for balance-of-power models in international relations. However, in the process Niebuhr's account became associated with both the strength and weakness of those theories. For example, the inability of interest-group theories to account for any good in common also seems to bedevil Niebuhr's account. That Niebuhr's justification of democracy was well-received in such circles is surely partly because, whether rightly interpreted or not, it nicely underwrote the interest of rising elites and their accompanying intellectual theories.

Nowhere can Niebuhr's accommodation to the changing politics of America be better seen than in his difference with the Social Gospel concerning economic relations. Gone entirely is any attempt to democratize economic institutions or relations. Now the object is to qualify power that comes through property with the power that comes through politics. The "property issue" can never be "solved," but rather it must be continuously adjusted to new developments. "The economic, as well as the political, process requires the best possible distribution of power for the sake of justice and the best possible management of this equilibrium for the sake of order" (p. 118). Thus, Niebuhr justified the distinction between economics and politics, as well as the distinction between those two "disciplines," because "justice" now means the qualification of the economic forces through political control. While such a policy was perceived as liberal at the time, it remains a remarkably conservative approach. Often forgotten, the very creation of "issues" as the center of political debate, a position integral to Niebuhr's account, means that any radical questioning of the political order is seen as "apolitical." Politics becomes the attempt to constantly adjust the balance of power among interest groups.

On what basis, however, are the various equilibriums to be judged? Niebuhr answers

> that there are no living communities which do not have some notions of justice, beyond their historic laws, by which they seek to gauge the justice of their legislative enactments. Such general principles are known as natural law in both Catholic and earlier liberal thought. Even when, as in the present stage of liberal democratic thought, moral theory has become too relativistic to make appeal to natural law as plausible as in other centuries, every human society does have something like a natural law concept; for it assumes that there are more immutable and purer principles of justice than those actually embodied in its obviously relative laws. (p. 68)

What we constantly must be on guard against is how such natural law theories, which try to base principles on reason, invariably introduce contingent practical applications into the display of the principle (p. 72). For example, equality is a transcendent principle of justice and, thus, one of the principles of natural law, but no society can insist on absolute equality as a possibility. In particular, equality cannot override the ultimate transcendence of the individual over communal and social processes. Democracy is the name for the ongoing struggle to reconcile the freedom of conscience beyond all laws and the requirements of human community (p. 80).

Note that Niebuhr simply asserts that equality and freedom of the individual are the primary content of natural law. Why that should be the case he feels no need to explain. That he does not do so is but an indication that like Rauschenbusch he simply assumes that liberal social orders, with their commitment to freedom of the individual and equality, are normative for Christian presumptions about social relations. Therefore, the Christian quest for justice, which always stands under the judgment of love, becomes the unending task of helping liberal social orders reconcile freedom with equality.

Niebuhr was explicit that any attempt to sustain this democratic project required religious presuppositions. First of all, religion is the final resource against idolatrous national communities that fail to acknowledge the law that resides beyond their power in the conscience of the individual (p. 82).[22] Such respect, moreover, is the only hope we have of dealing with the problem of religious and cultural diversity. In short, Niebuhr thinks only a religious justification is possible to sustain the ethos necessary for democracy. As he says:

> Religious ideas and traditions may not be directly involved in the organization of a community. But they are the ultimate sources of the moral standards from which political principles are derived. In any case both the foundation and the pinnacle of any cultural structure are religious; for any scheme of values is finally determined by the ultimate answer which is given to the ultimate question about the meaning of life. (p. 125)

Niebuhr argues that there are three primary approaches to the problem of religious and cultural diversity: (1) the Catholic, in which religious diversity is overcome by attempting to restore the original unity of culture; (2) the approach of secularism, which attempts to secure unity through a disavowal of historical religions; and (3) a religious approach, which seeks to maintain religious vitality within the conditions of religious diversity (p. 126).

He recognizes the second option to be the operative one in our society. Indeed, he notes that toleration in religion probably could not have been achieved in modern democratic society without a decay in traditional religious loyalties. That creates the pathetic character of bourgeois tolerance that must regard itself as having universal validity just at the time such tolerance is being unmasked as the peculiar convictions of a special class. As a result, bourgeois secularism does not have the capacity to recognize that it is a covert religion.

Secular defenses of democracy become but a less vicious version of the Nazi creed. It is less vicious because secular justifications allow criticism of the creed's own life, which is thus prevented from becoming completely idolatrous. "The creed is nevertheless dangerous because no society, not even a democratic one, is great enough or good enough to make itself the final end of human existence" (p. 133).

The third solution to religious diversity is possible, though what must be acknowledged is the religious depths of culture as well as a high form of religious commitment. "It demands that each religion, or each version of a single faith, seek to proclaim its highest insights while yet preserving a humble and contrite recognition of the fact that all actual expressions of religious faith are subject to historical contingency and relativity" (p. 134). From many Jewish and Catholic perspectives, however, such an account of humility appears to be asking them to understand their convictions in terms laid down by Protestant liberal theology.

Therefore, democracy requires religious humility, which is the profound recognition of the difference between divine majesty and human creatureliness. According to Christianity, it is exactly our pride that would hide our conditioned character and is thus the quintessence of sin.

> Religious faith ought therefore to be a constant fount of humility; for it ought to encourage men to moderate their natural pride and to achieve some decent consciousness of the relativity of their own statement of even the most ultimate truth. It ought to teach them that their religion is most certainly true if it recognizes the element of error and sin, of finiteness and contingency which creeps into the statement of even the sublimest truth. (p. 135)[23]

So, ironically, Niebuhr's justification of democracy turns out to be a legitimation of Protestant liberalism.[24] His views appear less religiously specific than those of Rauschenbusch, but that is only because his account of Christianity has already been well-policed by the requirements of sustaining democracy as a universal achievement. His views in this respect are no less imperialistic than those of Rauschenbusch, for now

Judaism and Catholicism, if they are to be "profound" religions, must think of themselves as expressions of a more determinative human condition—that is, as a knowledge available to anyone. Only in this way do they become acceptable religions within the democratic marketplace. Thus, if democracy is a theory of conflict as Niebuhr suggests, it is a carefully controlled conflict in which the rules have been laid down by liberal political and theological presuppositions.

The continuing power of Niebuhr's views can be seen not only in Kecklike positions, but in sophisticated philosophical considerations like that of Robert Adams in "Religious Ethics in a Pluralistic Society." [25] Adams commends Niebuhr's views because of Niebuhr's perception of the inevitability of conflict in even the best of social orders. He rightly saw, according to Adams, that democratic social orders are a reasonably fair and honest, minimally coercive system for the nonviolent working through of social conflicts. Majority vote, the necessity of a loyal opposition, along with agreement on the constitution provide a reasonable space for different factions to achieve power.

Adams confesses that such a society cannot help but relativize religious faith. But such accounts of the faith are often simply nostalgic longings for a religiously homogeneous society. Therefore, by becoming home in democratic society, the church is simply being asked to give up Constantinianism. Yet what Adams fails to see is that Niebuhr's justification of democracy is but a form of Constantinianism in a liberal key. Though Niebuhr and Adams praise democracies' capacity to sustain conflict, in effect the conflict that democracy allows is well-policed. Nowhere is that more evident than in the exclusion from the politics of democracy of any religious convictions that are not "humble." [26] In the name of democracy, the church wills its death.

Do We, That Is, Christians, Have Any Alternative?

I have provided this background of Christian justifications of democracy because I am obviously extremely critical of them. I regard them as mystifications of the political process in which we find ourselves, and accordingly as failing to provide Christians with the skills of discernment to help us name those powers that rule us. In effect, the praise of democracy by Protestant Christians in the past has been only a justification for why we should rule. It now functions primarily to give Christians the illusion that we continue to rule, long after the practices of liberal societies have rendered our convictions as Christians puerile. In the name of supporting democracy, Christians police their own convictions to insure none of those convictions might cause difficulty for making democracy successful.

Does that mean I do not support "democracy?" I have to confess I have not got the slightest idea, since I do not know what it means to call this society "democratic."[27] Indeed, one of the troubling aspects about such a question is the assumption that how Christians answer it might matter. Such an opportunity of choice assumes that we are or should be rulers; that is, Christians are or should have the status that asking the question, "If you do not like democracy, then what form of government do you think best?" makes sense. Yet as Yoder points out in "The Christian Case for Democracy," that question represents an "established" social posture. It is a Constantinian question.[28]

In contrast to that posture, I would like Christians to recapture the posture of the peasant. The peasant does not seek to become the master, but rather she wants to know how to survive under the power of the master. The peasant, of course, has certain advantages since, as Hegel clearly saw, the peasant must understand the master better than the master can understand herself or himself. The problem with Christian justifications of democracy is not that alleged democratic social orders may not have some advantages, but that the Christian fascination with democracy as "our" form of government has rendered us defenseless when, for example, that state goes to war.

In this respect no aspect of democratic ideology has been more destructive to the church than the assumption that democracy is or should be that form of government in which "the people" rule. The empowerment of the "common man" has robbed the church internally of those forms of discipline through which people acquire the virtues that ironically may be of service to what people take to be democratic social orders. For, finally, the problem with American democracy is not the Congress, or the president, or the rule of law, or the market; the problem is simply the American people who believe, after two centuries of instruction, that at least in the realm of politics their task is to pursue their own interests. We are finding it hard to restrict that lesson to "politics," since nowadays people increasingly live it out in church and family.

Does that mean I am therefore an "elitist?" Am I committed to some account of hierarchy? Am I questioning the presupposition that freedom and equality are the fundamental principles of social life? The answer to each question is, "Yes." But that answer is not interesting, since such questions only make sense when contextualized by the polity in which one stands. The polity I serve is that which takes as its primary text of government—which Yoder describes not as a prescription but a provocative paradigm—Jesus' words at the last meal he shared with his disciples (Luke 22: 24–30):

> A dispute also arose among them, which of them was to be regarded as the greatest. And he said to them, "The kings of the Gentiles exercise lordship over them; and those in authority over them are called benefactors. But not so with you; rather let the greatest among you become as the youngest, and the leader as one who serves. For which is the greater, one who sits at table, or one who serves? Is it not the one who sits at table? But I am among you as one who serves. You are those who have continued with me in my trials; as my Father appointed a kingdom for me, so do I appoint for you that you may eat and drink at my table in my kingdom, and sit on thrones judging tribes of Israel.

If that is right, then the crucial question for Christians is not the justification of democracies but our relation with the Jews. For it is the Jews who rightly insist that salvation is not knowledge, is not a gnosis, but fleshly. To be saved is to be engrafted into a body that reconstitutes us by making us part of a history not universally available. It is a history of real people whom God has made part of the Kingdom through forgiveness and reconciliation. Only a people so bodily formed can survive the temptation to become a "knowledge" in the name of democracy. Only such a people deserves to survive.[29]

CHAPTER 5 ▼ CREATION AS APOCALYPTIC

A TRIBUTE TO WILLIAM STRINGFELLOW

with Jeff Powell

William Stringfellow never really quite fit. He is not really a theologian, but he had wonderful theological insights. He was not really a lawyer, though he certainly practiced the law. He was not really a social activist, though few did more on behalf of people who lacked power.[1] He tended to make everyone mad because he did not fit. For liberal Protestant social activists he sounded far too theological. Religious conservatives thought he sounded far too critical of America. That he did not fit is the reason (of course) that we like him.

The fact that Stringfellow did not fit has something to do with his theological perspective. For in many ways he was well ahead of his time in terms of being able to employ what we now call apocalyptic, and in particular the Book of Revelation, for informing his perception of the challenges confronting Christians today. We suspect that during String-fellow's lifetime many of his readers were simultaneously attracted and repelled by his apocalyptic language. On the one hand, Stringfellow seemed able to say things about, for example, the true character of the Great Society, American foreign policy, or the legal profession that few if any other critics could. On the other hand, Stringfellow's apocalypticism seemed overblown or even repellent. "Come on now," one almost instinctively wanted to reply, "there's a lot wrong with America, but the Beast of Revelation 13—that's going a bit too far, don't you think? Surely, you're exaggerating just a bit."

It was and is easy to explain discomfort with Stringfellow's apocalypticism as a reaction to his apparently unembarrassed use of mythical language. Conceptualizing Stringfellow's language as a primitive or poetic use of myth is a way of getting control of what he was saying, of fitting it into our neat intellectual categories. When Stringfellow tells us, for example, that "the principalities seem to have an aggressive, in fact possessive, ascendancy in American life,"[2] we can demythologize his words as a quaint or homiletic way of stressing the existence of corporate problems in American social life that require social engineering—Stringfellow as proponent of the welfare state. Stringfellow then can be located on the map of contemporary theological and political debate and invoked or disparaged according to the reader's preexisting predilections. In doing so, it is necessary, of course, to ignore Stringfellow's own clear belief that he was talking about the biblical "angelic powers and principalities [that] are fallen and are become demonic powers,"[3] not about the constructs of modern social and policy science. But that biblical imagery is just imagery, after all, not the social reality that even Stringfellow must surely have wished to address. Of course.

"Translating" Stringfellow's apocalypticism, we believe, is a means of evading what he was saying and avoiding what really disturbs the reader about him—the uncompromising character of his criticisms, his refusal to leave any common ground for dialogue (or put another way, his impolite insistence that the Gospel does not contain some broad space for hedging). If we do not find some way to translate his apocalyptic, we might be obliged to question our comfortable certainty that things are fundamentally okay (or at least well on their way to getting there) in American society. What is so remarkable about Stringfellow's use of apocalyptic is that he did not think it needed to be demythologized. Rather than seeing apocalyptic as an extravagant and overblown way of talking about matters that liberal politics and social science discuss more directly, Stringfellow was positioned in such a way that he could see how apocalyptic language was working to help us understand the way the world is. Stringfellow did not want to translate the language he used into some other language in order for it to be understood; instead, he wanted to help us see how apocalyptic language narrates our world in a manner that helps us not to be seduced by the world's ways of doing good. Stringfellow understood, we believe, that apocalyptic is the right mode of narrative for persons struggling as Christians to live in the kind of world in which we live.

By apocalyptic, Stringfellow did not mean speculative theories about the end of time, nor did he mean that apocalyptic was some kind of poetic expression that embodied the existential condition facing each person. Apocalyptic for him always was a way of reminding us of the intrinsically political character of salvation. Apocalyptic is not an unfortunate mythological excrescence on metaphysical and ethical truths; it is, instead, the truthful and unavoidable mode of language in which one must talk about a world that is created but fallen, that has been redeemed but does not acknowledge its Redeemer. The disavowal or explaining away of apocalypticism necessarily privatizes Christianity and converts the Christian hope for the coming of the Kingdom either into a symbol for liberal sociopolitical progress or into the ultimately gnostic speculations of "Rapture" theology about the future redemption of the privileged elect. Apocalyptic is Stringfellow's—and we believe the authentic Christian—mode of taking seriously Christ's Lordship over the public, the social, the political.

In particular, apocalyptic was Stringfellow's way of reminding us that history is not a seamless web of casual relations. In that respect, we think his arguments not unlike those of Wittgenstein, who wrote:

> The truly apocalyptic view of the world is that things do *not* repeat themselves. It isn't absurd, e.g., to believe that the age of science and technology is the beginning of the end for humanity; that the idea of great progress is a delusion, along with the idea that the truth will ultimately be known; that there is nothing good or desirable about scientific knowledge and that mankind, in seeking it, is falling into a trap. It is by no means obvious that this is not how things are.[4]

Both the "liberal" American academy and "conservative" American politicians are committed, of course, to the opposite proposition—that it *is* obvious that things repeat themselves, that the social world is a sealed network of causally determined functions, that ultimately there can be neither sin nor hope. As Wittgenstein also noted: "The insidious thing about the causal point of view is that it leads us to say: 'Of course, it had to happen like that.' Whereas we ought to think: it may have happened *like that*—and also in many ways."[5] Stringfellow's apocalypticism enabled him—and demands of us—that we reject the "causal point of view" for a construal of "how things are" as the creation of the God who cannot be excluded from creating new possibilities for our lives through our lives.

The practical consequences of accepting the implicit determinism of liberal dogma are predictable: shallow optimism followed by the exhausted hopelessness that underlies contemporary American political discussion. Stringfellow's rejection of the self-contained social universe presupposed by liberal politics and social science enabled him to see through the pretensions of the politicians and to reject the pieties of their advisors. The practical consequences of accepting his apocalyptic reading of history are a truthfulness beyond "realism" and a hope beyond optimism. "A Christian lives politically within time, on the scene of the Fall, as an alien in Babylon, in the midst of apocalyptic reality. [But] a biblical person lives politically, on the identical scene, as member and surrogate of Christ's Church, as a citizen of Jerusalem, the holy nation which is already and which is vouchsafed."[6]

Stringfellow's adoption of an apocalyptic narration of the world is rather surprising, given his location within the world of legal practice. Anything Americans would recognize as "law" is, of course, conservative in the sense that its fundamental social role is to protect the status quo. American law itself is doubly so. The rhetoric of the law asserts the sovereignty of a kind of practical and intellectual determinism: the correct resolution of today's problems must be portrayed as logically entailed by yesterday's decision or last century's statute. As L. H. LaRue (another iconoclastic lawyer) has argued, the substance of American law, even in times of change, is shaped by the overriding goal of preserving "the social order in which [lawyers and judges] had a stake and to which they pledged loyalty."[7] Much of the current angst within American law schools is the product of the recognition, by academic lawyers and law students who wish to see the law as a means of liberal social change, of the determinism built into law as an intellectual construct; the widely publicized signs of discontent in the practicing bar reflect practitioners' dawning awareness that the successful among them are highly paid residents of gilded prisons.[8]

Stringfellow's apocalyptic perspective protected him from any liberal optimism about the law's capacity for achieving true justice, and thus protected him from the despair that follows quickly when that optimism is shattered by reality. For Stringfellow, the law could be at most another of the powers and principalities, and the lives it seeks to freeze into predetermined patterns were necessarily open to the intervention of the eschatological Lord who alone creates true justice. With the pretensions of the law shattered, Stringfellow was freed to employ the crafts of the lawyer as witness and as servant, without the crushing need to be "effective" or to achieve "results." It became possible for him to practice law humanly, even in the face of great difficulty, and thus become effective in the only sense that Christians are called on to worry about.

Those who emphasize apocalyptic often are accused, of course, of failing to do justice to God as creator. Despite the apparent centrality of creation to Christian faith, as actually employed, creation talk often serves as a means for the domestication of the Gospel. Appeals to creation often are meant to suggest that all people, Christian or not, share fundamental moral commitments that can provide a basis for common action. These appeals to creation too often amount to legitimating strategies for the principalities and powers that determine our lives. This type of creation talk is fundamentally false to the biblical profession of faith in the Lord of creation because it implicitly underwrites the lordship of the principalities and powers. Such powers are all the more subtle exactly to the extent that we either think of them as myths or believe that we create them rather than are determined by them.

What is so remarkable about Stringfellow's apocalyptic construal of principalities and powers is how they are rightly understood to be part of God's created order but are now seen through the eyes of the Gospel in a way that we acquire power to resist them. Thus, he reminds us in *Free in Obedience* that "a principality, whatever its particular form and variety, is a living reality, distinguishable from human and other organic life. It is not made or instituted by men, but, as with men and all creation, made by God for his own pleasure."[9] Of course, it is exactly because the principalities and powers are God's good creation that their perversion is all the more terrifying. We mistake the powers for God, we worship the powers rather than God, with the result that they and we are consigned to the power of death.[10]

No pacifist himself, Stringfellow saw the worship of war through the power of the modern nation-state clearly as one of the most determinative signs of the perversion of the powers, but he identified the violence of war as but one of the "stratagems of the demonic powers" that aim at "the dehumanization of human life."[11] In "this fallen world as men know it in their ordinary lives . . . the ascendant reality, apart from the reality of God himself, is death."[12] Stringfellow rightly discerned the dominion of death in American society—in the lies of the government and of Madison Avenue, the false claims to expertise of business and professions, and in the trivialization of American public life. "All of these snares and devices of the principalities represent the reality of babel, and babel is that species of violence most militant in the present American circumstances." [13]

Therefore, Stringfellow saw God's creation caught in a dramatic and final battle. Apocalyptic is but the name we give for the struggle to live in accordance with God's good creation as those who no longer have to fear death, baptized as we are into Christ's death and resurrection. [14] We believe that is why Stringfellow was able to challenge our liberal idealism which assumed that if we could just get people of goodwill to work together, somehow we could solve our social problems. He knew that any such "solution" would be far too pale a response to the powers we confront. Yet exactly because he knew we were part of an apocalyptic drama, he never gave up hope despite his clear-eyed vision of the terrors of the struggle. The question was not whether as Christians we were going to accomplish much, but whether we were going to live faithfully. As he put it in *Free in Obedience,* "the Christian, and the whole company which is the Church, need not worry about what is to be done. The task is, rather, to live within the victory of all that has been done by God. For the Christian the issue is not so much about what she/he does in this world but about who she/he is in this world. There is no serious distinction between who the Christian is and what he does, between being and doing. These are virtually the same." [15]

As a person identified with political radicalism, Stringfellow's sense of the importance of the church might well seem odd. But of course that was part and parcel of his apocalyptic perspective. Stringfellow knew that the world could have a glimpse of the Kingdom of Christ only in seeing the gathered congregation. He wrote that "the only apparent image of the community reconciled with God in which the members are also reconciled to themselves, to each other, to all men, and to all of creation" is the witness of the worshiping community. Only that community for Stringfellow could give evidence of existence of God's Kingdom in the world. "No ambition or attainment of political, economic, or moral power by the church can substitute for the worshipping community as a portrait of the kingdom. On the contrary, the worldly pretension of the church is mainly to bewilder the world and hinder its recognition of the true society living already in this world in Christ." [16]

So the church becomes the necessary correlative of an apocalyptic narration of existence. It is the eucharistic community that is the epistemological prerequisite for understanding "how things are." Only as we stand in the reality of the Eucharist can we see that "the causal point of view" is not the final truth of our lives. Instead, we can see that our world is not determined by the powers, that we do not have to submit to the necessities that we are told are unavoidable. Stringfellow's social witness of presence, which could appear conservative at first glance, was in fact radical precisely because he refused to accept the presumption that the way things are is the way they have to be. Rejecting the suggestion that Christ's "resistance and renunciation of temptation to political authority" on Palm Sunday counsels political quietism, Stringfellow wrote:

> Quite the contrary, it is the example of utter and radical involvement in the existence of the world, an involvement which does not retreat even in the face of the awful power of death. The counsel of Palm Sunday is that Christians are free to enter into the depths of the world's existence with nothing to offer the world but their own lives. And this is to be taken literally. What the Christian has to give to the world is his very life.[17]

Stringfellow thus was careful to distinguish the ministry of witness, which is the distinctively Christian and evangelical task, with social good works. He was critical, for example, of those who saw the purpose of ministry in urban slums to be the improvement of residents' education, the renovation of their housing, the location of jobs, the alleviation of the drug problem, and other forms of social action. All of these are good things to do, but it is not as if you have to do them before you preach the Gospel. Stringfellow, who spent much of his life engaged in hard work directed toward just such social goals, flatly rejected the idea that the Gospel could be preached and received only by people in those slums after their "other" problems were addressed. Instead, those who live in such settings are ready to hear the Gospel because they know their lives are subject to powers over which they have no control. Because they understand the political reality of their lives, they grasp more easily the truth that without there being an alternative community that rightly challenges the powers with the truth of the Gospel, there can be no hope.

Stringfellow observed in *An Ethic for Christians and Other Aliens in a Strange Land* that those who learned to resist the Nazis are often romanticized. We wonder why they took the risks they did for a cause that seemed to lack any chance of success. The answer, Stringfellow concluded, was an unromantic human truth as relevant to American urban decay as to the anti-Nazi resistance. "Why did these human beings have such uncommon hope? And the answer to such questions is, I believe, that the act of resistance to the power of death incarnate in Nazism was the only means of retaining sanity and conscience. In the circumstances of the Nazi tyranny, resistance became the only human way to live."[18] The only human way to live in the American slum, similarly, is the life of resistance, a life that ultimately can have a social and political location only in the worshiping community.

The human way to live for Stringfellow is essentially a life of truth. The means by which one resists the lies of Babel, by which one confronts and resists the powers, is first and foremost by calling them to the truth of the Gospel. He quoted Aleksandr Solzhenitsyn's Nobel prize address: "Let us not forget that violence does not exist by itself and cannot do so; it is necessarily interwoven with lies. Violence finds its own refuge in falsehood, falsehood its only support in violence. Any man who has once acclaimed violence as his method must inexorably choose falsehood as his principle."[19] Truth is the way of apocalyptic resistance.

We therefore should not be surprised that Stringfellow located the most determinative political form of the church's resistance to the powers in the charismatic gifts of the Spirit. The charismatic gifts themselves are powers (in a somewhat different sense), and only such powers are sufficient to confront the principalities. "These gifts dispel idolatry and free human beings to celebrate Creation, which is, biblically speaking, integral to the worship of God. The gifts equip persons to live humanly in the midst of the Fall. The exercise of these gifts constitutes the essential tactics of resistance to the power of death."[20] So the charismatic gift of glossalia, a gift of eschatological speech, is necessary if the church is to speak truthfully to this world. At Pentecost the ecstatic utterances of the Spirit-filled followers of Christ broke the bonds of nation, culture, race, language, ethnicity. Such ecstatic worship is needed by the church today if the scandal of national vanity is to be challenged. For it is the ecstatic utterance that witnesses to the vitality of the word of God against the blasphemies of this world.[21]

William Stringfellow's apocalypticism, we believe, bears a crucial message for Christians and other aliens in the strange land of the United States at the turn of the millennia. The nonapocalyptic vision of reality that dominates American public life tempts American Christians, like other Americans, to accept, with despair and relief, the inevitability and thus the goodness of things as they are. Christians, unlike other

Americans, ought to know better. Our world lies under the shadow of the principalities and powers, but they are not its legitimate or ultimate lords. Our helplessness in their hands is merely one of the lies by which they deceive and seek to control us. Against their deceptions, the apocalyptic perspective invokes God's truth. Another of the charismatic gifts, exorcism, typifies the resistance of truth to falsehood: in the Lord's Prayer, the quintessential exorcism, we pray to be delivered from the evil one and have faith that it can be done because we know God's victory is secure and that now we live in the time between the times.

CHAPTER 6 ▼ CAN A PACIFIST

THINK ABOUT WAR?

The question laid before John [of the Book of Revelation] by his vision of the scroll sealed with seven seals is precisely the question of the meaningfulness of history. This is a question that, the vision says dramatically, cannot be answered by the normal resources of human insight. Yet it is by no means a meaningless question or one unworthy of concern. It is worth weeping, as the seer does, if we do not know the meaning of human life and suffering.

Speaking more generally, let us affirm, as numerous historians of philosophy are arguing, that to be concerned about history, to assume that history is meaningful, is itself a Judeo-Christian idea. The concern to know where history is going is not an idle philosophical curiosity. It is a necessary expression of the conviction that God has worked in past history and has promised to continue thus to be active among men. If God is the kind of God-active-in-history of whom the Bible speaks, then concern for the course of history is itself not an illegitimate or an irrelevant concern. No mystical or existentialistic or spiritualistic depreciation of preoccupation with the course of events is justified for the Christian.

But the answer given to the question by the series of visions and their hymns is not the standard answer. "The lamb that was slain is worthy to receive power!" John is here saying, not as an inscrutable paradox but as a meaningful affirmation, that the cross and not the sword, suffering and not brute power determines the meaning of history. The key to the obedience of God's people is not their effectiveness but their patience (13:10). The triumph of the right is assured not by the might that comes to the aid of the right, which is of course the justification of the use of violence and other kinds of power in every human conflict; the triumph of right, although it is assured, is assured because of the power of the resurrection and not because of any calculation of causes and effects, nor because of the inherently greater strength of the good guys. The relationship between the obedience of God's people and the triumph of God's cause is not a relationship of cause and effect but one of cross and resurrection.

—John Howard Yoder, *The Politics of Jesus*

On Representing Christian Nonviolence

For me to represent the tradition of Christian nonviolence feels odd. To put it in stronger language, I feel something of a fraud. I am, of course, a pacifist. I am even a member of a church that seems to be against war. For example, in Article 16 of the United Methodist Church's Confession of Faith, my church affirms: "We believe war and bloodshed are contrary to the gospel and spirit of Christ." Yet the *Book of Discipline* also says: "We support and extend the Church's ministry to those persons who conscientiously choose to serve in the armed forces or to accept alternative service."[1] Like many people who take the wedding vows with their fingers crossed, the Methodists seem to want to have it both ways.[2] I do not want to have it both ways. I want my church to be consistently pacifist, yet the fact that I am a Methodist indicates something of the ambiguity of my pacifism.

I became a pacifist primarily for intellectual reasons. Thus the ambiguity of my position: for, as I will try to show, any compelling account of Christian nonviolence requires the display of practices of a community that has learned to embody nonviolence in its everyday practices.[3] Therefore, as one intellectually committed to nonviolence, I distrust my own ability to provide a fair presentation of it.

My concern is not simply "personal," but it has to do with the problem of how one describes Christian nonviolence. For I must resist the idea that nonviolence or pacifism is a clear and self-contained position that can be usefully contrasted to just war, "realism," and other alternatives that appear as "theories" about the ethics of war. Indeed, the very reason I became a pacifist was because I awoke, through John Howard Yoder's help, from the dogmatic slumber, induced by Reinhold Niebuhr, that pacifism was just such a theory.

Like most Protestant liberals, I had assumed that pacifism was a position about violence and war that was meant to be intelligible to anyone. This pacificism was, of course, the kind that characterized Niebuhr's own thinking about war early in his career. Niebuhr rightly subjected this optimistic and naive account of nonviolence to a withering critique, thus convincing many of us that pacifism was not—nor could it be—a defensible position for anyone concerned with the responsible use of power.

Yoder's account of Christian nonviolence is not, however, so easily critiqued. For what Yoder made me see is that the Christian commitment to nonviolence is not separable from the very structure of Christian theology and, even more, Christian practice. That is why I began with the long quotation from *The Politics of Jesus*, as it makes clear to what extent Christian nonviolence involves extraordinary claims about the nature and telos of history—or as I would prefer, providence. That nonviolence cannot be isolated or abstracted from fundamental theological claims makes the problem of representing it more difficult than simply my own personal and intellectual limits.

For example, one cannot begin, as critics and defenders of pacifism so often try to do, by asking if the New Testament is a pacifist text. To give such a question legitimacy presupposes that the questioner and the one expected to answer share an appropriate understanding of pacifism. Yet the very assumption that such a shared understanding is possible is rendered problematic by the kind of nonviolence that Yoder has shown us is characteristic of Christians. Indeed, note how our grammar itself betrays us, since in the last sentence it appears that I might know what nonviolence is, separate from the qualifier, Christian.

Therefore, one cannot show that Christians are committed to nonviolence on the basis of this or that text of Scripture. That limitation does not mean that texts are unimportant or that some texts may not be particularly significant for learning how to live nonviolently. But no account of Christian nonviolence can be justified by any particular biblical text or group of texts. The text of the Bible in and of itself does not require pacifism. Rather, only a church that is nonviolent is capable of rightly reading, for example, Romans 13.[4] It is not an accident that Yoder, in his *Christian Attitudes to War, Peace, and Revolution: A Companion to Bainton*,[5] does not deal with the Bible until the book's last chapters. You can display the Bible only after you have told the history.

Equally problematic from this perspective are typologies—crusade, pacifism, and just war—developed by Roland Bainton in *Christian*

Attitudes Toward War and Peace.[6] The heuristic value of such typologies hides from us the complexity of Christian nonviolence (as well as the multivalence of violence). This concealment is not only because Bainton held to the kind of Constantinian liberal pacifism that I think is so doubtful, but more significantly such typologies result in a peculiarly ahistorical reading of Christian nonviolence. For the typology makes it appear that the three types are simply "there." Each, it seems, necessarily exemplifies how Christians can, have, or should think about war and/or violence. Yet that very assumption relies on the notion that we have a clear idea of what war and/or violence might be, apart from the practices of a community of nonviolence.

This is not the place to mount a full-scale critique of Bainton, but it is interesting to note that he begins his book by suggesting that for the first three hundred years of the church, Christians had no "politics." "Politics" come only after the Constantinian settlement. Confronted only then by the problem of war, Bainton argues, Christians discovered that they had no specifically Christian ethic of war. In such a circumstance the only alternative for Christians was to borrow ideas about peace and war from Judaism and the classical world, most notably, from Stoicism.[7] Bainton, of course, is simply repeating Ernst Troeltsch, but that he does so only confirms my contention that such accounts of Christian nonviolence do not do justice to the embeddedness of pacifism as a practice of the church.

In contrast to Bainton's (and Troeltsch's) account of pacifism, Yoder argues that Jesus had a politics that was embodied in the church. Yoder does so to challenge the presumption that Jesus' Lordship is but an apolitical ideal. Rather, as the proclaimer of the Kingdom, Jesus makes nonviolent resistance not only a possibility but a reality for those who are called to be his disciples. We are asked by Jesus to follow him to the cross. That cross,

> the believer's cross, is no longer any and every kind of suffering, sickness, or tension, the bearing of which is demanded. The believer's cross must be, like his Lord's, the price of his social nonconformity. It is not, like sickness or catastrophe, an inexplicable, unpredictable suffering; it is the end of a path freely chosen after counting the cost. It is not, like Luther's or Thomas Muntzer's or Zinzendorf's or Kierkegaard's cross or *Anfechtung*, an inward wrestling of the sensitive soul with self and sin; it is the social reality of representing in an unwilling world the Order to come.[8]

Christian nonviolence for Yoder is therefore unintelligible apart from Christological and ecclesiological presuppositions. Yet those very presuppositions are political exactly because they create and are created by a different polity. For you cannot know who Jesus is without the kind of community he gathered around him, since there is no Jesus without the church. Jesus thus called into existence a society that was voluntary, a society into which you could enter only by repenting and pledging loyalty to its King. It was a society mixed in its composition—religiously, law abiders and law deniers, rich and poor. In calling such a society into existence, moreover, he gave his followers a new way to live:

> He gave them a way to deal with offenders—by forgiving them. He gave them a new way to deal with violence—by suffering. He gave them a new way to deal with money—by sharing it. He gave them a new way to deal with problems of leadership—by drawing upon the gift of every member, even the most humble. He gave them a new way to deal with a corrupt society—by building a new order, not smashing the old. He gave them a new pattern of relationships between man and woman, between parent and child, between master and slave, in which was made concrete a radical new vision of what it means to be a human person. He gave them a new attitude toward the state and toward the "enemy nation."[9]

From this perspective, Christian nonviolence or pacifism does not name a position; rather, it denotes a set of convictions and corresponding practices of a particular kind of people. Of course, there may be continuities and similarities between Christian nonviolence and other forms of pacifism. Thus, Yoder goes to great lengths in his *Nevertheless: Varieties of Religious Pacifism* to delineate the strengths and weaknesses of eighteen types of pacifism. Yet he notes that the pacifism of the messianic community depends on the confession that Jesus is the Christ, since it depends on the conviction that the *kind* of nonviolence incumbent on Christians is rooted in Jesus' resurrection. Yoder does not deny the name "Christian" to the other forms of pacifism that he analyzes, but he observes that his account of Christian nonviolence is the "only position for which the *person* of Jesus is indispensable. It is the only one of these positions which would lose its substance if Jesus were not Christ and its foundation if Jesus Christ were not Lord."[10]

It is fascinating to compare and contrast Yoder's account of Christian nonviolence with that of Reinhold Niebuhr. In many ways they are similar, as they share a profound realism about the character of human existence and the extent to which our lives are constituted by violence.

Niebuhr, in the interest of making Christians act "responsibly" in the world, clearly saw that Jesus could not be followed.[11] Of course, it is not so much Jesus as Jesus' ethic that could not be followed, since Niebuhr had no place for Yoder's account of Jesus as the eschatological messiah. Yet Yoder does not need to follow Niebuhr's withdrawal from Jesus because, unlike Niebuhr, he does not separate Jesus from the church. For Yoder, contrary to Niebuhr, a society exists that is more moral than the individual. Indeed, it is exactly that society that makes nonviolence possible:

> When we speak of the pacifism of the messianic *community,* we move the focus of ethical concern from the individual asking himself about right and wrong in his concern for his own integrity, to the human community experiencing in its life a foretaste of God's kingdom. The pacifistic experience is communal in that it is not a life alone for heroic personalities but for a society. It is communal in that it is lived by a brotherhood of men and women who instruct one another, forgive one another, bear one another's burdens, reinforce one another's witness.[12]

The strong Christological center of Yoder's account of Christian nonviolence can give the impression that he thinks that Jesus and the church are in deep discontinuity with Judaism, but he assumes exactly the opposite. Once Christian nonviolence is not made into a "position" separable from the practice of a community, Christianity begins to look a good deal like Judaism.[13] For it is the Jews who have always had to learn how to live out of control. We should not, therefore, be surprised to discover that the question "Can the Christian or the Jew participate in war?" looks wholly different as soon as it is asked by those who assume that because of the kind of people they are, Christians and Jews already exist in tension with the wider society. Thus, in *Christian Attitudes to War, Peace, and Revolution* Yoder observes:

> The ethics of the Jews can be generally characterized as never justifying violence, as making much of frequent nonviolent martyrs who would not fight back against their persecutors, because it might be that God himself is the one who is chastising them at the hand of the persecutors, and because only God can save. It is a story of frequent emigration and occasional rare prosperity and privilege after the model of Joseph and Daniel. Judaism successfully kept its identity without ever using the sword; kept its community solidarity without ever possessing national sovereignty. In other words: Judaism through the Middle Ages demonstrated the socio-

logical viability of the ethic of Jesus. Judaism in terms of actual ethical performance represents the most important medieval sect living the ethic of Jesus under Christendom. Jews are dispensed from becoming "Christian" because of the racism and the anti-Judaism of official Christianity. The story thereby demonstrates, without wanting to, that the way to be a Christian sectarian minority is to live without the sword.[14]

By briefly presenting Yoder's account of Christian nonviolence, I have tried to represent the kind of position I think is theologically defensible. As I indicated at the beginning, I have been attracted to Yoder's account because I think he rightly shows why any account of nonviolence for Christians cannot be abstracted from practices that are Christologically shaped. In that respect, I think that part of the problem of many of those attempting to do Christian theology today is they want to maintain a "high" Christology with a Niebuhrian social ethic.[15] Niebuhr was more honest, seeing that such a combination simply will not work.

One of the great difficulties in representing an account of Christian nonviolence such as Yoder's is that you are always playing by your opponents' rules and on their playing field. For example, one of the first responses to such an account of Christian nonviolence is that it surely does not represent the mainstream of Christian witness. Yet it all depends on who gets to tell the story of who and what constitutes the mainstream. Yoder's reading of Judaism certainly represents a challenge to how the story is usually told.

Feminists in a similar manner are beginning to challenge the way in which the story is told. I once remarked that, as a pacifist, I represent the minority tradition in Christian history; but I was challenged by one of my feminist graduate students. She observed that most Christians through most of Christian history were nonviolent, since most Christians have been women who have been prohibited from warfare. That they had no choice, any more than the Jews under the hegemony of Christian power had no choice, makes the nonviolence that characterized their lives no less significant. Such observations require a much greater framework of support to be compelling, but they at least remind us that the church has never been devoid of nonviolent witness.[16] As I will suggest, at least on some readings, any account of just war in the Christian tradition owes its intelligibility to the presumption of the practice of Christian nonviolence in the church.

The primary problem with such an account of Christian nonviolence is that it seems that Christians can make little contribution to those who are morally attempting to understand and limit war. Obviously, Christians are against war, however war may be conceived. Moreover, since it seems that Christian nonviolence makes sense only for Christians, then Christians really cannot enter into conversations about these matters with those who do not share the practices and convictions of the Christian community. You are either responsible or you are not. Christians may be nonviolent, but by being so they are profoundly apolitical.

Yet I hope to show that the representation I have made of Christian nonresistance has resources to challenge such dismissals. Those who would dismiss Christian nonviolence in this manner often do so on the presumption that the central and/or "eternal" problem of politics is that of controlling violence. In an odd manner they assume the same kind of ahistorical account of "the political" that I was criticizing in those who assume that pacifism and just war are simply "there" as unchanging theories. As I hope to show, just because Christians are committed to the practice of nonviolence does not mean that the conversation is at an end. Rather, the conversation is just beginning, as it always must be "just beginning," since there can be no timeless account of what does and what does not constitute violence or war or the state. Nonviolent and just war Christians alike, as well as those committed to subjecting violence to some moral reflection, cannot avoid providing some account of what peace, as well as war, might look like.

In undertaking such a task, the nonviolent Christian cannot assume that she can write for anyone, but she certainly can hope that anyone might be interested in the reflection in which she must engage, reflection that enables her to live in greater faithfulness to and conformity with her practices. If such a task has any hope of success, of course, it depends on its ability to draw on communal practices such as forgiveness and reconciliation, which are at the heart of nonviolence. This contingent possibility concerns me, since I fear, as I indicated, that my intellectual commitment to nonviolence is inadequate for a faithful report of the practice.

Can a Pacifist Tell a Just from an Unjust War?

Paul Ramsey challenged James Douglass's use of the just war theory in Douglass's book, *The Non-violent Cross*.[17] Douglass had tried to use just war theory as a "point of reference." But Ramsey, "with all due respect to the Christian pacifist position," asked:

> Can a pacifist tell *the just-war tests* and reason with them to the end of clarifying the responsibilities of citizens and statesmen in the international system? Has he not abdicated from the beginning the task of searching out the true meaning of the just-war theory and the requirements this imposes upon us under the conditions of modern war, by giving himself the premise he wishes to fetch forth from it, namely, that the just-war doctrine can (by condemning all war in a nuclear age, just before it becomes a "relic" in governing political consciences) furnish a negative and transitional ground but not any "essential support" for a life of non-violence and suffering resistance? In my day, this would have been called a prejudiced line of reasoning, suspect from the beginning.[18]

Ramsey's question obviously raises the central challenge to the pacifist who does not want to be rendered "politically irrelevant" because of her commitment to nonviolence. Ramsey accuses Douglass of bad faith, but I think the issues are much more complex than such an accusation suggests. That such is the case can be seen by the way in which Ramsey must continue his argument. What Douglass fails to see, according to Ramsey, is that just war theory is not simply a list of criteria for testing whether a particular war is morally permissible, but rather just war theory is in fact a theory of statecraft. The problem with pacifists, like Douglass, is that they fail to see that their pacifism takes them "beyond politics."

Ramsey is candid that his position in this respect draws on the work of Reinhold Niebuhr. Ramsey's task was to accept Niebuhr's "realism" and discipline the utilitarian implications in that realism through the use of just war reasoning. As he notes: "There is more to be said about justice in war than was articulated in Niebuhr's sense of the ambiguities of politics and his greater/lesser evil doctrine on the use of force. That more is the principle of discrimination; and I have tried to trace out the meaning of this as well as the meaning of disproportion in kinds of warfare that Niebuhr never faced." [19]

Douglass's error, according to Ramsey, is to ask the nation as well as the individual to embrace the cross. But surely it is only "escalated religious language" that connects claims of the Lordship of Christ with "humanistic" grounds for optimism which fails to see that in politics Christians must operate in the shadows cast by the cross of Christ.[20]

Ramsey has a deep respect for those who choose to take the stance of nonviolence, as long as they understand that in prescinding from the history of warfare they are prescinding from the history of nations. The Christian pacifist "radically even if still selectively withdraws from politics; he makes in trust the venture that God has not committed to him (but perhaps to persons outside the perfection of Christ) the use of armed force in justice-making and in peace-keeping."[21] James Douglass and Menno Simons "may be quite correct," but Ramsey believes that he must side with those Christians who believe that the "nation" becomes "God's good servant" in protecting the neighbor from injustice.

Ramsey's position is widely shared, but I think there are serious questions about its coherence that go beyond Ramsey's peculiar defense of just war as an exemplification of Christian charity. For it is by no means clear, as Ramsey assumes, that you can marry just war reflection so justified to the kind of political realism defended by Niebuhr. Given a realist account of politics, and international politics in particular, why would you generate a theory of just war at all? Who would have an interest in the production of such a theory and to what end?

It is surely not implausible to suggest that just war, at least as produced and used by Christians, is the product of the Christian presumption against violence.[22] You develop an account of justified violence only on the assumption that those who would use violence bear the burden of proof. Just war theory, from such a perspective, can be interpreted as the attempt to develop a theory of exceptions within the general Christian presumption against the use of violence.

From the perspective of "realism," however, I see no reason why such a presumption ought to exist in the first place. If violence is the character of our relations, both individually and in groups, then surely no presumption against the use of violence to achieve certain ends is necessary. Limits on violence may be generated on grounds of self-interest, and it may be possible to generate something like a just war theory on such grounds, but I see no reason why the use of violence requires limits on realist presumptions.[23]

In spite of Ramsey's attempt to co-opt him, Niebuhr was consistent in maintaining that from a realist perspective violence cannot be prima facie immoral. Such an assumption is to be expected from those with a stake in the status quo, but there can be no moral argument to sustain the prohibition against violence.

If a season of violence can establish a just social system and can create the possibilities of its preservation, there is no purely ethical ground upon which violence and revolution can be ruled out. This could be done only upon the basis of purely anarchistic ethical and political presuppositions. Once we have made the fateful concession of ethics to politics, and accepted coercion as a necessary instrument of social cohesion, we can make no absolute distinctions between non-violent and violent types of coercion or between coercion used by government and that which is used by revolutionaries.[24]

In spite of his extraordinary effort, I do not believe that Ramsey was successful in his attempt to make Niebuhr's realism but a prologue for just war thinking.

Indeed, the very attempt required the presumption of a Christian civilization based on moral commitments to the protection of the innocent. I suspect that Niebuhr, in an odd way, shared Ramsey's presumption in this respect. What Ramsey objects to in Douglass is not that Douglass presumes, as a Christian pacifist, to speak to the politics in which he resides, but that he refuses to be the kind of Constantinian that Ramsey was.

Ramsey can well object, however, that my reading of the just war theory as a Christian casuistry of exceptions to the general practice of nonviolence is a mistake. He was clear that just war theory and pacifism do not share an equivalent rejection of violence.

Pacifism's presumption is in favor of *peace* (or else peace and justice are believed to conflict). Just war's presumption favors the defense of an ordered *justice* (which sometimes may not consist with peace). *Just cause* is overarching in just-war theory; *within that,* last resort comes into play. If and only if there is found in justice a possible cause of war is there a presumption against resorting to violence to be taken into account. Thus a presumption against *injustice* is a lexically *prior* presumption to the "presumption against going to war" under "last resort." Confusion, not clarity, comes from saying that this is *like* pacifism's rejection of any use of violent means.[25]

This "justice" that war is to serve, moreover, is not a "natural" justice for Ramsey. The state's function in the use of armed force is not based on "another morality" than that of the Gospel. Rather, it is a "generous" justice, "the work of love in restraint of evil to relieve and protect oppressed neighbors."[26] From Ramsey's point of view, to abandon such justice is to abandon the indiscriminate and disinterested care of one's neighbor that Jesus requires.

This is not the place to suggest how Ramsey's Christology is deficient exactly because it remains captured by the presuppositions of Protestant liberalism. It is sufficient instead to challenge Ramsey to show that the justice pursued by war is the justice of such "ordered love." Ramsey can accuse the pacifist of being apolitical, but given his own presuppositions about the "justice" that war serves, such an accusation makes the pacifist look almost like the realist. In effect, Ramsey's justification of just war as a theory of "statecraft" becomes a blanket justification for the "states" that exist and the present configuration of those states in the international arena.[27] Given Ramsey's account, it is difficult to see how just war might actually function to tell a state it could not go to war.[28]

This is particularly the case given Ramsey's continued commitment to realist accounts of international relations. He rightly argues that states should never go to war for peace, but rather to restore a more ordered justice. As he puts it:

> Order is not a higher value in politics than justice, but neither is humanitarian justice a higher value than order. Both are in some respects conditional to the other. Order is for the sake of justice since the only real political justice is an ordered justice; yet justice is no less for the sake of order, since the only real political order in which men may dwell together in community and peace is one that is *just* enough to command the love and allegiances of men, or at least their acquiescence and their compliance. Power, which is of the *esse* of political agency, may be a conditional value only; but order and justice, which are ever in tension yet in inter-relation, both are values that comprise the well-being, the *bene esse*, of political affairs and the common good which is the goal of political action.[29]

Ramsey simply seems to assume that such order as he is describing is equivalent to the "generous justice" entailed in the disinterested love required by the Gospel, but I see no reason why that assumption is justified.

It should be clear by now that Ramsey's account of pacifism is but the other side of his understanding of just war. He assumes that each is a "theory" that derives from Jesus' teaching and example of disinterested love. Accordingly, pacifism and just war are equally valid alternatives for Christians, as long as those that profess the former understand that they must, by being pacifist, become apolitical. Just war and pacifism become further implications that can be deduced from Christian belief. Nonviolence, as a characteristic intrinsic to Christian convictions and community, simply is not an alternative that Ramsey seriously considered. Such a community might well, as Yoder has suggested, use just war theory to communicate to those whose language it is (Christian or not) to call them to their own vision of their integrity as well as making them less violent.[30]

As Yoder long ago argued, just war can be understood as an attempt to discipline the power of the state. Just war is best thought of as the way in which the state's internal police power is kept limited. Police power is the attempt to control conflict so that the most limited form of coercion is necessary for cooperation, which is, in turn, required for achieving the good ends of the community. On such a reading it makes sense to ask if a Christian formed through the practices of nonviolence might be called to be a police officer—a peace officer. Yoder refuses to accept the automatic "no" of the pre-Constantinian church or the equally automatic "yes" of the post-Constantinian church.

Instead, he suggests that we ought not ask the question in a legalistic manner, as if the question can be determined in the abstract. Rather, the question should be posed on the Christian level:

> Is the Christian *called* to be a policeman? We know he is called to be an agent of reconciliation. Does that general call, valid for every Christian, take for certain individuals a form of a specific call to be also an agent of the wrath of God? Stating the question in this form makes it clear that if the Christian can by any stretch of the imagination find his calling in the exercise of state-commanded violence, he must bring us (i.e., lay before the brotherhood) the evidence that he has such a special calling.[31]

Yoder acknowledges that he has not met anyone testifying to such a call, but in principle it cannot be excluded. Everything depends on the character of the society in which one finds oneself as well as the correlative nature of the police.

For example, it might well be that in some social orders the police are prohibited from using weapons. In such a context it might be possible for Christians to believe they are called to exercise their service to their neighbor through some form of police service. Or, to put the matter even more forcefully, it becomes the duty of those committed to

Christian nonviolence to draw on the resources found in their own community to help those in the wider society to develop habits that make the society capable of supporting a more nearly nonviolent police force. It would be fascinating to ask what forms of economic relations need to be fostered to make the resort to coercion and violence less necessary. The exclusion of Christians from such political involvement seems based on the assumption that all politics presuppose violence—an assumption I see no reason to accept in principle.

Yet Ramsey does think that much is at stake at this point. He contends that the pacifist who believes he can continue to be relevant to the world of politics confuses nonresisting love with nonviolent resistance. Appealing to Niebuhr, Ramsey defends this distinction as follows:

> I do not mean that *agape* of the New Testament is *passive,* or that Christian pacifism is *passivism.* It is rather that simple and sound New Testament conjunction of the imperative "do not *resist* evil" (Matt. 5:29) with the imperative "*overcome* evil with good" (Romans 12:21). Overcoming evil with good is surely positive, active, ever alert in the service of God and of our neighbors in God. This does not say, however, always "overcome evil with good" when you can; but when you cannot, go ahead and "*resist* evil nonviolently!"[32]

Ramsey thinks that this is the crux of the matter between pacifists and those who advocate just war. He thus keeps asking where pacifists like Yoder and myself stand on "nonviolent resistance." As he puts it, "unless the love of nonresistance is purified of its twentieth-century alloy with 'nonviolence,' the grounding of pacifism in its account of the person and work of Jesus Christ would have to be corrected back to a sort of *legalism.*"[33] Again, Ramsey asks of Yoder:

> Is there a nonviolent resistance that is *not* political pacifism, that is *not* an impurity when encompassed in nonresistant love? Can we speak of a "nonviolent cross" without contradiction, in any other than the trivial sense of "not violent" as an outlying circumscription of taking up our cross, the cross Jesus bore, which is significantly circumscribed only more narrowly as nonresistance and overcoming evil with good?[34]

As we saw, Ramsey appeals to Reinhold Niebuhr as the originator of the distinction between nonresistance and nonviolence. Yet if we turn to Niebuhr's account of that distinction, I think it becomes even more problematic. Niebuhr notes that it is impossible to make a clear distinction between violent and nonviolent coercion. All social life by definition is coercive, for "society is in a perpetual state of war." [35] For Niebuhr, nonviolent conflict may be as destructive as violent conflict since it cannot avoid some forms of coercion. "The chief difference between violence and non-violence is not in the degree of destruction which they cause, though the difference is usually considerable, but in the aggressive character of the one and the negative character of the other. Non-violence is essentially non-co-operation. It expresses itself in the refusal to participate in the ordinary processes of society." [36]

Gandhi represented for Niebuhr the strategy of nonviolence, but Gandhi's strategy does not embody the nonresistance of Jesus. Rather, Gandhi's is nonviolent coercion and resistance that still tries to achieve political objectives. Niebuhr (and Ramsey) can admire and perhaps even recommend such strategies, as Niebuhr did for the "emancipation of the Negro race in America," but they both refuse to acknowledge that such strategy is what Jesus was about in being nonviolent. Jesus requires complete noncooperation with these structures of coercion and violence.

I think it is obvious that when Ramsey asks Yoder and me to say where we stand on "nonviolent resistance," he is imposing a distinction that we see no reason to accept. It is a distinction born of the assumption that pacifism, and in particular the pacifism of Jesus, is that of complete noncooperation with the "world." Ramsey and Niebuhr betray their commitments to an ahistorical account of violence and nonviolence that is presumably simply part of the human condition. Such a theory is necessary because they lack any sense that nonviolence is one of the characteristics of a historical community. Such a community has no stake in the assumption that a hard-and-fast distinction can be or needs to be made between what is violent and what is not. Rather, it is pledged to constantly explore, through internal as well as external challenges, how practices that at one time may well have been nonviolent have in fact become violent.

Christian nonviolence, in short, does not begin with a theory or conception about violence, war, "the state or society," and so on, but rather with practices such as forgiveness and reconciliation. Only by learning how to live through such practices can we as a people come to see the violence, often present in our lives, that would otherwise go unnoticed. Such seeing produces generalizations that can be used to help Christians discern their place within the societies in which they find themselves—

for example, war is the organized killing of some groups of people by other groups of people.

Ironically, those committed to Christian nonviolence, as I have presented it, do not have a stake in strong theories about "peace" in contrast to "war."[37] For example, we have no reason to deny the realist argument that often what is called peace is but the imposition of order by the strong on the less strong. We are well-aware that what Christians mean by peace is not that which usually comes through state agency.

In other words, Christians refuse to allow their understanding of nonviolence to be determined by the world. Christian nonviolence is not determined by the absence of war. Thus, my oft-made claim that Christians do not choose nonviolence because we believe that through nonviolence we can rid the world of war, but rather in a world of war we cannot be anything but nonviolent as worshipful followers of Jesus the Christ. Since we believe that the God we worship has created us to be nonviolent, we think what we have learned can be of help outside our community. Therefore, we seek to make the world less violent through the diverse and different "politics" in which we find ourselves. For we see no reason to accept the essentialized presumption that all social and political life is violent.

I confess that one of the most problematic aspects of recent just war reflection for me has been its confidence in claiming to know what constitutes the distinction between, for example, war and terrorism. It is by no means clear to me that terrorism is a clear set of behaviors discontinuous with war that can be condemned in a manner that war cannot be. I am not trying to render war problematic by suggesting that all forms of warfare are but forms of terrorism under a different name. Some distinction between war and terrorism may be possible, but I distrust such distinctions made in the abstract. It makes all the difference who is making the distinction, for what purposes, and how the distinction is informed by the historical context.[38]

For example, if the suggestion I made concerning just war as a way to think about the police function of the "state" has some validity, then it might make sense to suggest that the attempt to extend that function beyond the bounds of the state means you no longer are talking about war. Strong discontinuities exist between war and the police function, since the police function involves (1) a clear designation of what constitutes crime, (2) some sense of the appropriate punishment for that crime, (3) the catching of the criminal, and (4) the carrying out of the punishment. In war, all of these functions are exercised by the same agent, whereas the police generally do not carry out the punishment themselves. I do not want to make too much out of such discriminations, but they at least suggest the kind of reflection that might be useful to Christians in order that they might distinguish between different kinds of coercion. Nothing in the practice of Christian nonviolence commits us to the view that all violence is the same. Like those committed to just war, we think discriminations are necessary to help us better serve our neighbor through the witness of nonviolence. Accordingly, we obviously think it important for those who feel called to engage in the killing of others in the name of war do so in a discriminating manner. Yet again, it makes all the difference what a society may mean by war. If war is taken to be a response to an insult, then what "discriminating" may mean will differ from those wars aimed at making another people's lives so miserable that they would prefer peace on another's terms rather than to extend the conflict. Those engaged in the latter kind of war, which I take to be the kind of wars produced in modern times, make it increasingly difficult to distinguish terrorism from conventional warfare. Indeed, the kind of weapons developed to make allegedly democratic societies capable of pursuing war, insofar as they force all "citizens" to think of themselves as potential combatants, can reasonably be thought to make the distinction between war and terrorism increasingly problematic.

Can the Christian Be a Citizen?

Of course, it may be objected that given the position I have developed concerning Christian nonviolence, Christians should not consider themselves citizens of any society and/or state. Again, I cannot answer such a challenge in the abstract since any adequate answer depends on the kind of state or society in which we find ourselves. I see no reason why Christians need to develop a theory of political authority. Rather, we accept the realism of Romans 13 and assume that such authority will exist. As Yoder suggests:

> Affirmations like Romans 13 are made not to encourage Christians to help run the Roman empire (which was not a historical possibility, not even

imaginable), but to help Christians be at peace with the fact that they could not do anything about the Roman empire in its negative impact upon them. Paul wants the Christians in the capital city to see that the world that was not under their control was still not out from under God's control. God had a function for pagan power.[39]

The problem, therefore, is not Romans 13. The problem is how that text is read after Christians have begun to think they ought to be like Caesar. What needs to be said is that Christians simply do not have a theory of state power as such. Rather, we have an account of authority among us that has to do with servanthood. Thus, in Romans 12 we are told that we are to be servants.

> It says "you shall be transformed by the renewing of your mind." It says, "you shall not take vengeance, because God will take care of that," and draws from that the deduction, "so we do not fight back against the Romans. We let Caesar have his function." The fact that the kings of this world lord it over them, we shall let stand because that is under God and his providence. In the situation where persecution is active, still we do not fight back. Still we let Caesar do his thing, even though we see that it is idolatrous and cruel. This is a call for the patience of the saints.[40]

For some regimes the very presence of such a people may be thought to be subversive. As with Peggy Lee, who was faithful to her lovers "in her own way," so Christians will be subordinate to the states in which we find ourselves in our own way. It may be the case, for example, given the character of certain regimes, that the nonviolence of the church may appear violent. No doubt many Romans must have seen Christians in just such a light, since the church could not affirm the "peace and security" promised by the power of Rome. As Klaus Wengst observes, from the Christian perspective the peace secured by Rome could not help but appear to arise from

> an abyss of hatred and anxiety as the presupposition and at the same time the consequence of force: it is based on the promise of eternal Rome as an infinite extension of the history of violence and is thus simply the expression of deep hopelessness. Over against that, Christian sobriety as faith, love and hope is not to be seen in the calculations of power, in so-called realistic analysis as a projection of the existing situation. Rather, trusting in the crucified Christ, it renounces aggressive violence and makes its love specific in the demolition and the overcoming of hatred and anxiety. But Christian sobriety demonstrates itself in particular—and it is here that the

stress lies in I Thess. 5.1–11 in a perception of reality which tests it from the perspective of the interruption of history and the coming of Christ. Those who are sober in this way, who do not get drunk with power, will keep possibilities open and already set signs of the new world in the midst of the old." [41]

That Christians are so constituted means that states which will tolerate our presence have potential to be less violent. Of course, everything depends on the church's ability to maintain its integrity as a nonviolent people in such states. For the temptation is to turn "toleration" into status, thus believing that we, as Christians, have a stake in maintaining the existence of this state in preference to others.

In this respect, democracy has been a particularly subtle temptation to Christianity. Christians have never killed as willingly as when they have been asked to do so for "freedom." I take it, therefore, that one of the most important challenges facing Christians today is to remember that the democratic state is still a state that would ask us to qualify our loyalty to God in the name of some lesser loyalty.

Many use the radical nature of such a stance to disqualify the pacifist from political involvement. We are dismissed as hopelessly naive or idealistic. Such would be the case if pacifism were a theory about society and/or state power. But as I have tried to make clear, it is not a theory but rather the form of life incumbent on those who would worship Jesus as the Son of God. Given that stance, I see no reason why Christians cannot try to serve in the many activities in societies and states that do not involve violence.

In this respect I do not see why there is a deep difference between adherence to just war and pacifism. After all, just war theory surely requires its adherents to contemplate the possibility that they will find themselves in deep tension with the warmaking policies of their governments. The criteria that war be declared by "legitimate authority" does not in itself entail any account of what constitutes legitimacy. I suspect, in fact, that something like traditional monarchy may well be more appropriate to just war thinking exactly because a monarch can be held more directly accountable. I suspect that those who employ just war thinking as Christians are able to do so with integrity exactly to the extent that they assume a position of resistance to the state not unlike that of their pacifist sister and brother.

A Few Methodological Comments at the End

I do not know if I have convinced anyone that adherents of Christian nonviolence can think about war. I am not sure if I have convinced anyone that adherents of Christian nonviolence can think, period. I write against a background of presumptions about nonviolence that I have been intent on defeating. Those presumptions are fueled by the contemporary desire for theory that can be assessed by anyone.[42] Since I do not share the presuppositions that gave birth to that project, I cannot defend my position on "objective" grounds.

I think, in other words, that there is a natural affinity between a kind of historicism and the account of Christian nonviolence I have tried to represent. Christians do not believe in an "eternal truth or truths" that can be known apart from the existence of the people of Israel and the church. We know that the witness that we are called to make is such exactly because that to which we witness is unavailable apart from its exemplification in the lives of a community of people. That such a witness takes the form of nonviolence is necessary because we believe that the God who makes such a witness necessary is a God who would not be known otherwise.

For many, that seems but an invitation to relativism and, correlatively, war and violence. If we lack a standpoint that at least promises to secure agreement between people who otherwise share nothing in common, what chance do we have of making war less likely? Yet from my perspective, just such theories have made war likely. Christians do not promise the world a theory of truth that will resolve conflict. Rather, we promise the world a witness that we think is the truth of our existence. That witness requires the existence of a body of people who provide an alternative so that we may be able to see the violence that so grips our lives.

Given the violence of the world in which we live, it may be thought that that is not much. For those of us who believe that God has made us part of the Kingdom of peace through cross and resurrection, however, it is everything.

CHAPTER 7 ▼ WHOSE "JUST" WAR?

WHICH PEACE?

The story is told of the "old boy" in Mississippi who was called to the ministry when he was out plowing with his mule. He interpreted a skywriter's "GP" as "Go Preach" rather than "Grand Prize Beer." Using his barn, he began to preach to whomever would come—blacks or white. Seeing nothing in the gospels that required the separation of the races, he did not let threats from the Klan change his practice. As a result, he was severely beaten. A friend who had come to comfort him reports that he was undeterred by the beating since, as he said, "You know there is a lot more to this race thing than just race." He meant that sin was having its day.

In like manner, there is a lot more to this "war thing" than just "just war." Indeed, there is much more to the question of the moral evaluation of war than the question of whether a war conforms to just war criteria. Just as Christians think racism has to do with sin and repentance, so should we think of war. As will become clear from what follows, I certainly do not mean to disparage all attempts to discipline and evaluate war on just war grounds. Rather, I will try to show how such attempts concerning the Gulf War have failed to acknowledge "a lot more."

The "more" to which I want to direct attention are the assumptions behind the recent spate of just war thinking and, in particular, the assumptions that have dictated mistakenly, in my view, what have become widely regarded as the relevant questions for assessing the morality of the Gulf War. Put differently, it makes all the difference who is asking questions about the "justice" of the war and for what reasons. When questions of who and why are ignored, the history that has shaped just war reflection as well as the conflicting histories of the Gulf War are assumed irrelevant.

Since I will argue that the "who" is all-important, I must make clear who I am, or at least who I think I should be, and for whom I write. I am a Christian pacifist. From my perspective that is an unhappy description, since I believe the narrative into which Christians are inscribed means we cannot be anything other than nonviolent. In other words, Christians do not become Christians and then decide to be nonviolent. Rather, nonviolence is simply one of the essential practices that is intrinsic to the story of being a Christian. "Being a Christian" is to be incorporated into a community constituted by the stories of God, which, as a consequence, necessarily puts one in tension with the world that does not share those stories.

I write hoping to convince the many Christians who supported the Gulf War that on Christian grounds such support was a mistake. The so-called just war theory, rather than helping Christians discern where their loyalties should be, in fact made it more difficult for Christians to distinguish their story from the story of the United States of America. As a result, appeals to that theory led to an uncritical legitimation of the Gulf War by most American Christians. This outcome should not be surprising since most Christians in America continue to believe that this is a "Christian nation."

It may be suspected that as a pacifist I am trying to defeat the just war theory in principle by calling attention in this instance to its perversion. That is certainly not my intention. I do think the locution "just war theory" is misleading, since it not only presumes the theory has always had a coherence that it has in fact lacked, but, more importantly, it presumes that as a "theory" it can be used by anyone, anywhere. Nonetheless, the question of whether a coherent and viable theory of just war can be defended on Christian grounds is distinguishable from the question of whether the Gulf War conformed to just war criteria.

Yet I hope to show that these questions are in fact not so neatly separable if the just war theory is to avoid being used in an ideological fashion—that is, as a cover story that hides from us the reality of what was done in the Gulf War. And it is my contention that such a cover story is invoked whenever appeals to just war theory are used, as they have been in justifying the Gulf War, to create an illusory moral objectivity.

For example, in one essay after another we have been reminded of the standard just war consensus. A just war is one declared by legitimate authority, whose cause is just, and whose ultimate goal is peace; furthermore, the war must be fought with the right intentions, with a probability for success, with means commensurate to its end, and with a clear respect for noncombatant immunity. Questions about the justice of the Gulf War seem to be a matter of whether "the facts" fit these criteria. It is assumed by those who defend the war on just war grounds and those who oppose the war on the same grounds that they are in fact standing on the same ground. The just war theory has become a given that can be generated and applied by anyone, anywhere, from any point of view.

But just this presumption is the problem. The assumption that just war theory provides criteria of assessment that are straightforward, self-explanatory, and not requiring interpretation is, from a Christian perspective, a sinful illusion. It is the kind of illusion one has come to expect of those in modern societies who hide from themselves the violent nature of those societies by justifying them in "in principled," universalistic terms. Ironically, in such a context it is left to the Christian pacifist to challenge such universalistic illusions by reminding those who would use the abstractions of just war theory that the wars of liberal societies, simply put, involve the use of violence for state interest. Such an illusion is sinful exactly because it hides from Christians our complicity in patterns of domination and violence.

That is why the title of this essay is a play on the title of Alasdair MacIntyre's book *Whose Justice? Which Rationality?* [1] MacIntyre's argument that all theories of justice and rationality are, contrary to liberal pretensions of universality, tradition-dependent is equally a challenge to the use of just war theory to justify the Gulf War. It has been the hallmark of ethical theory since the Enlightenment to ground morality in rationality qua rationality; in other words, morality only has meaning when considered as a schema of laws or principles self-evident to any reasonable person. But such accounts of morality, by their own admission, can give only extremely thin material content to their standards of right and wrong; they can proclaim that certain kinds of behavior are wrong "in principle." But when forced to consider added parts of a person's history, the circumstances of a situation, the role of the community in an individual's life—these material conditions of morality are set aside in favor of a simple assertion of what "in principle" must be true anytime and anyplace. The loss of material content is a small price to pay for this assumed universality. The issue, then, for such systems of ethics becomes how such universally derived principles are to be applied in concrete cases.

Such theories of morality attempt to free moral convictions from their history and, in particular, from their Jewish and Christian roots. From this perspective, for a principle to be moral it must be capable of being held and applied by anyone, whether they be Christian, Muslim, or American. It should not be surprising, therefore, that just war criteria were used to justify the Gulf War as if it made no difference who was using them and for what ends. My contention is that when the just war theory is so used, it cannot avoid ideological distortion.

The nature of such distortion is exemplified by what happens when I acknowledge that I write as a Christian pacifist in opposition to those who assume a just war stance. It is assumed that I am in a disadvantaged position because "pacifism," particularly a pacifism such as mine that is based on Christian beliefs, lacks "universal" or public standing. So few are thought to adhere to it, and many people eschew commitment to Christian tenets that they believe are required to sustain it. Thus, even if I provide an analysis of the Gulf War as a pacifist, it is presumed that my arguments can be persuasive only to those in a community that worships God in the name of the Father, Son, and Holy Spirit.

It is certainly not my intention to deny that I write from as well as to a particular audience called Christian. Indeed my primary concern in this essay is to help Christians see how unfaithful we have been through our willingness to underwrite the ends of that entity called the United States of America. That I write with such purpose, however, does not mean that my argument is limited in ways that the argument of those who appeal to just war theory is not. Indeed, it is my hope that non-Christians might be interested in the analysis that I provide. But I am not willing to acknowledge that simply because others do not share my Christian convictions, they thereby represent a more general, practical, or realistic morality. Indeed, I mean to challenge those who do not share my Christian presuppositions by asking how they think war became or continues to be susceptible to moral analysis. For, after all, Christians created just war reflection because of their nonviolent convictions; they assumed that those who would use violence bore the burden of proof for doing so. Thus, the wide reach of pacifism becomes clear, for if you do not believe that nonviolence is required, then why assume that war needs justification and/or control?

For example, there are accounts of war that free us from such restraint and judgment. Though there are many different forms of political realism, political realists, in general, assume that war is neither good nor bad but simply a necessary part of human life, given the violent tendencies of "human nature" as displayed particularly in relations between groups. In such a view, war should not be sought, but at times war may be necessary, given the lack of any means short of war for resolving international disputes.

It is my contention that the Gulf War was conceived and fought by such political realists who found it useful to justify it on grounds of just war. No doubt, some have cynically gone about this project, but I suspect that many realists who have justified the war on those grounds genuinely believe that the war was conceived and fought as a just war. But from a realist perspective what must be acknowledged is that those with the biggest armies and the best technology can call any war just, if they so choose, when or if they have won it.

This reality is sobering for many of us who have argued for the importance of disciplining American reflection and practice of war on just war grounds. Even though I am a pacifist, I have presumed that it would be a great good if moral reflection by Americans concerning war could be formed by just war considerations. As has often been observed, Americans prefer to go to war only if the war is a crusade—that is, a war whose cause is so noble that the standard moral and political limits are set aside in the service of a vastly greater good. Thus, Americans always want to fight wars to defend such abstract concepts as freedom and democracy, or in a special fit of hubris, to fight wars to end all wars.

Those who think that wars should be governed by a nation-state's political interests, that is, realists, and those who are advocates of just war share a distaste for crusade justifications of war. The realists regret it because often the moral justifications given for a war make it difficult to end the war when our interests have been achieved—for example, the irrationality of forcing Germany to accept unconditional surrender. Just warriors abjure the crusade because the "good cause" often overrides both the limited moral purpose that originally justified the war and noncombatant immunity.

But in the Gulf War, both of these accounts of war tended to be submerged by the American penchant to fight a "good war." The realist account of the war was subtly shifted into a crusade mode by twisting tenets of just war theory into its service. So just war thinking proved powerless to rein in the grand ambitions of a realist war fought primarily to "make Americans feel good about themselves after Vietnam." And thus, surprisingly, it may be that pacifists are better served by realist wars—wars fought for strict self-interest and little moral pretension— than by wars of massively powerful nations that are cloaked in the universal pretensions of the just war theory. Of course, such universalism is what we expect from imperial nations, since their power protects them from recognizing that they are serving their own interests. And thus, the Gulf War was necessary to oppose aggression in the interest of building a "new world order."

In this respect, it is worth considering the history of how just war theory became a prominent discourse among mainstream Protestants. Recoiling from what they perceived to be the failure of the idealist aims of World War I, American Protestants took a more or less pacifist stance against war following the armistice of 1918. Their "pacifism" was "liberal" as it drew on humanistic presumptions that the human race had outgrown war as a method of resolving disputes. In other words, they thought the problem with war was not that it offended the God revealed in Christ but that war was irrational given the progress of the human race. In an interesting way, this kind of "pacifism" was the mirror image of crusade justifications of war—if wars could not accomplish great goods, then they should not take place.

This vague but influential pacifism was powerfully attacked by Reinhold Niebuhr during his tenure as professor of applied Christianity at Union Theological Seminary in New York. In the process of writing classics such as *Moral Man and Immoral Society,* Niebuhr became the most, and perhaps the last, influential Protestant public theologian in America. He achieved this status, however, exactly because he provided the theological justification to support the liberal ideology for the rising political elite whose self-interest was commensurate with making the United States a world power.

Niebuhr subjected liberal pacifism, based as it was on progressivist views of history, to a withering critique because of its failure to acknowledge the sinful character of human existence. In Niebuhr's hands, sin became not a condition from which we must turn away, but an explanation in advance to justify the necessity to do evil in the name of creating less evil social orders. Niebuhr prepared American Christians to acknowledge that war is an evil, but a necessary evil that we should accept if we are to be about achieving relative justice within this world—which is all the justice we should hope for in this life. He argued that no alternative exists to a world constituted by nation-state systems, and, accordingly, that war is a necessary constituent of those systems. Thus, "peace" for Niebuhr can never mean an attempt to rid the world of war; rather, it is a word for "order" that too often serves the interests of status quo powers. If you are for justice, therefore, you cannot exclude the use of violence and war. In effect, Niebuhr gave a theological justification for political realism.

It was a great project of Paul Ramsey, professor of theological ethics at Princeton University and author of *War and the Christian Conscience,* to accept the fundamental presuppositions of Niebuhr's account of politics and war, but to discipline it by just war reflection. Ramsey saw clearly that Niebuhr's account lacked the kind of discriminating criteria that would allow Christians to discern when a war was legitimate as well as how it should be fought. Ramsey argued that just war reflection is a necessary constituent of Western civilization's Christian presuppositions, which are especially exemplified in matters of war and peace by the commitment to protect the innocent neighbor—thus, the importance for Ramsey, in contrast to Niebuhr, of the protection of noncombatants.

Accordingly, Ramsey thought he was able to defend just war as a coherent theory in practice because of the presumption that we live in a Christian civilization. He did not assume that those who accepted just war in fact were Christians, but he did think they continued to share the habits and moral presuppositions that Christianity had instilled within the social milieu of the West. Not the least of those presumptions was that our social order was built on the conviction that we would rather die as individuals and even as a whole people than directly kill one innocent human being. For Ramsey, that conviction meant that war must be pursued in a manner which may require more people to die in order to avoid directly attacking noncombatants—the innocent neighbors of any war.

For example, in Ramsey's account of just war, dropping the atomic bomb on Hiroshima and Nagasaki was profoundly immoral. It would have been better for more Japanese and American soldiers to die on the beaches of Japan than for noncombatants to be killed at Hiroshima and Nagasaki. Such judgments are necessary if Ramsey is right that intrinsic to the practice of just war is the protection of noncombatants from direct attack. For Ramsey, such judgments are a morally necessary condition to distinguish the killing done in war from murder.

Just war thinking, at least in theory, presumes therefore that there are some things one cannot do to win a war. War undertaken on just war grounds requires those who prosecute it to consider the possibility of surrender rather than fight a war unjustly. Confronted by such requirements, the tension is apparent between those who would think of war in just war categories and those who accept the more realist account of war. Ramsey attempted to wed the just war criteria to Niebuhr's essentially realist account of nation-state relations; I fear that the Gulf War has revealed this effort to be an unstable marriage.

The example of Hiroshima and Nagasaki reminds us of how difficult it is in the American context to think in a morally disciplined fashion about war. In many respects, World War II continues to set a terrible precedent for American thinking. For that war is what most Americans think a just war is about—namely, a war you can fight to win using any means necessary because your cause is entirely just. Thus, we want to fight wars that have, either explicitly or implicitly, the condition of unconditional surrender because we believe we are confronting a thoroughly corrupt and evil enemy.

Niebuhr's realism was meant to chasten such views, since to fight a war for unconditional surrender means you are ill-prepared for the kinds of limited purposes that wars should serve, given the political realities of the world. Just war advocates such as Ramsey also challenged the endemic crusade mentality of America, since at the heart of just war reflection is the assumption that wars have only limited political purposes in response to clear cases of injustice. That is why it is so important on just war grounds that wars be declared, since the enemy must clearly understand what surrender means so that the war does not become more violent than necessary. In contrast to the popular conception of a *"good war,"* realist and just war advocates share the intention to make war serve limited political purposes.

Of course, Vietnam in this respect proved to be a disastrous moral experience for Americans. The policymakers who gave us that war may have been realists, but they justified it as a crusade—a defense of freedom and democracy along the Asian rim. As a result, prosecution of the war with proportionate force proved impossible—that is, the use of only the means necessary to accomplish the war's end. Exactly because the war had to be described as a defense of freedom and democracy, the means used in the war became disproportionate to what either a realist or a just warrior would have conceived as its more limited purposes. After Vietnam, Americans desperately needed a good war to fight— that is, they needed a war that could restore the American belief that we fight wars only when the cause is unambiguously good.

An essential episode in this history of just war thinking is the conflict we have had with the Soviet Union called the cold war. That war was fought on crusade grounds in which complete good was opposed to complete evil. One need not give more credence than is due to Ronald Reagan's presumptions of the "evil empire" to nonetheless realize that U.S. foreign and military policy since World War II has not been essentially determined by just war presuppositions. American nuclear-targeting policies, which would lead to massive civilian death tolls, are an obvious problem for just war reflection, as Paul Ramsey rightly saw. But even more problematic for just war thinking has been the overwhelming fact that America's military forces have been organized to fight a massive and technologically sophisticated war against another world power that sought, like the United States, to expand its influence as widely as possible.

Which brings us to the Gulf War and the attempt to justify that war in just war terms. The war in the Gulf was prosecuted by a military shaped by realist presuppositions, justified by the crusade rhetoric of the cold war, and determined not to repeat Vietnam. Americans were able to fight the war in the Gulf as an allegedly just war, not because America is a nation whose foreign and military policies are formed by just war doctrine, but because America is a nation whose military had been shaped by realists to serve the crusade against communism. American Christians, undisciplined as they are by any serious reflection on the morality of war, enthusiastically backed this war as simply a providential instance of good versus evil.

Against this background, the use of the just war criteria by President George Bush appears almost comedic. He used the criteria as if they had dropped from heaven. Questions about who is using the criteria, to what purpose, and when are simply ignored. Just war theory appears as a kind of law—the only issue seems to be whether the law has been "broken." I am not surprised by this use, as it has often been observed that in liberal societies such as America it is almost inevitable that the law becomes our morality—for example, witness the current enthusiasm for "ethical" behavior by those in Congress or those involved in business. By ethical, they mean that they have broken no law.

Such use of just war theory to justify the Gulf War is not unlike schoolyard morality. Children often assume that questions of right or wrong primarily turn on whether a rule has been broken. In like manner, the only question about the Gulf War is whether it met all the conditions of just war. To begin to evaluate the war on such grounds is to accept terms of analysis that are childish—that is, like children we are asked to begin thinking morally without any consideration from where a morality has come.

When just war is construed in such an abstract way, we forget the social, political, and economic considerations that are necessary for the serious use of the theory. It is no wonder that the administration found it useful to make just war criteria appear as if they are generally agreed-upon presuppositions used by any right-thinking people. Those who possess hegemonic power always claim to represent a universal morality. Such universal claims are meant to create a social and historical amnesia that is intended to make us forget how the dominant achieved power in the first place.

For example, consider this seemingly innocent paragraph from Richard John Neuhaus's article, "Just War and This War," in the *Wall Street Journal*. Neuhaus notes:

> Just war theory was formulated by Augustine (died 430), refined by Thomas Aquinas (died 1274), and Francisco de Vitori (died 1546), and developed in more or less its present form by Hugo Grotius (died 1645), who was often called the Father of International Law. Skeptics claim that just war theory is useless because it has not stopped wars. That is like saying the Ten Commandments should be discarded because they have not eliminated theft, lying, and adultery. The presumption of just war theory is against the use of military force. The theory erects an obstacle course of moral testing aimed at preventing the unjust resort to war.[2]

Ironically, Neuhaus is wrong to suggest that just war theory presupposes a prima facie commitment against the use of military force. At least, he is wrong if Paul Ramsey was right that just war thinking presupposes the necessity of war as an ongoing reality of nation-state systems. Indeed, it was Ramsey's project to help people realize that the aim of just war was not to eliminate war but rather to discipline war to serve only the end of ordered justice. In that sense, Ramsey saw clearly that a deep gulf exists between pacifism and just war: the primary end of just war is limiting injustice, not disavowing violence. Of course, Ramsey also saw that without the presupposition that the West is a Christian civilization, no basis within realism can support the development of just war considerations.

That issue aside, however, the kind of history Neuhaus provides of the settings of just war theory gives the illusion that just war criteria have been unchanging through the centuries. Why the criteria were produced and reproduced, their various status and emphases, seems irrelevant for assessing the theory's validity. For example, the fact that just war reflection in the Middle Ages was predominantly used to help confessors discipline Christians who participated in war is obviously different from the use of just war reflection by the princes of the Holy Roman Empire, who employed it in their many wars of expansion. Furthermore, there is a vast difference between the use of such thinking in the former circumstances and the application of just war theory in the developing nation-state system to which Grotius was responding; in the nation-state system the theory now served not Christian princes but secular politicians. Neuhaus and others seem to believe that such historical and political considerations are irrelevant to the theory's meaning for today.

John Howard Yoder has pointed out many of the problems implicit in such an ahistorical appropriation of the tradition. For instance, he has noted that just war thinking was not intended for use in democracies: "When the just war tradition said that the decisions to go to war belong to the sovereigns they did not mean the democratic sovereign, but rather the king or the prince primarily within the Holy Roman Empire." Yoder continues: "The democratic vision which makes decisions that are 'sovereign' changes how the system has to work. Disinformation and spin control invalidate the administrator's claim to legitimacy. Civilian and military administrators are not trained to distinguish dissent from disloyalty, secrecy from security. They thus can refuse to provide 'the people' with the wherewithal for evaluating the claimed justification." [3]

In the case of the Gulf War the moral problems arising from such disinformation have become clear. Through the methods by which the administration and military controlled descriptions of the war, Americans believed that they had prosecuted a war in which "no one got killed." The fact that there were thousands of Iraqi casualties is not thought to be morally relevant. As a result, the Iraqi war has put realist and just warrior alike in the difficult position of having to meet the unreal expectations of the public in the future. Now realist and just warrior must justify future wars to the American people who believe in the technological fantasy of a war in which no one gets killed—when "no one" means any U.S. soldiers. As a result of this spin control that has fired the crusade mentality, the fundamental question for advocates of just war theory or realism is how democracies are to develop virtues in their citizens to fight wars with limited purposes, not crusades.

The abstract presentation of just war criteria, as given by Neuhaus, also ignores when and how decisions to go to war are made. Again, Yoder points to the hidden problems in the use of the just war tradition. The just war paradigm for decisions about war, he notes, assumes a punctual conception of legal and moral decision-making. "What is either right or wrong is that punctual decision, based upon the facts of the case at just that instant, and the just war tradition delivers the criteria for adjudicating that decision. This procedure underevaluates the longitudinal dimensions of the conflict" (p. 296). In other words, what such a view of moral decision fails to see is that most of the important decisions already are well in place before the decision is made to initiate the actual conflict. For example, it is now clear that the decision to go to war—on a massive scale in the Gulf—was made long before most Americans knew about it.

Oddly enough, those who use the just war criteria as a set of general rules look very much like situation ethicists. Such ethicists often present moral dilemmas as if they were simply givens, the same things from any point of view, like mud puddles that you either have to step over, wade through, or go round. Situationists thrived on examples that poked holes in the general prohibitions against suicide, adultery, and killing by suggesting that at certain times such actions would produce the greatest good. Their examples had power exactly because they were divorced from any thick descriptions of actual people and the histories that had brought them to such contexts—for example, in order to save ten people in a cave, can you dynamite the one person stuck in the cave opening?

In like manner, we are asked by Neuhaus and others to decide whether the prosecution of the war in the Gulf was in accordance with just war theory. But that question assumes that a simple yes or no answer can be given, since the question makes it appear that the options before American foreign policy were only to go to war or to refrain from war. By framing the question in this way, we are led away from analyzing the policy presumptions that made such a war seem so necessary and inevitable. Much is made of congressional approval of the administration's decision to prosecute the war in the Gulf, for example, the implication being that the administration went well beyond the just war requirement that the war should be declared by legitimate authority. The fact that the administration already had put hundreds of thousands of troops in Saudi Arabia before the congressional debate is somehow not thought to have significantly prejudiced that decisive vote.

Furthermore, as has often been pointed out, the administration's supportive relationship with Iraq, and in particular, Saddam Hussein, before his invasion of Kuwait, must be seen as bearing some responsibility for the tragic events that followed. On good realist geopolitical grounds, the United States may have been smart in its policy to support Saddam Hussein as a counterbalance in the area to Iran. But such support obviously led him to believe that he could pursue certain foreign policy initiatives that the United States had no reason to oppose on self-interested or moral grounds. How could Hussein have known, given the administration's prior realist support, that the United States was so serious about being a just war nation?[4]

The purported justifications for going to war also have been discussed largely in an abstract fashion that denies many relevant, concrete questions. For example, the general presumption that the United States had to intervene because America is morally obligated to resist aggression wherever and whenever it occurs is at best an exaggeration and at worse a clear case of lying. It is clear that American foreign policy does not entail that the United States must intervene anytime there seems to be an unjust aggression. The United States did not militarily intervene when China invaded Tibet, when the former Soviet Union invaded Afghanistan, or when Indonesia invaded Timor. What made this aggression so peculiarly an affront to justice that it made our intervention necessary?

Indeed, a clear view of the entire war reveals a bewildering mix of realist politics, crusade appeals, and just war pronouncements. President Bush's description of Saddam Hussein as a Hitler is particularly perverse, given the president's avowed commitment to just war doctrine

148

that should abjure such descriptions of a foe. There is no question that this move was carefully calculated by an administration that invited the American people to think about the war in terms antithetical to just war aims. If you are confronting a Hitler, then your crusading aim must be to remove that which is thoroughly evil.

Ironically, the administration can claim that in spite of the description of Saddam Hussein as Hitler, it prosecuted the war justly. The declared U.S. purpose was to liberate Kuwait, and once that had been accomplished hostilities ceased. But the crucial question is whether that cessation was the result of just war considerations or realist questions of the policy toward other Arab countries. I do not mean to suggest that just war considerations and policy questions are always in principle separable, but I raise the question since it is by no means clear how they are interrelated in this instance. The Kurds seem clearly to have been sacrificed in the name of the U.S. interest to remain in good standing with Arab allies. In like manner, it is amazing to see how quickly Hafiz al-Assad of Syria becomes a "statesman" when it is in the interest of American foreign policy.

Advocates of just war reasoning explain away the problems inherent in such a mishmash of shifting attitudes and policies by arguing that we must distinguish between moral and prudential judgments. Such a distinction assumes that just war criteria are clear; the only question is how they are to be applied. Thus, Richard Neuhaus in his *Wall Street Journal* article notes that while the criteria of justice are clear—last resort, probability of success, proportionate means—they still depend on prudential judgments by political and military experts. Likewise, Bryan Hehir in "The Moral Calculus of War" argues that "the judgment about the last resort is by definition open to prudential calculations about what is possible, what is wise, and when all efforts have been exhausted."[5] Michael Walzer employs the same distinction between morality and prudence in his article on the Gulf crisis in the *New Republic* where he notes

> we must ask whether there are any means short of war for defeating the aggressor and whether defeat can be inflicted at cost proportional to values under attack. Unfortunately, neither just war theory nor any other perspective of moral philosophy helps much in answering these questions. Political or military judgments are called for, and here theologians and philosophers have no special expertise. War as a "last resort" is an end-

lessly receding possibility invoked mostly by people who prefer never to resist aggression with force. After all, there is always something else to do, another diplomatic note, another meeting.[6]

The distinction between morality and prudence looks innocent enough, but it is exactly the source of the fundamental difficulty in the use of just war theory in the Gulf War. This distinction derives from accounts of morality that assume "the moral" can be determined in a manner that is abstracted from concrete communities and corresponding practices—that is, the widespread modern belief that morality is a distinct realm distinguishable from religious convictions, social practices, manners, and so on. Moral principles presumably can be and indeed must be justified in abstract and historical arguments: What is right or wrong is right or wrong for all times and places. Such an account of morality is what creates the peculiar modern presumption that we must first conceive and justify something called morality and then we must ask how to apply it—thus, the recent enthusiasm for "applied ethics" concerning matters of medicine, business, and law. Ethics is derived from philosophical speculation as engineering is from theoretical physics. (A terrible analogy if you know anything about physics and/or engineering.) When you first have an ethic that requires further questions about how it is to be applied, then you know you have an ideology.

It is of course this paradigm of moral rationality that I have tried to counter by declaring that I am a pacifist writing as a Christian. I do not pretend that I can write about the war for anyone, anywhere, anytime, as if such a position would insure "objectivity." Such an "objective" point of view is but a form of imperialism that fueled the imperialism that produced the presumption that Americans "had" to intervene in the Gulf. There, an imperial power pursued a war on the presumption that all right-thinking people could not help but agree that the "facts" required a moral response that "unfortunately" meant war.

To understand the Gulf War, it is crucial to understand the interrelation of moral and political imperialism exemplified by American justification of the war. Imperialism derives from the hegemonic power of an empire that presumes, exactly because it is an empire, that anyone, anywhere if given the opportunity would want to be part of the empire. A false universalism is created that necessarily blinds the imperialists, since they believe that they represent the nonbiased view of humanity.

Iraq, as an Arab nation, was an ideal opponent because such a nation so clearly lacked the necessary characteristics of universality.

The distinction between morality and prudence is so inscribed into the self-interest of imperial powers that I do not presume it can be defeated by argument. The Reverend Michael Baxter, C.S.C., has at least suggested to me an interesting test for those who assume that the distinction is intelligible for assessing the Gulf War on just war grounds. They should ask themselves what they might possibly learn that might make them consider the Gulf War unjust. If, for example, our primary object was to make Iraq withdraw from Kuwait, then was the bombing policy pursued in Iraq itself just? Why was it necessary at the same time we pursued the war in Kuwait to also try to eliminate Saddam Hussein's nuclear capacity? Surely, the potential to make nuclear weapons is not itself unjust, as otherwise the American policy in that regard would be problematic. The implications of American bombing policy in Iraq, moreover, surely must raise questions about the principle of discrimination, since such policy clearly was meant to disrupt Iraq's social infrastructure.

The distinction between morality and prudence is invoked by many Christians who justify the Gulf War on just war grounds because it lets them avoid "a lot more." Their appeals to prudence excuse them from naming what difference how they think about this war might make for them as Christians. For example, Professor Stephen Fowl of Loyola College, Baltimore, observes that, in terms of the criterion of last resort, Richard Neuhaus

> rightly notes that any judgment that all previous options have been exhausted is a prudential one; it is a judgment call for which one must take responsibility. What he fails to mention, however, is despite the contingencies of any particular situation, what counts as a last resort is going to be different for those who are also committed to loving their enemies than for those who are committed to maintaining a certain standard of living for themselves. If Christians are to reason both prudentially and faithfully, they will need to understand that criteria for determining the justice of any particular war are deeply tied to their convictions about God, the cross, their neighbors and their enemy—convictions which many others employing the language of just war theories do not share.[7]

By challenging the distinction between morality and prudence, I am not calling into question the need of practical wisdom for moral guidance. But as Aristotle and Thomas Aquinas emphasized, only the person of virtue, that is, the person of prudence and charity (in Thomas's case), has the capacity for such wisdom. For prudence is not the application of moral principles to concrete decisions; rather, it is discernment about matters that matter but can be different. All moral judgments are contingent—including moral principles—and that is why principles and criteria are useless if they are not constituted in practices that form and are formed by good people. Moreover, that is why judgments of practical wisdom by those who call themselves Christians may be profoundly different from those who are not so formed.

If Christians can ever be just warriors, they can be so only with profound sadness. As just warriors, they can never kill gladly. Indeed, if Paul Ramsey was right in his defense of just war, the Christian soldier should not intend to kill the enemy but rather seek only to incapacitate him so as to prevent him from achieving his purpose.[8] In fact, the Christian soldier would rather die, or at least take greater risks, than kill unnecessarily. From a Christian perspective, these thoughts should make the Gulf War even more doubtful since there is every reason to believe that the strategy was to inflict as much destruction on the enemy by using means that would not risk American lives in order to avoid adverse domestic political consequences.

Surely, the saddest aspect of the war for Christians should have been its celebration as a victory and of those who fought it as heroes. No doubt many fought bravely and even heroically, but the orgy of crusading patriotism that this war unleashed surely should have been resisted by Christians. The flags and yellow ribbons on churches are testimony to how little Christians in America realize that our loyalty to God is incompatible with those who would war in the name of an abstract justice. Christians should have recognized that such "justice" is but another form of idolatry to just the degree it asked us to kill. I pray that God will judge us accordingly.[9]

CHAPTER 8 ▼ WHY GAYS

(AS A GROUP) ARE MORALLY SUPERIOR TO

CHRISTIANS (AS A GROUP)

I am ambivalent about recent discussions concerning gays in the military. I see no good reason why gays and lesbians should be excluded from military service; as a pacifist, I do not see why anyone should serve. Moreover, I think it a wonderful thing that some people are excluded as a group. I only wish that Christians could be seen by the military as being as problematic as gays.

The groundswell of reaction against gays performing military service no doubt results from many factors. The response, however, is not because of the threat that gays might pose to our moral or military culture. Discrimination against gays grows from the moral incoherence of our lives; people who are secure in their convictions and practices are not so easily threatened by the prospects of a marginal group acquiring legitimacy through military service.

Gay men and lesbians are being made to pay the price of our society's moral incoherence not only about sex, but about most of our moral convictions. As a society, we have no general agreement about what constitutes marriage and/or what goods that marriage ought to serve. We allegedly live in a monogamous culture, but in fact we are at best serially polygamous. We are confused about sex, why and with whom we have it, and about our reasons for having children.

This moral confusion leads to a need for the illusion of certainty. If nothing is wrong with homosexuality, then it seems everything is up for grabs. Of course, everything is already up for grabs, but the condemnation of gays hides that fact from our lives. So the moral "no" to gays becomes the necessary symbolic commitment to show that we really do believe in something.

But in some way this prejudice against gays has worked in their favor. They at least know more about who they are and who their enemy is. If only Christians could be equally sure of who they are. If only the military could come to view Christians as a group of doubtful warriors.

What if Catholics took the commitment to just war seriously as a discipline of the church? Just war considerations might not only raise questions about targeting strategies of nuclear weapons, but also question whether we should even have a standing army. A just war stance requires discussion in order to secure genuine conscientious participation. The very fact of our standing army means too often such discussion is relegated to politicians who manipulate the media to legitimate what they were going to do anyway. If Catholics challenged the presumption of a standing army, or at least one the size of the U.S. army, they might not be so quickly received into the military.

Consider the implications of Catholic Christians trained to press issues of discrimination in terms of battlefield strategy. Would the military welcome pilots who worried if bombing drops might incur civilian casualties? Even concern with the distinction between direct and indirect intention for dealing with such matter is, I suspect, more than the military wants to address on a daily basis.

Imagine Catholics, adhering closely to just war theory, insisting that war is not about killing but only incapacitating the enemy. They could participate only in wars designed to take prisoners and then, if that is not a possibility, only to wound. Killing the enemy is a last resort. What would military training look like if that were institutionalized?

Concentration on just war reflection is probably too abstract a way to imagine how Christians as a group might become suspect for military service. Far more likely are Christian behaviors and practices. Christians, for example, might be bad for morale in barracks. For example, non-Christians may find it disconcerting to have a few people gathering nightly holding hands with heads bowed. God knows what kind of disgusting behavior they might be engaged in.

Even more troubling is what they might say to one another in such a group. Christians are asked to pray for the enemy. Could you really trust a person in your unit who thinks the enemy's life is as valid as his own or his fellow soldier's? Could you trust someone who would think it more important to die than to kill unjustly? Are these people fit for the military?

Prayer, of course, is a problem. But even worse is what Christians do in corporate worship. Think about the meal, during which they say they eat and drink with their God. They do something called "pass the peace." They even say they cannot come to this meal with blood on their hands. People so concerned with sanctity would be a threat to the military.

Having them around is no fun. They think they ought to keep their promises. They think that fidelity matters. They do not approve of the sexual license long thought to be a way of life and legitimate for those facing the danger of battle. Their loyalty is first to God, and then to their military commanders. How can these people possibly be trusted to be good soldiers?

Finally, consider the problem of taking showers with these people. They are, after all, constantly going about the business of witnessing in the hopes of making converts to their God and church. Would you want to shower with them? You never know when they might try to baptize you.

If gays can be excluded as a group from the military, I have hope that it could even happen to Christians. God, after all, has done stranger things.

However, until God works this miracle, it seems clear to me that gays, as a group, are morally superior to Christians.

CHAPTER 9 ▼ COMMUNITARIANS

AND MEDICAL ETHICISTS

OR "WHY I AM NONE OF THE ABOVE"

In our time it is not unusual for students in divinity school to say something like: "I'm not into Christology this year. I really am into relating." In response they are told: "Well, then, you ought to take some more courses in Clinical Pastoral Education. After all, that is what the ministry is really about today [i.e., relating]. So take some courses that will teach you better how to relate."

It is interesting to contrast that kind of response to someone who might enter medical school thinking, "I'm not really into anatomy this year. I'm really into relating. I'd like to take some more courses in psychology." The response in medical schools is radically different from that in divinity schools. Such a student is usually told: "We're not really interested in what you're interested in. You either take anatomy or you can simply ship out!"

It is interesting to ask what accounts for these differences. I think they derive from the fact that no one anymore really believes that an incompetently trained priest might threaten his or her salvation, since no one really believes that anything is at stake in salvation; but people do think that an incompetently trained doctor might in fact do them serious harm. People no longer believe in a God that saves, but they do believe in death, and they know that they want to put it off as long as possible. They assume, wrongly, but no less dogmatically, that medical care can add significant years to their lives. Accordingly, the social power of medicine continues to increase in our society, and the power of religion diminishes.

That medicine has such social power explains why medical education is so much more morally serious than the education of people going into the ministry. In medical education students are subjected to a rigorous discipline that trains them to attend to others in a way that gives them skills of attention and care. Thus, we continue to expect physicians to study and train themselves even after graduation in a manner that we do not expect of those in the ministry. What skills and knowledge do ministers have that anyone else does not already have?

The contrast between the ministry and medicine is nicely exhibited in our respect for how each discipline structures its time. Physicians can be late for appointments, not show up at all, be curt in certain situations without the need for apology or explanation. It is simply assumed that such behavior is excused because they are attending to patients, studying to know how to better care for patients, or are under great stress. In contrast, those in the ministry have to be on time, always be available, and perpetually act pleasant.

I begin with these contrasts in training and conduct in order to challenge the assumption that I represent a communitarian alternative to the liberal presuppositions that have shaped most of the work in recent medical ethics. While I have drawn on some motifs derived from communitarian thinking, my concerns always have been how to exhibit the power that theological convictions have had, can have, and should have for how Christians should understand their care for one another through the office of medicine. Indeed, I think that underwriting the commonly made contrast between liberalism and communitarianism can result in blurring the theological issues. For Christians should have as many difficulties with most communitarian alternatives as they do with liberal alternatives.

I am uneasy with the contrast between liberalism and communitarianism because those alternatives are produced by the very liberal presuppositions that I think are so problematic. I am, accordingly, very sympathetic with Charles Taylor's suggestion that the very terms "liberal" and "communitarian" need to be scrapped. Rather, we need much thicker accounts of the different positions embraced by those two terms and the infinite variety of differences between those positions.[1]

For example, too often communitarianism is identified with a nostalgia for small-town America and the correlative "family doctor" who no longer exists. While I think nostalgia can be an extremely important form of social criticism, I certainly do not hanker after small-town America or that kind of medicine. I am not sure if such an America ever existed, and even if it did, whether it was a good thing.

The longing for community so prevalent in our time is, from my perspective, but the working out of liberal theory and practice. Thus, I fear all appeals for community as an end in itself. For communities formed by the alienated selves who are created by liberalism too quickly can become a kind of fascism. No one should want community as an end in and of itself, but one should want to be part of communities because the forms of cooperation offered by them provide for the achievement of goods otherwise unavailable—such as the worship of God.

I fear appeals to community in the abstract, just as I fear appeals to "family values" in the abstract. I was called by a reporter during the 1992 Republican national convention and asked what I thought about family values. I replied that since I am a Christian I have, of course, a deep distrust of the family, since for Christians the family is one of the great sources of idolatry. Christians believe our first loyalty is to the God who constitutes us first by making us part of the church rather than of the family. I soon discerned that the reporter was having trouble understanding these basic theological points, so I changed my tactics. I noted that people suggest that when fascism comes to America it will come with a friendly face. I then suggested that the form that face will take is, of course, family values. "Family values," it turns out, is how Americans talk about "blood and soil."

I fear that appeals for community as a good in and of itself in liberal societies too often mask rather than expose exactly those conflicts that we need to have in order to locate goods which we might come to share. In many ways the development of medical ethics as a strategy in liberal political practice has been a communitarian enterprise. The creation of a formal discipline called ethics, displayed concretely over medical practice, results in the comforting illusion that this society can sustain an intelligible practice of medicine, even though we have no way of determining what purposes medicine should serve—other than the prolonging of each individual's life. That is why I think that the most determinative communitarian thinker in medical ethics is H. Tristram Engelhardt.[2]

That also is why, of course, I am not a communitarian. I do not want community as an end in and of itself; instead, I want us to be the kind of people who can sustain, for example, practices as significant as baseball.

Baseball represents the kind of shared practice that I think is morally important. Charles Taylor illumines this point by telling the story of Jacques, a man who lives in Saint Jérôme, Quebec. It seems that Jacques had for years listened to the Montreal Symphony, directed by Charles Dutoit. He desperately wanted to hear the symphony live, but because he cared for his aged mother, who suffered from acute anxiety when he left town, he was not able to do so. Refusing to let these circumstances thwart his desire, he recruited other music lovers in Saint Jérôme, organized a campaign, and succeeded in bringing the Montreal Symphony there. Taylor notes that when Jacques actually experienced his first live concert: "He was enraptured not only by the quality of the sound, which was as he had expected quite different from what you get on records, but also by the dialogue between the orchestra and the audience. His own love of the music fused with that of the crowd in the darkened hall resonated with theirs, and found expression in an enthusiastic common act of applause at the end. Jacques also enjoyed the concert in a way he had not expected, as mediately common good." [3]

The significance of Taylor's story can be seen by attending to Christopher Lasch's suggestion that at the heart of the communitarian criticism of liberalism is the significance of practices. For good communities result from shared judgments derived from skills acquired through the training necessary to pursue certain practices—such as architecture, medicine, baseball, or writing. Different practices require different virtues; for example, hitting a baseball requires great dexterity. Moreover, appreciating the dexterity required to hit a baseball is a skill of its own.

Lasch suggests that the real difference between liberalism and communitarians is not about abstract appeals to the importance of community, but the communitarian understanding that the state's responsibility is to protect practices rather than privacy. All attempts to protect privacy that are not subordinate to the end of securing practices that have become goods in common cannot help but corrupt the polity. As Lasch observes:

> Liberalism assumes that men and women wish only to pursue their private purposes and that they form associations only in order to advance these purposes more effectively. Its solicitude for individual rights extends to the right of association, but it finds it hard to conceive voluntary associations except as pressure groups seeking to influence public policy in their own favor. This blindness deprives liberals of any perspective from which to

criticize corruption of practice by external groups. Pressure groups are by definition interested in external goods alone—quite appropriately, from a liberal point of view—and the task of politics, accordingly, is merely to decide among their competing claims. Internal goods, on the other hand, are no business of the state, in the liberal view. The state obviously has no authority to tell doctors how to practice medicine or baseball players how to field their positions. It steps in only when these practices acquire a public interest, when they affect the distribution of external rewards in other words, or—not to put too fine a point on it—when there is money involved. My objection to the liberal view of things can be simply summarized by saying that this is too narrow a conception of the public interest.[4]

Lasch goes on to argue that the distinction between the public and private so integral to liberal accounts of state and society fails to give an appropriate account of the public interest. Even worse, it trivializes those activities that need to be protected and nourished. The problem with the liberal protection of privacy is that, exactly because it equates freedom with the absence of constraint, it has no moral content. Once one takes the view of practice, such as that articulated by Lasch, one sees that freedom is in fact submission to the exacting discipline of learning to play and appreciate baseball—and/or becoming a minister or physician.

What does all of this have to do with medical ethics? I think what it helps us see, as MacIntyre pointed out in "Patients as Agents," is that the problem is not community but authority.[5] Like Lasch, MacIntyre notes that judgments about matters that matter are seldom like the exercise of a mechanical skill. For often judgments require one to go beyond existing precedent and presumptions about "what usually is the case." For those who can act with authority, often judgments have to be made about particular cases in a way that necessitates the reformulation of rules about those cases. Therefore, authority cannot exist "without institutionalized respect; authority cannot exist unless we are prepared on some occasions to accept its judgement as superior to our own, even when our own differs."[6]

For such authority to flourish requires, of course, a tradition for the display of the skill of giving reasons. Only within a degree of moral consensus derived from past judgments can those engaged in a practice have confidence in one another in a way that the tradition can be extended.

That is why all rational practices, according to MacIntyre, require the recognition of authority. The very suggestion that what is needed is moral authority challenges the presuppositions of American liberalism, which assumes that freedom consists in having individuals freed from all commitments other than those they have freely contracted.

Yet not only is such an account of authority necessary for the good functioning of medicine, but there must be a sense of a hierarchy of goods for medical as well as other forms of authority to function well. MacIntyre argues that the authority of a doctor over a patient is not simply that which derives from the technical skills of the physician or the surgeon, but that which stems from a whole set of beliefs and practices based on a sense of the hierarchy of human goods. Thus, he asks us to consider a culture where

> a variety of human practices is normatively ordered in terms of the goods which are internal to them and for each practice there are professions specifically intrusted with the pursuit of that good and with the cultivation of those virtues necessary to achieve it. So the good of national independence is intrusted to the military profession, along with the virtues of courage and strategic thinking. The goods of rational inquiry are intrusted to learned professions, along with the virtues of intellectual honesty, self-criticism, and theoretical thinking. The good of health is intrusted to the medical profession with its concomitant virtues. There is a moral division of labor and each part of the society has to repose trust in the other. The distribution of powers is justified by the relationship of the professions, goods, and virtues.[7]

MacIntyre's picture of a well-ordered society is, of course, far too "ordered." He is well-aware that good societies will be constituted by conflict between various authorities, since the goods may well conflict. The contrast between a well-ordered society and our society is not between harmony and order, but that we do not live in a society in which conflict between authorities can be acknowledged. For to acknowledge such conflict means we would have to expose the empty center of our politics.

In such a polity MacIntyre doubts that authority of the physician can any longer be vindicated as moral authority. Accordingly, physicians, who still must make decisions about what is good for patients, are forced to derive their authority from their technical expertise. Correlatively, the patient is made even more powerless in order to legitimate the illusory authority derived from technique. Patient autonomy is therefore asserted as the only alternative to redress the unjust power of the physician over the patient.

Which of course brings me back to my opening account of the difference between the kind of training undertaken by a physician and by a person studying for the ministry. Our problem is simply that in the absence of any good beyond our basic physical survival, we lack any sense of what limits might be placed on the good that medicine serves—thus, the subordination of those in the ministry to those in medicine. Any attempt to limit medical care in such a context cannot help but appear arbitrary and cruel. As a result, medical care becomes increasingly just another form of liberal bureaucracy that must be subject to the same kinds of rules so characteristic of the wider political life.[8] I therefore take medical ethics to be but one form which that kind of bureaucratic maintenance assumes. That, of course, is why I do not aspire to be a medical ethicist.

Such a claim surely may seem disingenuous for me since I have written about medicine and in particular medical ethics. I have done so, however, not because I am a communitarian but because I am a theologian. Medical practice remains, I believe, more like baseball than bureaucracy. Just to the extent medicine is an activity—practice—that morally transforms its practitioners means that the power that accrues to it has the potential to create as many problems as it solves. Yet exactly to the extent that medical care has remained committed to those it cannot cure, medicine provides one of the more profound practices on which we can draw in our culture for moral example. I suspect, moreover, that so many of us who have been associated with ethics have been drawn to medicine—that is, the actual practice of medicine rather than the theory of medicine—because we have discovered in medicine what a substantive moral practice actually looks like. Accordingly, we have been turned into a community called medical ethicists, who now threaten to destroy what we are allowed to observe because our theories are not rich enough for us to understand why we should care for those we cannot cure.[9]

As a theologian, I have been drawn to medicine because it provides the issues where we might see again what difference Christian convictions or their absence might have for how we live. To be a Christian is to be made part of a community through which I am trained to die early.[10] What difference that training might make for how the hierarchy of goods that shapes our living and our dying and correlatively the authority of medicine, I take to be one of the most interesting questions before us.

Compassion: The Liberal Virtue

I first became aware that compassion can kill when watching a film sponsored by the National Association for Retarded Citizens. The film shows a couple looking into a crib. The room is dark, and we do not see who is in the crib. The young mother looks up and says, "Don't let this happen to you. Our baby was born retarded. Our lives are crushed and we do not know where to turn. Do not let this happen to you. Get prenatal counseling. Help us eliminate retardation."

I was absolutely stunned by that commercial. It had been developed with the best intentions. The National Association for Retarded Citizens thought this was a way to mobilize support for research monies from the government to help find cures for retardation. Just as people think we ought to try to eliminate cancer, so they think we ought to eliminate retardation. Of course, there is one difficulty. We can care for the cancer patients by trying to alleviate their cancer without destroying the patient, but you cannot eliminate retardation without destroying the person who is retarded.

I began to reflect on what possibly could fuel this extraordinary desire to eliminate the retarded in the name of caring for them. For there is no question that the most compassionate motivation often lays behind calls to eliminate retardation, for helping the old to die without pain, for insuring that no unwanted children are born, and so on. Such policies seem good because we assume compassion requires us to try to rid the world as much as possible of unnecessary suffering. Those born retarded seem to be suffering from outrageous fortune, cruel fate, that if possible should be eliminated. Ironically, in the name of responding to suffering, compassion literally becomes a killer.

Nowhere do we see this fact more powerfully than in issues raised through the practice of medicine. For modern medicine has had its task changed from care to cure in the name of compassion—a killing compassion. For example, the recent discussion of doctor-assisted death, or what perhaps should be called doctor-assisted suicide, surely must be seen in this context.[1] Unable to cure those who are dying, we then think it is the compassionate alternative to help them to their death. Euthanasia thus becomes but the other side of the medical and technological imperative to keep alive at all cost.[2]

A kind of madness erupts in our modern souls when we confront the suffering of our world. How do you work to care for some when not all can be cared for? We thus work to save starving children, and by keeping them alive they have even more children who cannot be fed. Thus, compassion perpetrates cruelty, and we are driven mad by such knowledge. Some in their madness turn to strategies that require them to sacrifice present generations in the hope of securing a better future for those who are left. All in the name of compassion.

The philosophical name we give to this compassion as an ethical alternative is sometimes called utilitarianism.[3] Even though utilitarianism is often thought to be a radical secular philosophical alternative, in fact it can be seen as a form of Christianity gone mad. For the utilitarian is radically self-denying exactly to the extent that consistent utilitarians give themselves or those near them no more value than anyone else. So each person is equal to every other person—that is, each person is viewed as simply another unit seeking to maximize his or her self-interest. Utilitarians, with the greatest compassion, are thus willing to sacrifice some, who may include themselves, so that the greater number may flourish. Of course, you have the difficulty of knowing who is to count as one of the greater number and over how long a time.

Confronted with this kind of killing compassion, one is tempted to literally kill compassion. Years ago I published an article called "Love's Not All You Need" in which I attacked those who construed the nature of the Christian moral life primarily in terms of love.[4] When compassion becomes the overriding virtue, linked with liberal political practice, it cannot help but be destructive. As Oliver O'Donovan observes in his book *Begotten or Made?*:

> Compassion is the virtue of being moved to action by the sight of suffering—that is to say, by the infringement of passive freedoms. It is a virtue that circumvents thought, since it prompts us immediately to action. It is a virtue that presupposes that an answer has already been found to the question "what needs to be done?," a virtue of motivation rather than of reasoning. As such it is the appropriate virtue for a liberal revolution, which requires no independent thinking about the object of morality, only a very strong motivation to its practice.[5]

It is not my intention to try to defeat the overdetermined emphasis on compassion by suggesting the negative results of this position in societies like our own. No question that charity is, in Aquinas's phrase, the form of all the virtues.[6] But that charity is first and foremost disciplined by the witness of our God who would have us die, yea even our children die, rather than to live unworthily.[7] Therefore, Christians are formed by a harsh and dreadful love, but one we think truthful, rather than the generalized forms of sentimentality that we call compassion.

I call attention to compassion as the central norm and virtue that characterizes our lives as a way to help us locate those stories that hold us captive.[8] For there can be no question that the generalized commitment to compassion characteristic of Enlightenment societies forms the Christian as well as the non-Christian soul. My way of putting the matter is that today we are all liberals, and we are such because we have no choice but to be such.

It was the project of modernity to create social orders that would produce something called the free individual. The powerful institution of the division of labor makes it almost impossible to escape the fate of being an individual whose sole moral focus is that of compassion. Put simply, the story of modernity is that you should have no story except the story you have chosen when you had no story. Thus, the modern presumption is that one never should be held responsible for commitments that we have not freely chosen, even if we thought at the time we were freely choosing. Compassion and the creation of compassionate societies try to make it possible for each person in a society of individuals to have the social, economic, and political status to choose who they want to be. The project of liberal societies is simply to make the freedom of choice a necessity. Thus, we achieve the goal of making freedom the fate of each individual.

That, of course, creates the peculiar form of self-deception at the heart of the modern project. For, ironically, what liberal societies cannot acknowledge is that we did not choose the story that we should have no story except the story we have chosen from the position where we allegedly had no story. Therefore, modern liberal societies cannot acknowledge that they are coercive, since they derive their legitimation from the presumption that no one, if they have appropriate social and economic power, is coerced to be a member of such social orders. Our task, our social idealism, is now to work for societies where everyone has the economic power to be whatever they want.[9]

This compassionate ideal renders problematic some of our most basic practices, as they cannot help but appear unintelligible on liberal and compassionate grounds. For example, at the University of Notre Dame, where I once taught part of the normal course offerings in the theology department, a course on marriage was given. I did not want to miss the opportunity to teach such a course, but I knew how I taught it would be a disappointment for both the parents who wanted their children to take the course as well as for the students who took it. For I knew they would want the course taught from the perspective of "how to do it," and I could only teach the course from the perspective of "why would you want to?" Marriage for Christians, after all, is not a necessity, since we believe our lives as Christians do not require marriage for the simple reason that the true family is the church.[10]

However, trying to satisfy as many students as possible, I knew that they had been sent to Notre Dame because it had the reputation of being a relatively conservative school. By conservative, most people meant that students at Notre Dame would be taught some absolutes. Not wanting to disappoint those expectations, I always taught what I called Hauerwas's law: you always marry the wrong person. Though such a law sounds cynical, it is not in fact meant to be, since it is also reversible: you also always marry the right person.

I did not teach Hauerwas's law simply to challenge the romantic conceptions of marriage shared by both my students and their parents. Rather, I taught Hauerwas's law to challenge some of the basic liberal presuppositions that I thought were destroying the very notion of marriage as an institution and practice characteristic of Christians. For it is the peculiar sensibility of modernity to think that if our marriages have gone bad, it is because we did not know what we were doing when we "chose" the person we married. If we just become more intelligent and more thoughtful, we surely will get it right the second time.

The anomaly behind this set of presumptions is that one could ever know what one was doing when one got married. I take it that the wisdom of the Christian tradition has been that the church witnesses a couple's marriage, not because we think they know what they are doing, but because they do not. That is why we as Christians (should) insist that we can only have marriage witnessed in the church among people who will hold us to our promises. Marriage provides the set of practices and expectations that allow us over a lifetime to name our lives together as love. Without the time that fidelity in marriage creates, there is no possibility of love.

The other anomaly is that liberal presuppositions create an unintelligibility with regard to how we feel for our children as well as how our children view their responsibility to their parents. But why should we be responsible for people whom we did not choose as part of our life? Rather, we discover that our parents as well as our children are simply given to us, and we must learn to be stuck with them and in being so stuck we learn that our lives graciously are not our own. Yet it is exactly such limits to create a society where we are freed from such "fate" that the compassionate imperative of liberalism renders problematic.

That is why compassionate liberals have so much difficulty understanding why we may have obligations to near neighbors who come in the form of our children that cannot be overridden for the good of future generations.[11] The kind of obligation we have to our own children does not mean that they can have computers while children in Somalia are starving. The difficulty we face, however, is that we do not know how to say or express our care for children in Somalia without underwriting the liberal project of compassion. We thus throw up our hands, acknowledging that if we cannot do everything necessary to make the world free of starving children, then we might as well do nothing.

Failing to meet the demands of compassion leads many to adopt the other virtue of modernity, cynicism. I realize that it is odd to think of cynicism as a virtue, but I believe it to be at the heart of the liberal moral project. For in the absence of any agreed-upon goods, we are forced to create our own values. The difficulty is that we do not trust any values we have chosen exactly because we have chosen them. So we adopt a cynical stance toward our own and others' projects—that is, we believe we must always preserve our autonomy by being able to step back from our engagements by describing them as self-interested pursuits. That is why we are so hesitant to ask others, and in particular our own children, to make sacrifices for our convictions.[12]

Perhaps in no place is this peculiar set of virtues better exhibited than in education. Thus, the task of education in most liberal societies becomes that of providing information for students to "make up their own minds." The most feared perversion of such education we call indoctrination. It never seems to occur to us that in the name of respecting students' individual desires, we indoctrinate them to believe that their own individual desires should matter. Any education that is worthy is obviously indoctrination. Our inability to acknowledge it as such in the name of respect and love for the student is but a sign of our corruption.

The Discovery of Everyday Life: Charles Taylor's *Sources of the Self*

Rather than continue to describe the anomalies created by the domination of compassion in our lives, I want to try to help us understand how this has happened by drawing on Charles Taylor's *Sources of the Self: The Making of Modern Identity.*[13] In this book Taylor makes some extremely acute observations about the discovery of the significance of ordinary life, discoveries that are the necessary background for the ethics of compassion. By ordinary life he means "those aspects of human life concerned with production and reproduction, that is, labor, the making of the things needed for life, and our life as sexual beings, including marriage and the family" (211).

Taylor is not making the absurd claim that before modernity people did not love their children or marry for love. Nor is he saying that prior to modernity did they value less their everyday work. People of all ages and in all societies have cared for their children, though what "care" meant obviously varied. It is not the actual place of affection that Taylor is calling to our attention, but the sense of its importance. As he says:

> what changes is not that people begin loving their children or feeling affection for their spouses, but that these dispositions come to be seen as a crucial part of what makes life worthy and significant. For whereas pre-

viously these dispositions were taken as banal, except perhaps that their absence in a marked degree might cause concern or condemnation, now they are seen as endowed with crucial significance. It is of course true that beginning to make something of them also alters these dispositions. (p. 292)

Taylor notes that Aristotle managed to combine in his account of the eudaemonistic life two activities—theoretical contemplation and participation as a citizen in the polity. Yet Plato looked unfavorably on the second, and the Stoics challenged both sets. At least for some of the Stoics the sage should be detached from the fulfillment of his vital and sexual needs. Taylor calls our attention to Aristotle, Plato, and the Stoics to note that, in contrast to the valuing of ordinary life, stand those forms of social existence that are intrinsically hierarchical. It is the life of contemplation and political participation, the latter often exemplifying the aristocratic ethic of honor, that render the minor householder as inferior.

Taylor suggests that the transition he thinks so significant is when these hierarchies are displaced in favor of labor and production, on the one hand, and marriage in family life, on the other. All previous "higher" activities are now rendered problematic. For example, under the impact of the scientific revolution, the intellectual project of grasping the order of the cosmos through contemplation is now seen as vain. Instead, the object now is to engage in the detailed work of discovery. Accordingly, Frances Bacon reorientates science to be about relieving the condition of man, not about understanding the beauty of planetary motion. Science is not a higher activity that ordinary life should subserve; on the contrary, science should benefit ordinary life.

According to Taylor, inherent in this new evaluation of ordinary life is a commitment toward social leveling. The good life is about what everyone can and/or should achieve. The elitism of the ethic of the gentleman, the ethic of honor, is slowly eroded in favor of the virtues necessary to sustain the life of commerce, the science that serves that commerce, and for the goods of work and family. Even, or especially, revolutionary thought such as Marxism has as its goal the realization of our highest dignity in labor and the transformation of nature in the service of life (p. 215).

Taylor argues that rightly to understand this transformation of the significance of ordinary life, we cannot attribute it to the process of secularization. Indeed, Taylor suggests that the origin of this discovery of the everyday came first of all from the Reformation. For it was one of the central points of the Reformation to reject hierarchy and mediation. In particular, the Reformation criticized the Catholic presumption that some in the corporate body of Christ could be more dedicated, thereby making them capable of winning merit and salvation for others who were less so.

The rejection of mediation was interconnected with the reformers' denial that the sacred could be found in some places and times more than in others—no holy objects, land or people.[14] Salvation is now the exclusive work of God, requiring the rejection of the Catholic understanding that the church is the necessary mediator of God's salvation. The very idea that there were special places or times for actions, where the power of God is more intensely present, became the hallmark of those people called Protestant.

When salvation is no longer thought to be mediated, then the personal commitment of the believer becomes all-important. No longer does one belong to the people of God by one's connection to a wider order that sustains a sacramental life; now one's wholehearted personal commitment is required. Monasticism accordingly is rendered problematic. Monasticism flourished when members of the church drew

> on the merits of those who are more fully dedicated to the Christian life, through the mediation of the church, and because I am accepting this lower level of dedication, I am settling for less than a full commitment to the faith. I am a passenger in the ecclesial ship on its journey to God. But for Protestantism, there can be no passengers. This is because there is no ship in the catholic sense, no common movement carrying humans to salvation. Each believer rows his or her own boat. (p. 217)

Accordingly, the very notion of vocation changes. While in Catholic cultures the term vocation is usually used in connection with the priesthood or the monastic life, for the Puritans vocation becomes any employment understood as useful to mankind and imputed to use by God. "The highest life can no longer be defined by an exalted *kind* of activity; it all turns on the *spirit* in which one lives what everyone lives, even the most mundane existence" (p. 224). Such a view of vocation assumes that the creator intends the preservation of all creatures. "Humans serve God's purposes in taking the appointed means to preserve themselves in being. This doesn't mean that we are called upon to preserve others at our own expense; it is no question of renunciation. Rather, we are called upon to serve both ourselves and others as being equally humans and God's creatures" (p. 225). Vocation thus is alleged to have intrinsic rules, determined by the order of creation or sovereign spheres, to which the believer must submit as part of her or his service to each neighbor.[15]

Taylor argues that it was not accidental that the Puritan discovery of ordinary life, articulated through a theology of work, provided a hospitable environment for the scientific revolution. Bacon's outlook on science was in fact made possible by those Puritan presuppositions. Baconian science and Puritan theology equally "rebelling against a traditional authority which was merely feeding on its own errors and as returning to neglected sources: the Scriptures on one hand, experimental reality on the other. Both appealed to what they saw as living experience against dead received doctrines—the experience of personal conversion and commitment, and that of direct observation of nature's workings"[16] (p. 230).

Baconian science thus institutionalized the shift from contemplation as the goal of science to science becoming the means for humans to be stewards of God's creation. Accordingly, Baconian science served to legitimate an instrumental stance toward the world, which, ironically, made science all the more powerful as it is now filled with spiritual meaning. Now our task through science is to gain rational control over ourselves and the world for the good of the world. Instrumentalizing is crucial to this approach to the world, since we are constantly reminded to treat the things of creation merely as instruments and not as ends valuable in themselves. Taylor argues that as a result

> the tremendous importance of the instrumental stance in modern culture is overdetermined. It represents the convergence of more than one string. It is supported not just by the new science and not just by the dignity attaching the disengaged rational control; it has also been central to the ethic of ordinary life from its theological origins on. Affirming ordinary life has meant valuing the efficacious control of things by which it is preserved and enhanced as well as valuing the detachment from purely personal enjoyments which would blunt our dedication to its general flourishing. (p. 232)

The rationalized form of Christianity called deism resulted from those developments. The Puritan emphasis on work for the common good becomes the Enlightenment assumption that a way of life exists that can conciliate self-service and beneficence. Just to the extent that our service to the self can take a productive form, such service can be furthered without invading others' rights and property. The Puritan assumption that our purpose was to worship God is now translated into living rationally, that is, productively.[17] Instrumental rationality becomes the avenue of participation in God's will. This is not an abasement of God's will to the status of a factor in our game; rather, it exalts our reasoning to a level of collaboration in God's very purpose (p. 244).

Thus, the affirmation of ordinary life went hand in hand with the notion that the very purpose of God's creation was for the human good. This belief took its form from the good order of nature. Miracles, in fact, had to be excluded not simply because the assumptions of an ordered universe required that they be eliminated, but because if miracles were a possibility then we were less sure of developing predictable sciences necessary for serving the human good.[18] Of course, as Taylor observes, to construe the order of nature in terms of mechanistic causes not only excludes miraculous interventions, but it also marginalizes history. The great historical events of Exodus and the cross require that Christians maintain unbroken continuity with these moments through tradition.

> Once the notion of order becomes paramount, it makes no more sense to give them a crucial status in religious life. It becomes an embarrassment to religion that should be bound to belief in particular events which divide one group from another and/or in any case open to cavil. The great truths of religion are all universal. Reason extracts these from the general course of things. A gap separates these realities of universal import on the particulate facts of history. These latter cannot support the former. (p. 273)

What is extraordinary about Taylor's analysis is how it helps us see why any Christian account of love necessarily suffers a loss of a Christological center, not because of science, but because of the moral presuppositions commensurate to the valuation of everyday life. If we are to create compassionate societies in which the value of each individual is thought to be equal to other individuals, then we must devalue the extraordinary. The extraordinary, of course, comes in the form of extraordinary people as well as extraordinary events. But in the interest of creating compassionate societies, that is, societies driven by the imperative of technology to render existence as much as possible free of suffering, we discover that we must live in a world in which the ordinary reigns. Ironically, the story of modernity is that modernity was created by Christianity, which then rendered its creator irrelevant—trivial at best, perverse at worst.

Patience: The Christian Virtue

Which brings us back to Oliver O'Donovan's worries in *Begotten Or Made?* For O'Donovan has seen clearly how the technological imperatives driven by the ethics of compassion can only end, ironically, in murder. What do we as Christians have to offer as an alternative to this set of events? According to O'Donovan, we can do four things. First, Christians should confess their faith in the natural order as the good creation of God.

> To do this is to acknowledge that there are limits to the employment of technique and limits to the appropriateness of "making." These limits will not be taught thus by compassion, that only by the understanding of what God has made, and by discovery that it is complete, whole and satisfying. We must learn again the original meaning of the great symbolic observance of Old Testament faith, the Sabbath, on which we lay aside our making and acting and doing in order to celebrate the completeness and integrity of God's making and acting and doing, in the light of which we can dare to undertake another week of work. Technique, too, must have its Sabbath rest. (p. 12)

Secondly, according to O'Donovan, Christians must confess at this juncture our faith in the providence of God as the ruling power of history. To make this confession, we must make clear the limits to our responsibility with regard to the future. The future is not an artifact that we can mold to our will. Rather, we must see that ways of acting contribute to the course of events, a deed, which, whatever its outcome, is fashioned rightly in response to the reality that confronts the agents as they act.

Third, Christians should confess that our faith is in a transcendent ground if we are to affirm human community at all.

> In our time the notion of brotherhood has broken up into two inadequate substitutes: on the one hand, the notion of bearing responsibility for

someone, which implies care for the other's freedom without mutuality of action, and on the other the notion of association in a common project, which implies mutuality of action without care for the other's freedom. If we are to recover the mutual responsibility between doctor and patient, we need to think of their quality as co-operating human agents, in ways that only the Christian confession can open up to us. (p. 13)

Fourth, Christians should confess their faith that creation from beginning to end is made through the word that we call Jesus. Only on that understanding are we capable of acknowledging the kind of order that is rightly to be found in the world.

O'Donovan's suggestions for how we as Christians are to respond to the ethos of compassion are wise and profound. I wish that I thought them adequate. But I fear such appeals to order, and the correlative confessions in God's creation that sustain them, because I do not believe such order is knowable apart from cross and resurrection. O'Donovan seeks an account of natural law that is not governed by the eschatological witness of Christ's resurrection. We cannot write about *Resurrection and Moral Order* because any order that we know as Christians is resurrection. I am not denying that we are creatures of a good creator; I am simply suggesting that as Christians we know nothing about what we mean by creation separate from the new order we find through the concrete practices of baptism and Eucharist, correlative as they are to Christ's resurrection.[19]

What this means is, in short, that in no way can we protect ourselves from the ethos of compassion by appeals to the order guaranteed by God's good creation. I do not care whether you call it orders of creation, or sphere sovereignty, or common grace. What must be recognized is that the ethos of compassion that currently threatens to destroy us will not be checked by appeals to the integrity of creation but by people who know that their lives have meaning only as they are called to serve one another through the body and blood of Jesus of Nazareth. Only such a people can know how to love some people when not all can equally be cared for.

Albert Borgmann notes that our lives are characterized by a kind of addiction to hyperactivity. Since we believe that we live in a world of endless possibilities secured through technology, we find ourselves constantly striving, restless for what—we are not sure. Such hyperactivity creates, according to Borgmann, a kind of sullen leisure resentful of our inability to be satisfied.[20]

Borgmann does not think it possible or wise to deny that technology is now our "postmodern destiny." Rather, he suggests that our task is to shape that destiny through a recovery of the virtue of patience as an alternative to power.

> When power prevails in its paradigmatic modern form, it establishes order on the ruins of inconvenient circumstances and on the suppression of un-cooperative people. Regardless, power rests on destruction and remains haunted by it. Patience has the time and strength to recognize compli-cated conditions and difficult people, to engage them in cooperation and conversation. The powerful provoke envy and fear; the patient earn admi-ration and affection. By patience I do not mean passivity but endurance, the kind of strength we admire in an athlete who is equal to the length of a run or the trials of a game. (p. 124)

Borgmann notes that such patience is required not only by our need to learn the limits of the land, but by the frailties of our bodies that call for social and individual patience. Noting that this country is ter-ribly confused about health care, Borgmann suggests that little hope of clarification about such matters is possible

> until we learn a common and, indeed, communal patience with the pains of fatal diseases, the debilities of old age, and the aches and pains of daily life. Only a shared understanding will encourage the individual to endure and society to agree on explicit and reasoned limits to medical interven-tion. More properly put, it is only when society becomes something like a community and the individual more of a member in that community that health and patience will be reconciled. (p. 125)

Borgmann ends his powerful book noting that such patience is possible only through communal celebration. Christians call such cele-bration worship, believing as we do that placed in a world of deep agony we can do nothing more important than to take the time to worship a God whose patience took the form of a cross.[21] It is to be hoped that if we can learn to live out such patience, we might help ourselves and others learn better how medicine might be patiently ordered to care for the ill and the dying.

CHAPTER 11 ▼ THE CHURCH AND

THE MENTALLY HANDICAPPED

A CONTINUING CHALLENGE TO THE

IMAGINATION

The "Problem" of "the Problem" of the Mentally Handicapped

The challenge of being as well as caring for those called "mentally handicapped" is to prevent those who wish they never existed or would "just go away" from defining them as "the problem" of the mentally handicapped. It is almost impossible to resist descriptions that make being mentally handicapped "a problem," since those descriptions are set by the power of the "normal." For example, parents who have a mentally handicapped child often were and sometimes still are told that such a child will be happier "institutionalized." Such roadblocks continue when parents try to get adequate medical care and often find that doctors assume it would be better for everyone if this child would die. The adversity continues as parents face the hundreds of silent slights contained in the stares of people in grocery stores and service stations, stares that communicate—"thank God that is not me."

Such roadblocks and slights are destined to get worse as our society seeks and finds ways to eliminate the mentally handicapped. What will happen, for example, if this society starts requiring amniocentesis? The human genome project is a potential threat to the mentally handicapped as it will encourage the presumption that people should regulate their sexual and marital behavior to avoid having handicapped children. What will our society say to those who decide to challenge the presuppositions that we ought to avoid having mentally handicapped children? It is possible to envision that society may well put legal and financial penalties on people who decide to have children who are less than "normal."

Of course, implicit in these projects is the false assumption that most of the mentally handicapped are primarily born rather than made. Thus, even if this society decides to eliminate the birth of mentally handicapped children, they will continue to be confronted by those who are environmentally handicapped—that is, those whose condition is the result of pollution, nutritional deficits, and poverty rather than genetics. The care of those children whose handicaps result from such environmental causes may be even worse, since on the whole this society already has decided that such "unfortunate accidents" should not exist.

There are, moreover, roadblocks interfering with adequate training of the mentally handicapped. Schools are not set up to handle mentally handicapped people because such individuals do not learn as we learn. Mentally handicapped folks are segregated, not because they cannot learn, but because they are segregated for being not like us. Furthermore, we fear those who are not like us. It is said that they will slow other children down, and well they might, but it is never thought that they might morally speed up other children.

Faced with such obstacles and challenges, those who have and care for the mentally handicapped often feel their most immediate task is to try to overcome the immediate threats to the mentally handicapped. They become advocates of normalization and fight for the "least restrictive alternatives" for the mentally handicapped. These strategies, to be sure, have much to recommend them, but too easily they can become part of the agenda of those who basically want to deny the existence of the mentally handicapped. Ask yourself, for example, would you want to be pressured to be normal? Who is to say what that entails? Since I am a Texan I would not have the slightest idea what it means to be normal. While I do not disagree with most of the recommendations put forward in the name of normalization, I do worry that that concept does not in itself specify what we need to say on behalf of the mentally handicapped; or perhaps better put, it does not focus on what we need to make possible for the mentally handicapped to say on their own behalf.

Particularly disturbing are the ways in which our confrontation of the challenges facing the mentally handicapped tend to put the burden of care entirely on the family. Our society seems to say, "Your luck was bad, and now you are stuck with this kid. We will help you so long as you do not ask for too much." Therefore, the family becomes the only agent representing the mentally handicapped, since absolutely no one else is there to represent them.

Many who care for the mentally handicapped then get caught up in contradictions that seem unavoidable. For example, in the interest of supporting families in their care of the mentally handicapped, often against unfeeling bureaucracies, we maintain that families have all rights regarding the mentally handicapped. The family can serve the interest of the child on the assumption that parents best know the child's needs.

However, we then feel at a loss when we encounter families who do not want to care for the child. Those who refuse to provide basic medical care for a Downs Syndrome baby who needs further surgery is only one dramatic example. As a result, we have institutions filled with mentally handicapped people who are there because they have been abandoned by the only people this society thinks can care for them—their parents.

The Mentally Handicapped and the Christian Imagination

These examples challenge our imaginations concerning how we are to act with the mentally handicapped. What has gone wrong is not that we lack goodwill, but that we simply do not know how to care because we need the challenge of real people who will teach us how to care. Such people really are the imagination of a community, for we must remember that imagination is not something we have in our minds. Rather, the imagination is a pattern of possibilities fostered within a community by the stories and correlative commitments that make it what it is. Necessities force us out of our paths of least resistance, and, as a result, they make us more likely to form communities that know how to care for one another.

Our imaginations, when driven by little more than the logic of our desires, easily can lead us astray. As Christians, this fact should not surprise us, since we have learned that those aspects of our lives that offer the greatest resources for good also offer equivalent resources for evil. This is why human imagination, like any other human capacity, must be ordered by something more determinative.

For Christians, that something is both the story of who God has called us to be and our concrete attempts to faithfully embody that calling. For a community with such a self-understanding, imagination is not a power that somehow exists "in the mind"; instead, it is a pointer to a community's constant willingness to expose itself to the innovations required by its convictions about who God is. Similarly, the world is seen differently when construed by such an imaginative community, for the world is not simply *there,* always ready to be known, but rather is known well only when known through the practices and habits of community constituted by a truthful story.

The Christian imagination forces us to acknowledge that the world is different from what it seems. That difference requires Christians to be willing to explore imaginative possibilities in ways not required of those who do not share the narratives and practices that both make us Christian and, concomitantly, shape our view of the world. Of course, stating the matter in this way is dangerous, for it easily can be interpreted to mean that Christians refuse to acknowledge the world as it "really is." In other words, we open ourselves to the charge that by failing to live in the world "as it really is," our view of the world remains "fantastic"— that is, that it arises out of fantasy or illusion.

Yet Christians hold that the so-called world-as-it-really-is is itself fantastic, and so we must learn to live imaginatively, seeing what is not easily seen, if we are to faithfully embody the character of the God we worship. Christians are well-aware of how easy it is to live as if the world had no creator. In short, it is easy to live as if we, as well as "nature," had no purpose other than survival. But to live in such a way is not to live in the world "as it is." For to live in the world "as it is" is to be the kind of people who can see that everything has been created to glorify its creator—including the mentally handicapped. To fail to live in such a way is to deny the way the world "is." This is why Christians believe that imagination formed by the storied practices of the church constitutes the ultimate realism.

"Realism" often is used in epistemological contexts to denote that position whose advocates believe objects exist that can be known "in and of themselves." Realists often contrast their views with those who emphasize the importance of the imagination, associating the imagination with fantasy. Imagination is fiction; but knowledge, it is alleged, describes the world "as it is." There is no question that common usage underwrites this kind of distinction between knowledge and imagination—that is, the kind of distinction whose advocates can say, "It's all in her imagination." But as Garret Green observes, it is also the case that people think imagination is essential for helping us know what would otherwise go unnoticed. Thus, we often praise people who demonstrate "insight and imagination."[1]

Much can be said for those like Green who want to rehabilitate imagination as a mode of knowing essential to how Christians think about the world. According to Green, "imagination is the means by which we are able to present anything not directly accessible, including *both* the world of the imaginary *and* recalcitrant aspects of the real world; it is the medium of fiction as well as of fact."[2] Imagination, therefore, seems to be central to the kind of claims that Christians make about God.

However, one problem with proposals like Green's is that such accounts of imagination appear to be too abstract and disembodied. Such accounts accept the assumption that the status of imagination is fundamentally an epistemological issue divorced from the practices of particular communities. On the contrary, however, the Christian imagination is constituted by practices such as nonviolence and learning how to be present to—as well as with—the mentally handicapped—who we hopefully know not as mentally handicapped, but as Anna and Boyce, our sister and brother in Christ.[3]

On Children, the Church, and the Mentally Handicapped

Of course, learning to live joyfully with the Annas and the Boyces draws on the resources of other practices that make their presence intelligible in relation to other practices that constitute who we are and desire to be. For example, consider an issue that at first may seem foreign to the question of how we should care for the mentally handicapped—namely, why we have children in the first place. I often used to begin a course in the theology and ethics of marriage with the question: "What reason would you give for yourself or someone else for having a child?" Few students had thought about the question, and their responses were less than convincing: that is, children should manifest their love for one another as a hedge against loneliness, for fun, and/or to please grandparents. Often, one student finally would say that he or she wanted to have children to make the world better. The implicit assumption behind this reason was that the person who spoke up would have superior children who, having received the right kind of training, would be enabled to help solve the world's problems.

Such reasoning often appears morally idealistic. However, its limitations can be revealed quickly by showing its implications for the mentally handicapped. For people who want to have superior children in order to make the world better are deeply threatened by the mentally handicapped. If children are part of a progressive story about the necessity to make the world better, these children do not seem to fit. At best, they only can be understood as deserving existence insofar as our care of them makes us better people.

Such attitudes about having children reveal a society with a deficient moral imagination. It is an imagination correlative to a set of practices about the having and care of children that results in the destruction of the mentally handicapped. The fundamental mistake regarding parenting in our society is the assumption that biology makes parents. In the absences of any good reason for having children, people assume that they have responsibilities to their children because they are biologically "theirs." Lost is any sense of how parenting is an office of a community rather than a biologically described role.

In contrast, Christians assume, given the practice of baptism, that parenting is the vocation of everyone in the church whether they are married or single. Raising children for Christians is part of the church's commitment to hospitality of the stranger, since we believe that the church is sustained by God across generations by witness rather than by ascribed biological destinies. Everyone in the church, therefore, has a parental role whether or not they have biological children.

For Christians, children are neither the entire responsibility nor the property of parents. Parents are given responsibility for particular children insofar as they pledge faithfully to bring up those children, but the community ultimately stands over against the parents reminding them that children have a standing in the community separate from their parents. Therefore, the ways in which mentally handicapped children are received in such a community should be strikingly different from how they are received in the wider society. For the whole burden of the care for such children does not fall on the parents; rather, the children now are seen as gifts to the whole community.

At the very least, the church should be the place where parents and mentally handicapped children can be without apologizing, without being stared at, without being silently condemned. If others act as if we ought to be ashamed for having such children among us, then those others will have to take on the whole church. For this is not the child of these biological parents, but this child is the child of the whole church, one whom the church would not choose to be without. Moreover, as this child grows to be an adult, she, just as we all do, is expected to care as well as to be cared for as a member of the church.[4]

Such a child may add special burdens to the community but on the average not more than any child. For every child, mentally handicapped or not, always comes to this community challenging our presuppositions. Some children just challenge us more than others as they reveal the limits of our practices. Christians are people who rejoice when we receive such challenges, for we know them to be the source of our imaginations through which God provides us with the skills to have children in a dangerous world. The church is constituted by a people who have been surprised by God and accordingly know that we live through such surprises.

The church, therefore, is that group of people who are willing to have their imagination constantly challenged through the necessities created by children, some of who may be mentally handicapped. The church is constituted by those people who can take the time in a world crying with injustice to have children, some of whom may turn out to be mentally handicapped. We can do that because we believe this is the way God would rule this world. For we do not believe that the world can be made better if such children are left behind.

I am aware that this view of the church's treatment of the mentally handicapped is overly idealized. But I believe I am indicating the potential contained in common Christian practice. Moreover, the presence of the mentally handicapped helps Christians rediscover the significance of the common, because the handicapped call into question some of our most cherished assumptions about what constitutes Christianity.

For example, often in Christian communities a great emphasis is placed on the importance of "belief." In attempts to respond to critiques of Christian theology in modernity, the importance of intellectual commitments often is taken to be the hallmark of participation in the church. What it means to be Christian is equivalent to being "ultimately concerned" about the existential challenges of human existence and so on. Yet the more emphasis that is placed on belief, particularly for individuals, the more the mentally handicapped are marginalized. For what the mentally handicapped challenge the church to remember is that what saves is not our personal existential commitments, but being a member of a body constituted by practices more determinative than my "personal" commitment.

I suspect this is the reason why mentally handicapped people often are better-received in more "liturgical" traditions—that is, traditions which know that what God is doing through the community's ritual is more determinative than what any worshiper brings to or receives from the ritual. After all, the God worshiped is the Spirit that cannot be subject to human control. The liturgy of the church is ordered to be open to such wildness by its hospitality to that Spirit. What the mentally handicapped might do to intrude onto that order is nothing compared to what the Spirit has done and will continue to do. Indeed, the presense of the mentally handicapped may well be the embodiment of the Spirit.

Nowhere is the individualistic and rationalistic character of modern Christianity better revealed than in the practice of Christian education. For example, religious education is often the attempt to "teach" people the content of the Christian faith separate from any determinative practices. What it means to be Christian is to understand this or that doctrine. Yet if the church is the community that is constituted by the presence of the mentally handicapped, we know that salvation cannot be knowing this or that but rather by participating in a community through which our lives are constituted by a unity more profound than our individual needs. From such a perspective the mentally handicapped are not accidental to what the church is about, but without their presence the church has no way to know it is church—that the church is body. If the word is preached and the sacraments served without the presence of the mentally handicapped, then it may be that we are less than the body of Christ.

Mentally handicapped people are reminders that belief and faith are not individual matters, but faith names the stance of the church as a political body in relation to the world. We are not members of a church because we know what we believe, but we are members of a church because we need the whole church to believe for us. Often, if not most of the time, I find that I come to be part of the community that worships God not as a believer or as a faithful follower of Christ, but as someone who is just "not there." I may not be a disbeliever, but I am by no means a believer either. By being present to others in church I find that I am made more than I would otherwise be—I am made one in the faith of the church; my body is constituted by the body called church.

The mentally handicapped remind us that their condition is the condition of us all insofar as we are faithful followers of Christ. The church is not a collection of individuals, but a people on a journey who are known by the time they take to help one another along the way. The mentally handicapped constitute such time, as we know that God would not have us try to make the world better if such efforts mean leaving them behind.[5] They are the way we must learn to walk in the journey that God has given us called Kingdom. They are God's imagination, and to the extent we become one with them, we become God's imagination for the world.

Of course, worshipping with the mentally handicapped can be no easy matter. Such worship can be disorderly, since we are never sure what they may or may not do. They create a "wildness" that frightens because they are not easily domesticated. Yet exactly to the extent that they create the unexpected, they remind us that the God we worship is not easily domesticated. For in worship the church is made vulnerable to a God that would rule this world not by coercion but through the unpredictability of love. Christians thus learn that the mentally handicapped are not among us because we need someone to be the object of charity, but because without these brothers and sisters in Christ whom we call retarded, we cannot know what it rightly means to worship God.

So through the prism of worship, Christians discover the mentally handicapped as brothers and sisters in Christ. They are not seen as victims of our society. For the great strength of the mentally handicapped is their refusal to be victimized by the temptations to become victims. Through their willingness to be present in church, they provide the church with the time to be the church. We thus learn that we can take the time for someone who does not talk well to read the Scriptures. We can take the time to walk slowly together to the communion table when one of our own does not walk well or not at all. We can take the time to design our places of gathering so that they are open to many who would otherwise not be able to be there. We can take the time to be a people open to children who always will distract us from the projects that seem so promising for making the world "better."

A community formed imaginatively by the presence of the mentally handicapped should, however, provide ways to respond to the challenges and roadblocks mentioned earlier. For if the wider society lacks the basis for knowing how to care for the mentally handicapped, it does so because it is devoid of examples to help it spur its imagination.

185

What we need to exhibit is that it is not simply the question of how to "care" for the mentally handicapped, but how to be with the mentally handicapped in a way that we learn from them. What any community needs to learn is that the mentally handicapped are not among us to be helped, though like all of us they will need help, but rather by their being among us we learn how we are all more able to be a community. It is interesting, for example, how quickly communities forget how certain practices designed for the "handicapped" become accepted as ways of life for everyone. Thus a study at the University of Kansas asked why slopes had been put into sidewalks. Most respondents said that they thought that they were there to make bicycling easier. So the access for the handicapped becomes an opportunity for the whole community.

Certainly the ignorance and cruelty of the wider society toward the mentally handicapped needs to be constantly challenged. But more important is the witness of those who have learned that it is not simply a matter of caring for the mentally handicapped but of learning to be with the mentally handicapped. Only when we learn how to be with those different from us can we learn to accept the love that each of us needs to sustain a community capable of worshiping God. It should not be surprising, therefore, that Christians may well be seen in the future as a people who have learned how to be with the mentally handicapped. We may accordingly be thought very odd indeed if our society continues in the direction of the threats discussed above. Yet we believe that nothing could be more significant for a world that assumes that God has not given us the timeful imaginations to be with the mentally handicapped.

INTRODUCTION
Positioning: In the Church and University but Not of Either

1. In the introduction to *Doing What Comes Naturally: Change, Rhetoric, and the Practice of Theory in Literary and Legal Studies* (Durham, N.C.: Duke University Press, 1989), Fish identifies himself as "white, male, a teacher, a literary critic, a student of interpretation, a member of a law faculty, a father, a son, an uncle, a husband (twice), a citizen, a (passionate) consumer, a member of the middle class, a Jew, the oldest of four children, a cousin, a brother, a brother-in-law, a Democrat, short, balding, fifty, an easterner who has been a westerner and is now a southerner, a voter, a neighbor, an optimist, a department chairman" (p. 30). Though I cannot confirm all of these self-descriptions, since I live next door I know he is a neighbor and on the whole a good one. I do, however, think it pretentious for him to claim to be a southerner, since he will never know how to "talk right."

This series of self-identifications Fish uses to make the important point that his critique of foundationalist claims for transcontextual rationalism should not be taken to invoke an alternative totalizing structure. He names his membership in the various interpretative communities to indicate his enterprise is not "pure" and to note that conflict can occur between these various "roles." I mention this because my identification as "Christian" can invite a far too monochromatic account of what it means to be Christian. I certainly think being Christian has a distinct character, but the lives of the saints make clear that there are many ways to be Christian. That does not mean I am in agreement with Fish's way of putting the matter, since I know being a southerner should never be described as a "role." You can never play at being southern, anymore than you can play at being a Texan. Southern and Texan are ontological categories.

2. The difficulty with putting the matter this way is it makes it appear that theology is a first-order enterprise when in fact the work of the theologian is parasitical on faithful practice of Christian people. That does not mean theologians reflect on what most Christians are currently doing, but what Christians have done through the centuries. Such an appeal to the "past" does not mean that Christians will be faithful today by doing what was done in the past, but by attending to how Christians did what they did in the past we hope to know better how to live now. Of course, since we believe in the communion of saints it is a comfort to know that our past forebearers are present with us.

As one as critical as I am of the Christian complicity with the order of violence that in shorthand is called "Constantinianism," the significance of this I hope will be duly noted. I do not believe that God ever abandons the church even in its unfaithfulness. So the "Constantinian" church remains "my" church as I know, even in the Constantinian strategies, that within it lie aspects of the Gospel. After all, behind the Constantinian attempt to rule lay the presumption that all is God's good creation. I am well-aware that in many ways my theology is no less imperialistic than are many forms of Constantinianism. I certainly would, if I could, have as many be nonviolent as possible. The problem, of course, is that since I am committed to nonviolence, I cannot coerce anyone to so live.

3. Pacifism no more names a position that one can assume than does the name Christian. Both name a journey that is ongoing and never finished in this life. For the pacifist, nonviolence is not a "given," but an activity that hopefully helps us discover the violence that grips our lives in ways we had not noticed. Such discoveries require the use of the art of causistrical comparison through which descriptions are tested by analogy. Though I find it tiresome to be constantly subjected to "But what would you do if . . ." by those convinced that violence and war are moral necessities, I still must count them blessed insofar as they help me see what I may have missed.

4. Of course, there are all kind of conversions. I want my reader to submit to the discipline of the church, but that means they first will have to be converted from being a liberal. In *Whose Justice? Which Rationality?* (Notre Dame, Ind.: University of Notre Dame Press, 1988), MacIntyre characterizes the liberal self as "the person who finds him or herself an alien to every tradition of enquiry which he or she encounters and who does so because he or she brings to the encounter with such tradition standards of rational justification which the beliefs of no tradition could satisfy. This is the kind of post-Enlightenment person who responds to the failure of the Enlightenment to provide neutral, impersonal tradition-independent standards of rational judgment by concluding that no set of beliefs proposed for acceptance is therefore justifiable" (p. 395). Mac-

Intyre rightly observes that only "by a change amounting to a conversion, since a condition of this alienated type of self even finding a language-in-use, which would enable it to enter into dialogue with some tradition of enquiry, is that it becomes something other than it now is, a self able to acknowledge by the way it expresses itself in language standards of rational enquiry as something other than expressions of will and preference" (pp. 396–97).

5. More than twenty years ago I wrote an article called "Situation Ethics, Moral Notions, and Moral Theology," that argued that descriptions are more determinative than decisions. I drew on Julius Kovesi's wonderful and unfairly overlooked book, *Moral Notions* (New York: Humanities Press, 1967) to suggest that notions like humility or murder are more morally important than words like right or good. Everything I have written since has presupposed this argument which I still find as persuasive now as I did then. I wish I could find more convincing ways to persuade others. The essay now appears in my *Vision and Virtue: Essays in Christian Ethical Reflection* (Notre Dame, Ind.: University of Notre Dame Press, 1981). The essay was first published in the *Irish Theological Review* (1983).

6. For example, Ronald Thiemann in *Constructing a Public Theology: The Church in a Pluralistic Culture* (Louisville, Ky.: Westminster/John Knox Press, 1991) suggests that the challenge before Christians is to "develop a public theology that remains based in the particularities of the Christian faith while genuinely addressing issues of public significance. Too often, theologies that seek to address a broad secular culture lose touch with the distinctive beliefs and practices of the Christian tradition. On the other hand, theologies that seek to preserve the characteristic language and patterns of Christian narrative and practice too often fail to engage the public realm in an effective and responsible fashion. (He means Hauerwas.) Either they eschew public discourse altogether in order to preserve what they see as the uniqueness of Christian life, or they enter the fray with single-minded ferocity, heedless of the pluralistic traditions of our democratic polity. (He means fundamentalist.) If Christians are to find an authentic public voice in today's culture, we must find a middle way between these two equally unhappy alternatives" (p. 19). The rhetorical strategy of this paragraph would take an essay to analyze, but note that Thiemann assumes that there is a "public discourse" that is simply "out there." Christians cannot eschew the use of that discourse if we are to work within the "pluralist traditions of our democratic polity." It is unclear to me from where the justifications for such descriptions come. They probably sound a good deal more convincing at Harvard—namely, that institution dedicated to producing the people who would rule the world in the name of "freedom." I find the language of pluralism particularly puzzling, since it would seem if we really value pluralism, then I do not see why those who enter the fray with "single-minded ferocity" are doing anything wrong. Thiemann later says my attacks

on liberalism blind me "to the resources that liberalism might provide for the reconstruction of a political ethos that honors the pluralism of contemporary public life" (p. 24). I simply have no idea what it means or why Christians have a stake in honoring "the pluralism of contemporary public life." Why should we call this social world "pluralistic?" and if we do in what sense is it "public?" From my perspective "public" and "pluralism" are simply words of mystification that some people use when their brains are on automatic.

7. In their recent book, *Fullness of Faith: The Public Significance of Theology* (New York: Paulist Press, 1993), Michael Himes and Kenneth Himes, O.F.M. go to great lengths to show that the Christian belief in the Trinity, which "is the summary grammar of our most fundamental experience of ourselves," is not incompatible with a commitment to human rights (p. 59). They do try to distance themselves from liberal theories of rights by suggesting that rights gain their intelligibility from our capacity of self-gift. Yet even with such a qualification the conceptual relations between their considerations of the Trinity and human rights are vague at best. Even more puzzling is why they think it matters. Who are they trying to convince? Liberal rights theorists could care less. Are they trying to convince Catholics who may believe in the Trinity that they also ought to support human rights? Do they think American Catholics need to be convinced of that? One cannot help but feel the pathos of such projects as they strive to show that Catholics too can be good liberals. For example consider their suggestion that "in his teaching Jesus emphasized the value his Father placed on human life and the extent of God's concern which embraced all people irrespective of distinctions such as class, race, gender or nationality" (p. 92). We needed Jesus to reveal that God is the great liberal bureaucrat? I leave without comment that the cover of the book has a picture of the White House with the Washington Monument in the background. I assume they did not choose the cover.

8. For those anxious for an adequate characterization of liberalism, I can do no better than that offered by Ronald Beiner in his *What's the Matter With Liberalism?* (Berkeley: University of California Press, 1992). My own characterization is best-found below under the chapter heading "Killing Compassion." The interrelation between liberal political, social, and ethical theory is complex. MacIntyre in *Whose Justice? Which Rationality?* has presented that complexity as well as anyone.

9. Liberalism as a politics and morality has been made possible by its continued reliance on forms of life it could not account for within its own presuppositions. There is nothing wrong about it having done so except the power of liberal practices has increasingly undermined just those forms of life for which it could not account—such as why we have children. For example, T. M. Scanlon recently noted in a review of Ronald Dworkin's *Life's Dominion: An Argument About Abortion, Euthanasia, and Individual Freedom* that "if, as

most contemporary moral philosophy suggests, morality can be simply identified with the sphere of rights, interests, duties, and obligations (i.e., with 'what we owe to others') then there is no distinctive morality of sex. Sexual activity is judged to be right or wrong by the same categories that apply to every other sphere of life, categories such as deception, coercion, consent, and injury." "Partisan For Life," *New York Review of Books,* July 15, 1993, p. 46. The problem is that such a view of morality is insufficient to account for why such everyday activities such as friendship and having children make any sense at all.

The influence of liberal moral theory can be seen insofar as some now think that murder is wrong because it robs the one killed of his or her rights. Such accounts derive from the presumption that you need a theory to tell you what is wrong with murder. I have no doubt that liberals do need such a theory, which is but an indication why they are in such desperate need of retraining.

10. No doubt many people are oppressed as well as victimized in this society as well as in others, but the current cult of victimization has clearly gotten out of hand. I attribute this development to liberal egalitarianism, which creates the presumption that any limit is arbitrary and thus unjust. As a result, we are all victims who must compete to show who has been more decisively victimized. The difficulty with such a process is that nothing more victimizes us than accepting the description that we have been victimized.

11. The biographies of Trollope by Hall and Glendinning make clear that try as he would to be an English gentleman, Trollope's gregariousness as well as his inability to look well-dressed, no matter how expensive his clothes, always hindered his rise in society. See N. John Hall, *Trollope: A Biography* (Oxford: Clarendon Press, 1991) and Victoria Glendinning, *Anthony Trollope* (New York: Alfred Knopf, 1993). Trollope's current "popularity" is puzzling but gratifying for many of us who have long enjoyed his work.

For a particularly interesting reading of Trollope, see J. Hillis Miller, *The Ethics of Reading* (New York: Columbia University Press, 1987), pp. 81–99. Drawing on Trollope's *An Autobiography,* Miller argues that in spite of Trollope's attempt to portray the production of novels as a reinforcement of the normal exchanges of his time, he undermined that official doctrine. Miller suggests that Trollope's self-description of "being impregnated with my own creations" indicates a kind of "auto-fecundation" that made him a solitary, alien, inassimilable to the world of Victorian production. As Miller puts it, Trollope "wants to show how the writing of novels was a means of legitimate entry into society. He wants to show that his novels are moral in the sense of affirming the values of that society. He wants to show that his readers have got their money's worth when they have purchased his novels. In spite of himself he shows the opposite. He shows that he has perpetrated a kind of fraud, that he has secretly undermined the values of his society, and that for their shillings his readers have purchased books which are for that reason dangerous or subversive" (p. 96).

I am sure Trollope would enjoy Miller's account of the "subversive" character of his work, but I think he knew that his work was even more subversive than Miller's depiction. He knew the world was changing in ways that undermined his world of honor and love. Yet he loved his characters, people caught in such a changing world, with a love that would not rob them of their ambiguity. As I try to show, it was a love that was formed by the practice of forgiveness that will always prove subversive to the world of violence.

For a profound account of the substance, as well as the limits, of the ethic of the gentleman for the practice of the law, see Thomas L. Shaffer and Mary Shaffer, *American Lawyers and Their Communities: Ethics in the Legal Profession* (Notre Dame, Ind.: University of Notre Dame Press, 1991). Jack Sammons puts it wonderfully when he asks how Professor Shaffer's gentleman is to act in a culture he must reject if he is to continue to be a gentleman. He suggests that Shaffer's truthful gentleman "would not trust his own judgment in these circumstances because he knows too well what happens to good people in bad cultures. The true gentleman in a corrupt society, in other words, knows he should not trust his own instincts and, because he should not, he cannot continue being a gentleman." "The Professionalism Movement: The Problems Defined," *Notre Dame Journal of Law, Ethics, and Public Policy* 7 (1993): 289.

12. I confess, also, that I strongly identify with Trollope's desire to be well-liked—at least by his fellow authors. Trollope, I believe, had an extraordinary capacity for friendship which I should also like to emulate. At the same time he could not stand cant and was quite capable of telling his friends the hard truth. Trollope understood that candor and honesty, though closely related, are not the same thing. His novels often exhibit the hard work required to be able to say honestly what has happened and is happening to us.

13. In her wonderful book, *Parallel Lives* (New York: Alfred Knopf, 1983), Phyllis Rose notes: "We tend to talk informally about other people's marriages and to disparage our own talk as gossip. But gossip may be the beginning of moral inquiry, the low end of the platonic ladder which leads to self-understanding. We are desperate for information about how other people live because we want to know how to live ourselves, yet we are taught to see this desire as an illegitimate form of prying. If marriage is, as Mill suggested, a political experience, then discussion of it ought to be taken as seriously as talk about national elections. Cultural pressure to avoid such talk as 'gossip' ought to be resisted, in the spirit of good citizenship" (pp. 9–10). It is my hunch that the novel became our primary form for the instruction of the moral imagination once we lacked the cultural consensus to make the kind of instruction exemplified by Samuel Johnson in the *Rambler* papers coherent. When I am asked who should one read for moral instruction, I recommend Ms. Manners.

14. MacIntyre notes that "insofar as the internationalized languages-in-use of late twentieth-century modernity have minimal presuppositions in respect of possibly rival belief systems, their shared criteria for the correct application of such concepts as 'is true' and 'is reasonable' must also be minimal. And in fact truth is assimilated, so far as is possible, to warranted assertibility, and reasonableness, so far as possible, is relativized to social context. Hence when texts from traditions with their own strong historical dimension, are translated into such languages, they are presented in a way that neutralizes the conceptions of truth and rationality and the historical context" *Whose Justice? Which Rationality?,* p. 384. Such language is necessary to preserve what MacIntyre characterizes as one of the defining beliefs of the culture of modernity—namely, the belief "in its ability to understand everything from human culture and history, no matter how alien" (p. 385). It is not easy to insult people with such presumption, but I am trying.

15. In *Arendt, Camus, and Modern Rebellion* (New Haven, Conn.: Yale University Press, 1992), Jeffrey Isaac observes that anarchism is frequently misunderstood. He notes that the Russian revolutionary Voline (Vsevolod Eichenbaum), who argued that anarchism is antipolitical only in the state, and in the forms of political activity that support state sovereignty, is considered the sine qua non of politics (pp. 148–50).

16. It seems odd, but the contemporary university appears to be intent on excluding people with strong views. You can "entertain" ideas that seem out of fashion, but you had better not be caught taking them seriously. Accordingly, university administrators seem to be people who have from birth talked in circumlocutions. Like people considered for the U.S. Supreme Court, the last thing with which they would want to be caught is a strong position from the past. It turns out the "vision thing" is not just a problem for George Bush, but for most aspiring "leaders" in this society who think leadership means "management." I should say I do not blame them for becoming managers but rather assume that such a character type is required by the politics of liberalism. See, for example, Alasdair MacIntyre's account of the manager in *After Virtue,* 2d ed. (Notre Dame, Ind.: University of Notre Dame, 1984), pp. 74–78.

17. For a welcome analysis of abortion that offers an alternative to the current sides, see Elizabeth Mensch and Alan Freeman, *The Politics of Virtue: Is Abortion Debatable?* (Durham, N.C.: Duke University Press, 1993), as well as Kathy Rudy, "Mapping the Moralities of Abortion" (Unpublished Ph.D. dissertation, Duke University, 1993).

18. I am in the process of writing a book that will tell the story of the rise and fall of Christian ethics as a discipline in the United States. My way of putting the matter is to have the book ask the dramatic question: how did a tradition that began with Walter Rauschenbusch's *Christianizing the Social Order* end with a book by James Gustafson entitled *Can Ethics Be Christian?* My

answer is simple: just to the extent that we got the kind of society the Social Gospel wanted, that outcome made Christianity unintelligible. An overview of this story can be found in my *Against the Nations: War and Survival in a Liberal Society* (Notre Dame, Ind.: University of Notre Dame Press, 1992), pp. 23–50. For a very different account of this development, see Harlan Beckley, *Passion for Justice: Retrieving the Legacies of Walter Rauschenbusch, John A. Ryan, and Reinhold Niebuhr* (Louisville, Ky.: Westminster/John Know Press, 1992). Susan Curtis's account of the Social Gospel rightly argues: "With their focus on the improvement of society in the here and now, social gospelers had helped lay the ideological and moral foundations of a society and culture dominated by secular institutions, standards, and values. The evolution of the social gospel and of American culture occurred simultaneously, each influencing the nature of change in the other. By 1920 the message of the social gospel had helped create and legitimize a new culture in the United States that effectively marginalized historical Protestantism. Social gospelers, in their effort to be part of the changing culture they served, adopted the secular language, methods, and standards of commerce in their religious belief and practices. The success of the social gospel writers in articulating a new social understanding of work, family and polity also had the ultimate effect of undermining its originating religious impulse" *A Consuming Faith: The Social Gospel and Modern American Culture* (Baltimore: John Hopkins University Press, 1991), pp. 228–29.

19. For more extensive reflection on how preaching as a truthful practice might look, see William Willimon and my *Preaching to Strangers* (Louisville, Ky.: Westminster/John Knox Press, 1992).

20. The most determinative form of that politics being the implicit contract between liberal intellectuals and those they serve that nothing will take place at the university that might challenge "democracy." That is done by intellectuals allowing themselves to be characterized as agents of the world of "ideas," which by definition are nonpolitical. The American university thus remains safe from political control, since it is already well self-policed.

21. John Murray Cuddihy delivered the decisive critique of the idea of civility in his *No Offense: Civil Religion and Protestant Taste* (New York: Seabury Press, 1978). It may seem odd for one who defends an ethic of honor to be critical of civility, but the person of honor is committed to a hierarchical understanding of the moral goods that may require them to act in less than a civil fashion for the preservation of those goods. For example Cuddihy quotes Chesterton to the effect, "The sentimentalist is the man who wants to eat his cake and have it. He has no sense of honor about ideas; he will not see that one must pay for an idea as for anything else" (p. 49).

22. Charles Taylor observes that it was the collapse of social hierarchies, which used to be the basis of honor, that forms the background of the current preoccupation with identity and recognition. The democratic notion of

"dignity" replaced honor, which certainly seemed to be an advance insofar as honor was linked to inequalities. Yet the politics of dignity has given rise to the politics of difference, but without a clear basis on which the "difference" is to be determined. Using the example of Quebec, Taylor argues that the liberal politics of equal respect articulated and enshrined in the language of rights does in fact seek to abolish cultural difference. He wisely offers no easy solution other than suggesting that liberalism must recognize that it is not a "possible meeting ground for all cultures, but is the political expression of one range of cultures, and quite incompatible with other ranges. Moreover, as many Muslims are well aware, Western liberalism is not so much an expression of the secular, postreligious outlook that happens to be popular among liberal *intellectuals* as a more organic outgrowth of Christianity—at least as seen from the alternative vantage point of Islam. The division of church and state goes back to the earliest days of Christian civilization. The early forms of the separation were very different from ours, but the basis was laid for modern developments. The very term *secular* was originally part of the Christian vocabulary. All this is to say that liberalism can't and shouldn't claim complete cultural neutrality. Liberalism is also a fighting creed" *Multiculturalism and "The Politics of Recognition,"* ed. Amy Gutmann (Princeton, N.J.: Princeton University Press, 1992), p. 62. Taylor's sensitivity to the hegemonic character of liberalism makes him quite unsympathetic with the general denunciation of the Islamic condemnation of Rushdie. As he observes, we—that is, secular liberals—simply can no longer imagine why blasphemy—that is, insult against God's honor—might matter. He notes that "Rushdie's book is comforting to the western liberal mind, which shares one feature with that of the Ayatollah Khomeini, the belief that there is nothing outside their world-view which needs deeper understanding, just a perverse reflection of the obviously right. To live in this difficult world, the western liberal mind will have to learn to reach out more" "The Rushdie Controversy," *Public Culture* 2 (Fall 1989): 121.

For a nice example of one Western liberal mind's inability to make the kind of reach for which Taylor calls, see Gutmann's introduction to the book that contains Taylor's essay. As she puts it, "liberal democracy enriches our opportunities, enables us to recognize the value of various cultures, and thereby teaches us to appreciate diversity not simply for its own sake but for its enhancement of the quality of life and learning. The liberal democratic defense of diversity draws upon a universalistic rather than a particularistic perspective" (p. 10). The implications for the university are apparent to Gutmann as "no university curriculum can possibly include all the books or represent all the cultures worthy of recognition in a liberal democratic education. Nor can any free society, let alone any university of independent scholars and teachers expect to agree on hard choices between competing goods. The cause for concern about the ongoing controversies over multiculturalism and the curriculum is rather that the most vocal parties to these disputes appear unwilling to defend their views before people with whom they disagree, and to entertain seriously the possibility of change in the face of well-reasoned criticism. And so they create two mutually exclusive and disrespecting intellectual cultures in academic life, evincing an attitude of unwillingness to learn anything from the other or recognize any value in the other. In political life writ large, there is a parallel problem of disrespect and lack of constructive communication among spokespersons for ethnic, religious, and racial groups, a problem that all too often leads to violence" (p. 21). The sheer arrogance of these passages is almost beyond belief. Note that Gutmann assumes that she does not need to change her mind in the "face of well-reasoned criticism." Moreover it is clear that she probably is not capable of that feat since she is still able to write as she does even though I assume she probably heard and even read Taylor's essay. I would have thought Taylor's arguments might have made her think twice that she represents the universal and, thus, "peaceful" solution.

23. For a wonderful critique of free speech absolutism see Stanley Fish, "There's No Such Thing as Free Speech and It's a Good Thing Too," in *Debating P.C.: A Controversy Over Political Correctness on College Campuses,* ed. Paul Berman (New York: Laurel/Dell, 1992), pp. 231–45. Kathryn Pyne Addelson makes a similar point about academic freedom. She observes with specific reference to the authority of philosophers to publish and teach their opinions that such authority is a professional authority; "it was politically won and it is politically maintained. Philosophers cannot simply assume that 'academic freedom' allows them to teach and publish whatever definitions of the moral institution their graduate schools supported. Academic freedom is a political instrument, and it should not be used unless academics make explicit their moral, social, and political responsibilities. At a minimum, that requires knowing the implications of our work, and it requires asking by what authority we define the moral institution of life." *Impure Thoughts: Essays on Philosophy, Feminism, and Ethics* (Philadelphia: Temple University Press, 1991), p. 104.

24. For further reflections as honor codes, see my "Honor In The University," *First Things* 10 (February 1991): 26–31.

25. For a nice example of this genre, see Beverly Asbury, "Campus Life in a Time of Culture War," *Soundings* 75 (Winter 1992): 465–76. I respond to Asbury in the same issue in an essay called "A Non-Violent Proposal for Christian Participation in the Culture Wars" (pp. 477–92).

26. See, for example, Jon D. Levenson's *The Hebrew Bible, the Old Testament, and Historical Criticism: Jews and Christians in Biblical Studies* (Louisville, Ky.: Westminster/John Knox Press, 1993). Levenson contends that the "historical-critical" method was largely the work of liberal Protestants to replace the traditional study of scripture by Jews and Christians. Moreover, this project served the interests of the liberal state. As Levenson notes "historical criticism

is the form of biblical studies that corresponds to the classical liberal political ideal. It is the realization of the Enlightenment project in the realm of biblical scholarship. Like citizens in the classical liberal state, scholars practicing historical criticism of the Bible are expected to eliminate or minimize their communal loyalties, to see them as legitimately operative only within associations that are private, nonscholarly, and altogether voluntary" (p. 118). For my more extended critique of fundamentalism and historical criticism, see my *Unleashing the Scripture: Freeing the Bible from Captivity to America* (Nashville, Tenn.: Abingdon Press, 1993).

27. For a helpful account of Islam and Western misperceptions, see John L. Esposito, *The Islamic Threat: Myth or Reality* (New York: Oxford University Press, 1992). Esposito observes: "modern notions of religion as a system of belief for personal life, and separation of Church and State, have become so accepted and internalized that they have obscured the beliefs and practice of the past and come to represent for many a self-evident and timeless truth. As a result, from a modern secular perspective the mixing of religion and politics is regarded as abnormal, dangerous, and extremist. Thus when secular minded peoples in the West encounter Muslim individuals and groups that speak of Islam as a comprehensive way of life, they immediately dub them 'fundamentalist' with the connotation that these are backward-looking individuals, obstacles to change, zealots who are a threat" (p. 199).

28. Those who practice Christian nonviolence cannot avoid the possibility that they make the world more violent through nonviolence. For often the violence that is hidden in what we have come to call the "normal" will be all the more violent if it is exposed. Advocates of nonviolence should be particularly sensitive to such violence, since we are committed to discovering the violence that always is part of our lives.

29. The classic statement of this criticism was made by my teacher James Gustafson in "The Sectarian Temptation: Reflections of Theology, the Church, and the University," *Proceedings of the Catholic Theology Society* 40 (1985): 83–94. I responded in the introduction to my *Christian Existence Today: Essays on Church, World, and Living In-Between* (Durham, N.C.: Labyrinth Press, 1988). I confess that I am extremely tired of answering this charge, but it forces me to find different ways to put matters, through which I discover implications I had not known I knew; when you have a position that is out of the "mainstream," you cannot repeat yourself too often. Repetition, it turns out, is a necessary moral practice to resist domination. Karl Barth's *Church Dogmatics* is a wonderful example of the importance of repetition for Christian theology. The repetitious character of Christian worship is a resource seldom appreciated— by doing the same thing we become always new.

30. I have no "theory" about the secular. All I mean by the "secular" is that many, including many who count themselves "religious," are quite capable of

living lives of practical atheism. If pressed for an account of this development I certainly think that by Charles Taylor in *Sources of the Self: The Making of Modern Identity* (Cambridge, Mass.: Harvard University Press, 1989) tells much of the story. People obviously still "believe in God," but the relation of that "belief" to any "sources" of that belief is the problem. From my perspective the problem in modernity is not that people are not religious, but they are too religious. Secularists too often think when Judaism and Christianity are destroyed that people will then learn to live "rationally." Rather what happens is people live religiously in the most dangerous ways—romanticism, as depicted by Taylor, being one form of such religious resurgence. As a Christian I confess I think we live in a very frightening time religiously. For a more critical perspective on Taylor's account see David Matzko and my "The Sources of Charles Taylor," *Religious Studies Review* 18 (October 1992): 286–89.

As one who has a reputation as an unapologetic Enlightenment basher, I am quite well aware that the Enlightenment in many ways grew from Christians' presuppositions. Indeed, I think Leszek Kolakowski is right to suggest that the Enlightenment emerged from a reconsidered Christian heritage, but in order to take root, crystallized and ossified forms of that heritage had to be defeated. "When it does begin to take root, in an ideological humanist or reactionary shape, that is, in the shape of the Reformation, it gradually drifts away from its origins to become non-Christian or anti-Christian. In its final form the Enlightenment turns against itself: humanism becomes moral nihilism, undergoes a metamorphosis that transforms it into a totalitarian idea. The removal of the barriers erected by Christianity to protect itself against the Enlightenment, which was the fruit of its own development, brought the collapse of the barriers that protected the Enlightenment against its own degeneration, either into a deification of man and nature or into despair. It is only today that a spiritual movement on both sides is taking shape: Christianity and the Enlightenment, both gripped by a sentiment of helplessness and confusion, are beginning to question their own history and their own significance. From this doubt a vague and uncertain vision is emerging, a vision of new arrangements of which, as yet, we know nothing" *Modernity On Endless Trial* (Chicago: University of Chicago Press, 1990), p. 30. There is no question of excepting or rejecting the Enlightenment en toto. I have no idea what that would even look like. That I often seem to side with the "nihilistic, deconstructionist, relativist," should not be surprising, however, as they are the kind of "atheist" only the Enlightenment could produce. Christians are also "atheist" when it comes to humanism, but our atheism is, of course, Trinitarian.

For the account of "the secular" I think most compelling, see John Milbank, *Theology and Social Theory: Beyond Secular Reason* (Cambridge: Basil Blackwell, 1990). My general indebtedness to Milbank's argument I hope is obvious.

31. I confess that I still have enough Yale in me that I find it difficult to write "autobiographically" particularly if by doing so I might suggest that being from Texas might make a difference for how I think. I am well schooled in that form of academic discourse that teaches us that we deserve to be read only when we represent an "objective" or "detached" point of view. As a Christian and Aristotelian I should know how to avoid the unhappy alternatives of "subjectivism" and "objectivity," but it remains hard. Some of what follows was done only because I was asked to write in the *Christian Century* series "How My Mind Has Changed." I tried to shape my account to defeat the notion I have a "my mind." For a set of extraordinary reflections on the place of our histories for the doing of philosophy, see Addelson, *Impure Thoughts*.

32. For a rejection of the category genius to characterize theologians as well as an answer to the question, "where have all the great theologians gone?" see William Willimon and my, "Why *Resident Aliens* Struck Such a Chord," *Missiology: An International Review* 19 (October 1991): 419–29.

33. "Constantinianism" gains its original meaning from the legitimation of Christianity by Constantine, but in many ways the church at that time was less Constantinian since it still had habits of memory derived from persecution. The current disestablishment of Christianity has created neo-Constantinian strains that are in many ways more insidious than the legal establishment of Christianity. See, for example, John Howard Yoder's account of the various kinds of neo-neo-Constantinianisms in his *The Original Revolution: Essays on Christian Pacifism* Scottdale, Pa.: Herald Press, 1971), pp. 148–82.

If liberal theology is the inevitable result of the Protestant Reformation, it is equally the case that theology was fated, if it was to have academic respectability, to become history which would survive only so long as there was an audience of those interested in the subject investigated; or it would be reduced to being nothing more than the personal creations of individual professors. Any sense that the theologians occupy an office of authority with correlative responsibilities could not be sustained. Part of the pathos of my work is that it cannot help but appear as but another "position," since I am but a "professor." For a fascinating study in this respect, see Michael Hollerich, "Retrieving a Neglected Critique of Church, Theology and Secularization in Weimar Germany," *Pro Ecclesia* 2 (Summer 1993): 305–32. The characterization of academic theology I borrow from Hollerich, who learned it from his study of Eric Peterson.

34. Charles Taylor provides a powerful defense of ad hominem argument in "Explanation and Practical Reason," *The Quality of Life*, ed. Martha Nussbaum and Amartya Sen (Oxford: Oxford University Press, 1993), pp. 208–31. Drawing on MacIntyre, Taylor is particularly good in showing that modern skepticism and subjectivism have been the result of trying to rule out ad hominem modes of practical reasoning in the name of objectivity.

35. For more extended reflections about what it meant for me to teach at Notre Dame, see my "A Homage to Mary and the University of Notre Dame," *South Atlantic Quarterly* (forthcoming).

36. John Howard Yoder, *The Priestly Kingdom: Social Ethics as Gospel* (Notre Dame, Ind.: University of Notre Dame Press, 1984), pp. 3–4.

37. Ibid., p. 7.

38. John Howard Yoder, *The Politics of Jesus* (Grand Rapids, Mich.: Eerdmans, 1972).

39. Ibid., p. 132.

40. Eccentric he may be, but I believe Harold Bloom is closer to the truth than many wish to believe when he argues that American Christianity is actually a form of gnosticism—that is, the American religion "is a knowing, by and of an uncreated self, or self-within-the-self, and the knowledge leads to freedom, a dangerous and doom-eager freedom: from nature, time, history, community, other selves. I shake my head in unhappy wonderment at the politically correct younger intellectuals, who hope to subvert what they cannot begin to understand, an obsessed society wholly in the grip of a dominant Gnosticism" *The American Religion: The Emergence of the Post-Christian Nation* (New York: Simon and Schuster, 1992), p. 49. What Bloom misses, I think, is how this kind of "gnosticism" is almost endemic in Protestantism once salvation is freed from the church. Niebuhr, of course, would be aghast at being identified with Bloom's heroes, the Mormons and the Southern Baptists, but that simply makes him all the more interesting as an exemplification of Bloom's narrative.

41. This interpretation of Niebuhr is obviously controversial, though I think it is less so as Niebuhr's theological liberalism is increasingly recognized. Only a liberal culture could have identified Niebuhr as "neo-orthodox" because of his emphasis on sin. Niebuhr had a much better self-understanding, as he was aware he stood squarely in the heritage of Protestant liberalism. For Niebuhr's most explicit account of the "symbolism" of the cross, see *The Nature and Destiny of Man* (New York: Charles Scribner's Sons, 1949), pp. 70–76.

42. Fredric Jameson, *Postmodernism or, The Cultural Logic of Late Capitalism* (Durham, N.C.: Duke University Press, 1991), p. 390.

43. For a more extended discussion of friendship, see my "Happiness, the Life of Virtue, and Friendship: Theological Reflections on Aristotelian Themes," *Asbury Theological Journal* 45 (Spring 1990): 5–48.

44. This view of history can properly be called apocalyptic since it challenges the view that history is a web of causal relations going nowhere. The latter view of history is meant to give us control of the world. Apocalyptic requires we learn to live acknowledging that God's providence is a more determinative category than history.

45. Scott Davis observes that "War pits one fighting force against another

in a test of strength and ability on the field of battle. The measure of success is disabling the opponent, and this is accomplished by destroying his forces. Soldiers are trained to kill other soldiers. The killing is intended, planned, and practiced. It is, nonetheless, not murder. Murder, as Aristotle remarked, is always and everywhere recognized to be wicked, but no blame accrues to the soldier who kills because this killing is just, undertaken in support of a lawful authority" *Warcraft and the Fragility of Virtue: An Essay in Aristotelian Ethics* (Moscow, Idaho: University of Idaho Press, 1992), p. 61. As a committed Aristotelian, Davis provides the most compelling defense of war as a moral institution we have. The only difficulty, as he recognizes, is that given his Aristotelian commitments to polities of virtue few contemporary regimes have the moral capacity to conduct just wars. In one of the haunting passages in his book, Davis observes: "The most brutal irony of war is that conducting it justly demands, on the one hand, the firmest and most self-disciplined exercise of the virtues and, on the other, war does everything in its power to shatter the very virtues it demands. Even if we do not wish to call the individual soldiers 'murderers,' reserving this perhaps for their superior officer, we're still inclined to think that a world made up of such men would not, unlike Pericles' Athens, be worth living in, much less dying for" (p. 88). And, of course, that is why we should not be willing to die for a state like the United States. One of the many virtues of Davis's book is his account of Yoder's pacifism in the first chapter.

46. For an attempt to suggest how medicine has become the primary institution to insure the theodicy required by liberalism, see my *Naming the Silences: God, Medicine, and the Problems of Suffering* (Grand Rapids, Mich.: Eerdmans, 1990).

47. In his *Ethics After Babel: The Languages of Morals and Their Discontents* (Boston: Beacon Press, 1988), Jeffrey Stout provides what I think is the strongest account of a substantive ethic for liberal social orders. Whether his *bricoleur* can give an account, or whether they need an account, of the relation between the virtues, I take to be, one of the most interesting questions raised by his position. For a more extended account of Stout's position, see Philip Kenneson and my "Flight from Foundationalism, or, Things Aren't as Bad as They Seem," *Soundings* 71 (Winter 1988): 683–99.

CHAPTER 1

Constancy and Forgiveness: The Novel as a School for Virtue

1. Alasdair MacIntyre, *After Virtue* (Notre Dame, Ind.: University of Notre Dame Press, 1981), p. 223.

2. Ibid., p. 189.

3. Ibid.

4. Ibid., p. 171.

5. Ibid., p. 225. There is a significant relation between an emphasis on constancy and an appreciation for the temporal nature of the moral life. The connectedness between otherwise contingent events and actions comes as an agent intends the unity of past and present commitment through the mutability of action. I am indebted to Mr. Philip Foubert for making this point clear to me.

6. Ibid., p. 225.

7. Ibid.

8. Ibid., p. 224.

9. Shirley Letwin, *The Gentleman in Trollope: Individuality and Moral Conduct* (Cambridge, Mass.: Harvard University Press, 1982), pp. 3–21. My general indebtedness to Letwin's fine book will be obvious. I do not mean to suggest a complete correlation between constancy and Trollope's (or Letwin's) account of a gentleman, though I think there are obvious similarities. Being constant is a more inclusive moral description than that of being a gentleman. Thus one may be a gentleman without being constant in the full sense. It may well be, moreover, that the "English gentleman" lacks a certain "hardness" necessary for constancy. MacIntyre thinks Austen had such hardness.

10. Ibid., p. 17.

11. Ibid., p. 16. Letwin later makes a suggestion that further illumines the role of manners in the ethics of a gentleman: "What remains constant is the manner in which gentlemen conduct themselves—their agreement that what matters most is maintaining integrity. And this agreement is expressed in a readiness to observe certain formalities in their intercourse with one another. Formalities consist in outward forms of behaviour, whether of speech or of gesture, which are established by convention and by law. A gentleman's respect for formalities has given plausibility to the common misconception of a gentleman as someone who is governed mechanically by 'a code.' But the real reason a gentleman respects formalities is that it enables him to distinguish between agreeing with others on fundamentals, on a certain manner of conducting oneself, and a substantive agreement on what to do here and now. This distinction makes it possible for gentlemen to live together amicably without committing themselves to approving of all that the others do and think. Gentlemen need not therefore dissimulate when they disagree. They can differ and remain friends without hypocrisy because their concord is not founded on either a real or a feigned uniformity" (p. 91).

12. Ibid., p. 21.

13. Ibid., p. 58. Of course, this is one reason that one of the marks of a gentleman is his tolerance for the differences in other gentlemen. Since "being moral" is a matter of judgment worked out through the contingencies of our

existence, the gentleman must often withhold judgment about behavior on the part of another gentleman.

14. Ibid., p. 60. For how this account of character differs as well as develops my earlier analysis see the "Introduction" to the second edition of my *Character and the Christian Life: A Study in Theological Ethics* (San Antonio, Tex.: Trinity University Press, 1985). This book is now distributed by the University of Notre Dame Press. My earlier emphasis on character as a qualification of agency owed too much to the "liberal self." The display of the self through narratives helped me see that character does not qualify agency, but insofar as agency language works at all, character constitutes agency.

15. Letwin, *The Gentleman in Trollope*, p. 61.

16. Ibid., p. 64.

17. Ibid., p. 65.

18. No doubt social class was used as a decisive indicator for making the initial judgment whether someone was or was not a gentleman. Moreover, Trollope seems to have assumed that England had a stake in maintaining the tradition, property, and status of certain families to insure that some would always carry the ethics of public spiritedness he thought crucial to England's survival. Yet he was far too honest an observer of the social scene not to appreciate how many who did not come from such a class in fact were better representatives of what it meant to be a gentleman than those that did so. This was true not only of such characters as Mr. Monk, but of John Crumb in *The Way We Live Now*.

19. Letwin, *The Gentleman in Trollope*, p. 67. It is interesting to reflect on how different this sense of respect is from that defended by Kant. For Kant we respect the other, not because he or she is different, but because we respect the moral law which obliterates differences. In Trollope, respect required because of differences goes with an ethics of constancy. This respect generates the great scene in *The Last Chronicle of Barset* in which Archdeacon Grantley answers poverty-stricken Mr. Crawley that they are equal in terms of the only thing that matters—they are both gentlemen.

20. Letwin, *The Gentleman in Trollope*, pp. 68–69.

21. Anthony Trollope, *Barchester Towers* (Oxford: Oxford University Press, p. 225. Trollope's fascination with power, particularly political power, has often been noted, but he was equally interested in the relinquishment of power. Septimus Harding is, of course, a study in the divestiture of power, but there are many others—for example, Mr. Fenwick's refusal to use his power against the dissenters of his parish or Phineas Finn's resignation from Parliament. Trollope seems to have held the view that power should be exercised in the name of a social rather than a personal good. If one lived with integrity the latter would take care of itself.

22. Trollope's depictions of such people are among his finest portraits. Particularly memorable is Sir Roger Scatcherd in *Doctor Thorne*. Letwin makes the particularly interesting observation that what prevents Scatcherd from being a gentleman is finally not the roughness that survives from his past as a stone mason, but his lack of self-sufficiency, manifested by his ambition to be recognized by the great. See *The Gentleman in Trollope*, p. 96. No doubt Trollope drew on his own experience for the portrait of Scatcherd, as he suggests in his *Autobiography* that one of the greatest failings was a desire to be liked.

23. The relation between this sense of fortune and the development of character has not been sufficiently explored. Character, both for the novel and for morality, requires a recognition of contingency which becomes part and parcel of "who we are." In a sense, character makes the contingent necessary by providing a narrative construal that allows us to make sense out of "our" luck.

24. Letwin, *The Gentleman in Trollope*, p. 70.

25. Ibid., p. 71.

26. Anthony Trollope, *An Autobiography* (Oxford: Oxford University Press, 1980), pp. 354–55.

27. Ibid., p. 178.

28. Anthony Trollope, *The Small House at Allington* (Oxford: Oxford University Press, 1980), p. 331.

29. Anthony Trollope, *The Last Chronicle of Barset* (Oxford: Oxford University Press, 1980), p. 360.

30. Ibid.

31. Thus late in *Phineas Finn* (Oxford: Oxford University Press, 1982), in confessing his involvement with Lady Laura and Violet Effingham to Mary Flood, Phineas says:

> "Love is involuntary. It does not often run in a yoke with prudence. I have told you my history as far as it is concerned with Violet Effingham. I did love her very dearly."
>
> "Did you love her, Mr. Finn?"
>
> "Yes;—did love her. Is there any inconstancy in ceasing to love when one is not loved? Is there inconstancy in changing one's love, and in loving again?"
>
> "I do not know," said Mary, to whom the occasion was becoming so embarrassing that she no longer was able to reply with words that had a meaning in them.
>
> "If there be, dear, I am inconstant." He paused, but of course she had not a syllable to say. (p. 266)

Trollope clearly does not try to answer whether Phineas finally is or is not inconstant. Clearly, however, the judgment depends on how one interprets his final faithfulness to Mary.

32. Trollope, *Last Chronicle,* p. 236. Though Trollope wrote nothing but comedies, one cannot help but feel how the tragic is often close to the surface of his novels. For often the good cannot be done because of a person's limits—limits that under different circumstances might be strengths. Thus, Lily knows she can never have Crosbie back because the limits of his character make it impossible for him to be forgiven.

33. Anthony Trollope, *The Prime Minister* (St. Albans: Panther Books, 1975), p. 558. Trollope says Mr. Wharton, Emily Lopez's father, "had already formed his hopes in regard to Arthur Fletcher. He had trusted that the man whom he had taught some years since to regard as his wished-for son-in-law, might be constant and strong enough in his love to forget all that was past, and to be still willing to redeem his daughter from misery. But as days had crept on since the scene at the Tenway Junction, he had become aware that time must do much before such relief would be accepted" (p. 558). Trollope never assumed that forgiveness was easy. Mr. Wharton, of course, had from the first distrusted Lopez, not thinking him a gentleman, but he had no evidence for his hunch other than Lopez's foreignness. He was right, of course, but he could not be shown right until it was too late and the marriage had already occurred.

34. Trollope, *Prime Minister,* p. 637. In *Ralph the Heir* (London: Oxford University Press, 1951), Clarissa overcomes her love for Ralph Newton by being forced to recognize his complete lack of constancy. She becomes constant by changing her mind and accepting a proposal of marriage from Gregory, Ralph's brother. Though a less romantic figure than Ralph, Gregory has proven his worth by remaining constant to Clarissa even though she had twice rejected him. In *Ralph the Heir* Trollope's narrator muses: "Whether marriages should be made in heaven or on earth, must be a matter of doubt to observers;—whether, that is, men and women are best married by chance, which I take to be the real fashion of heaven-made marriages; or should be brought into that close link and loving bondage to each other by thought, selection, and decision. That the heavenly made prevails the oftenest there can hardly be a doubt. It takes years to make a friendship; but a marriage may be settled in a week—in an hour" (p. 328). That such is the case makes it particularly important that constancy precedes rather than follows marriage.

35. Trollope, *Autobiography,* pp. 183–84. Here again, we see Trollope concerned with the necessity to renounce power, and yet how often it is restored to the constant exactly because they are constant.

36. Interestingly, even though in his *Autobiography* Trollope says that if Plantagenet Palliser is not a perfect gentleman then he is unable to describe a gentleman, in *The Duke's Children* (Oxford: Oxford University Press, 1973) he has Palliser say the following in response to Mary's claim that Tregear is a gentleman even if he has no money:

"So is my private secretary. There is not a clerk in one of our public offices who does not consider himself to be gentleman. The curate of the parish is a gentleman, and the medical man who comes here from Bradstock. The word is too vague to carry with it any meaning that ought to be serviceable to you in thinking of such a matter."

"I do not know any other way of dividing people," said she, showing thereby that she had altogether made up her mind as to what ought to be serviceable to her.

"You are not called upon to divide people. That division requires so much experience that you are bound in this matter to rely upon those to whom your obedience is due. I cannot but think you must have known that you were not entitled to give your love to any man without being assured that the man would be approved of by—by—by me." He was going to say, "your parents," but was stopped by the remembrance of his wife's imprudence.

She saw it all, and was too noble to plead her mother's authority. (pp. 67–68)

Later in the same novel, Trollope records a conversation between Lord Silverbridge, the Duke's son, and Mr. Boncassen, the rich American whose daughter Silverbridge wants to marry. In response to Mr. Boncassen's suggestion that he could not blame the Duke for objecting to such a marriage just as Mr. Boncassen would object if his daughter wanted to marry a mechanic in America, Lord Silverbridge says:

"He wouldn't be a gentleman."
"That is a word of which I don't quite know the meaning."
"I do," said Silverbridge confidently.
"But you could not define it. If a man be well educated, and can keep a good house over his head, perhaps you may call him a gentleman. But there are many such with whom your father would not wish to be so closely connected as you propose." (p. 424)

37. Anthony Trollope, *Orley Farm* (Oxford: Oxford University Press, 1950), pp. 62–63.

38. Ibid., p. 63.

39. Letwin provides a particularly useful discussion of Lady Eustace. See *The Gentleman in Trollope*, pp. 96–105.

40. Anthony Trollope, *The Vicar of Bullhampton* (New York: Dover, 1979), p. 450.

41. Anthony Trollope, *The Way We Live Now* (Oxford: Oxford University Press, 1982), p. 467. The relationship between forgiveness and repentance is

never straightforwardly presented in Trollope's novels. While he often suggests that before forgiveness can take place the sinner must show repentance, he was obviously never satisfied with that formula. He knew well that repentance was not simply a matter of deciding or trying to do better; often forgiveness must create conditions that make repentance possible. As we will see, he explored this theme relentlessly in *The Vicar of Bullhampton*. Trollope knew, as Lady Mason says in *Orley Farm*, that "it is easy to talk of repentance, but repentance will not come with a world" (p. 198).

42. Trollope, *The Way We Live Now,* p. 471.

43. Trollope, *Autobiography,* p. 333.

44. Ibid., pp. 329–30.

45. Ibid., pp. 333–34.

46. Trollope, *The Vicar,* pp. 30–31.

47. Ibid., p. 6.

48. Ibid., p. 259.

49. Ibid., p. 112.

50. Ibid., p. 359. It is typical of Trollope to make his hero or heroine have the same problem he or she is suffering from at the hands of others.

51. Ibid., p. 275.

52. Ibid., p. 251.

53. Ibid., pp. 113–14. It is interesting that Mr. Fenwick is willing to confront Mr. Puddleham about this but not about the chapel. It may be he wanted the latter to feel the need for forgiveness, but I suspect even more that Mr. Fenwick thinks finally nothing morally at stake in the building of the chapel whereas Carry's life is at stake in Puddleham's attitude.

54. Ibid., p. 301.

55. Ibid., pp. 303–4. Though the author obviously liked Mr. Fenwick immensely, Trollope cannot help but poke some fun at his "meddling." Indeed after the disaster of his joint attempt with his wife to arrange a match between Mary Fenwick and Mr. Gilmore, they resolve never to interfere at matchmaking again (p. 399).

56. Trollope as usual plays on the necessity of chance as crucial for the movement of the novel. It is only by a series of unconnected events that Carry is discovered by the Vicar and ultimately finds her way home.

57. Ibid., p. 348. Trollope never tires of exploring the relationship between pride and constancy, for true constancy cannot finally be built on pride, since that would make us subject to the judgment of others. Humility is crucial if constancy is to derive from a steadfastness not determined by the judgment of others.

58. Ibid., pp. 432–33.

59. Ibid., p. 434.

60. Ibid., p. 367. Later Trollope has the Vicar muse that "The truth is, that the possession of a grievance is the one state of human blessedness. As long as the chapel was there, *malgre moi,* I could revel in wrong. It turns out now that I can send poor Puddleham adrift tomorrow, and he immediately becomes the hero of the hour" (p. 398).

61. Ibid., p. 390.

62. Ibid., p. 229.

63. The implications of this for interpreting Trollope's "political novels" are far-reaching. His increasing cynicism about the possibility of constancy in politics should never blind us to his unfailing assumption of the necessity of a politics capable of sustaining truthful discourse—whether it be the politics of the family or the nation. For a particularly insightful treatment of Trollope's ability to connect "personal" and "political" relations see John Halperin's *Trollope and Politics* (New York: Barnes and Noble, 1977).

64. Trollope, *Autobiography,* pp. 228–29.

65. Ibid., p. 233.

66. Though Trollope could appreciate the traditional role that required some to spend most of their time in leisure, he distrusted the corrupting influence of those who literally had nothing to do. Thus Plantagenet Palliser's love of work, his sense that work is necessary for saving us from our muddles, reflect Trollope's own views. It is certainly true that Trollope was tied to his work and could not stop working even when it was no longer financially necessary. In *Ralph the Heir,* Trollope characterizes men's attitude for work: "There are idle men who rejoice in idleness. Idleness, even when it is ruinous, is delightful to them. And there are men who love work, who revel in that, who attack it daily with renewed energy almost wallowing in it, greedy of work, who go to it almost as the drunkard goes to his bottle, or the gambler to his gaming-table. These are not unhappy men, though they are perhaps apt to make those around them unhappy. And again there are men, fewer in number, who will work though they hate it, from sheer conscience and from conviction that idleness will not suit them or make them happy. Then there are they who love the idea of work, but want the fibre needful for the doing of it" (pp. 277–78). Trollope was clearly the second type.

67. Trollope, *Autobiography,* p. 145.

68. Ibid. In *Ralph the Heir* Trollope defends making a figure such as Ralph Newton the hero: "The reader of a novel—who had doubtless taken the volume up for amusement, and who would probably lay it down did he suspect that instruction, like a snake-in-the-grass, like physic beneath the sugar, was to be imposed upon him,—requires from his author chiefly this, that he shall be amused by a narrative in which elevated sentiment prevails, and gratified by being made to feel that the elevated sentiments described are exactly his own. . . . It is the test of a novel writer's art that he conceals his snake-in-

the-grass; but the reader may be sure it is always there. No man or woman with a conscience,—no man or woman with intellect sufficient to produce amusement, can go on from year to year spinning stories without the desire of teaching" (p. 338).

69. Letwin provides an excellent analysis of Trollope's religious views, *The Gentleman in Trollope,* pp. 216–46.

70. I cannot pretend to be an expert on Trollope or Trollope criticism, and I am therefore particularly indebted to David Solomon and Thomas Shaffer for reading and criticizing an earlier draft. You know they are in a different league, as the former told me he leaves a few Trollope novels unread just to have something to look forward to. As he observed: "He only wrote forty-seven." I am also indebted to Philip Foubert, Jack McDonald, Joe Buttigieg, Dave Burrell, and Jim Burtchaell for their good criticism.

I particularly regret that I was not able to incorporate in the revision of this essay the criticism I received from my good friend, Dr. Ralph Wood. Dr. Wood argues that I have been too uncritical of Letwin's account of the gentleman insofar as she claims the character of a gentleman "is a purely human property which enables men to make of themselves what they will." Hence, the gentleman's refusal to conform is based on nothing outside the self. Dr. Wood suggests that his is a stoicism that my emphasis on the centrality of forgiveness refutes. He says: "Forgiveness is a virtue rooted in a reality larger than the gentlemanly code. Neither does one have to be a gentleman to practice it. Moreover, it is this complexification of character—seeing both its contradictions and its transcendental possibilities—that makes Trollope so much more than a Victorian moralist." While I think that Dr. Wood may be a bit hard on Letwin, his general point seems to me right.

CHAPTER 2

On Honor: By Way of a Comparison of Karl Barth and Trollope

1. Gerhard Sauter, "Shifts in Karl Barth's Thought: The Current Debate Between Right and Left Wing Barthians," unpublished paper presented at Barth symposium, State University of New York, Buffalo, 1986.

2. David Ford's *Barth and God's Story* (Frankfurt am Main: Peter Lang, 1985), is certainly the best treatment of this aspect of Barth's work.

3. Hans Frei, "An Afterword: Eberhard Busch's Biography of Karl Barth," in *Karl Barth in Re-View,* ed. Martin Rumscheidt (Pittsburgh: Pickwick Press, 1981), pp. 110–11.

4. For the development of this theme, see Peter Berger, "On the Obsolescence of the Concept of Honor," in *Revisions: Changing Perspectives in Moral Philosophy,* ed. Stanley Hauerwas and Alasdair MacIntyre (Notre Dame, Ind.:

University of Notre Dame Press, 1983), pp. 172–81; and my "Truth and Honor: The University and Church in a Democratic Age," in *Christian Existence Today: Essays on Church, World, and Living In-Between* (Durham, N.C.: Labyrinth Press, 1988), pp. 221–36. I also discuss the importance of honor codes in "Honor at the Center," in *Jesuit Education and the Cultivation of Virtue*, ed. William J. O'Brien (Washington, D.C.: Georgetown University Press, 1990), pp. 73–88.

5. William Werpehowski, "Command and History in the Ethics of Karl Barth," *Journal of Religious Ethics* 9 (Fall 1981): 298–320. Werpehowski is responding to my treatment of Barth in *Character and the Christian Life: A Study in Theological Ethics* (San Antonio, Tex.: Trinity University Press, 1981). A third edition of that book has been published with an introduction that indicates the mistakes I made in the earlier edition of that book.

6. Werpehowski, "Command and History," p. 300.

7. R. H. Roberts, "Barth's Interpretation of Time: Its Nature and Implications," in *Karl Barth: Studies of his Theological Method,* ed. Stephen Sykes (Oxford: Clarendon Press, 1979), pp. 107–8.

8. Werpehowski, "Command and History," p. 305.

9. Ibid.

10. Ibid., p. 316.

11. In his *The Hastening That Was: Karl Barth's Ethics* (Oxford: Clarendon Press, 1993), Nigel Biggar defends Barth against this charge as well as my earlier criticisms of Barth. He allows that my complaint about Barth's abstractness is not "entirely wide of the mark." More interestingly Biggar suggests my criticisms of Barth's failure to consider how Christian character is formed derives from the subtle differences in our Christologies—namely Barth's Christology in Nicaean and Chalcedonian and mine in Anabaptist. As a consequence, Barth gives far more prominence to the "moral normativity of Jesus' relationship with his divine Father" than I do. I believe my work has at times been insufficiently Trinitarian, but I still find Biggar's criticisms odd since an "Anabaptist Christology," even though I am unclear to its material content and/or if I represent that alternative, assumes, at least if Yoder is right, that Nicaea and Chalcedon remain normative benchmarks.

12. Berger, "On the Obsolescence of the Concept of Honor," p. 173.

13. Barth does not explain how all are equally honored by God without that kind of egalitarianism undermining the specific nature of the honor of this or that man. Of course, Barth has an easy response as he can say God honors each person differently without in any way qualifying his honoring each person—that is, for God honor is not a scarce resource or a zero-sum game.

14. Barth does little to explain how something can at once be unmixed yet interrelated.

15. Trollope tells us that Dr. Wortle "left his position at Eton because the head-master has required from him some slight change of practice. There had been no quarrel on that occasion, but Mr. Wortle had gone." *Dr. Wortle's School,* ed. with introduction by John Halperin (Oxford: Oxford University Press, 1984), p. 3. All references to the novel will appear within parentheses in the text.

16. Trollope makes clear throughout the novel that Dr. Wortle was a man who was quite able to locate his interests.

17. It is interesting that Trollope does not try to say that what the Peacockes or Dr. Wortle did was right, but only that it was understandable. He is acutely aware of how good communities must be able to maintain standards while forgiving the sinner.

18. Barth fails to provide any extended treatment of friendship in his work. Certainly his discussion of honor could have provided the context for that, but, like so many moderns, he tends to overlook the moral significance of friendship.

19. One cannot help but think that Barth is thinking of his isolation resulting from his refusal to take the oath of obedience to Hitler and thus losing his university position. That isolation, of course, was bounded as it would have surely been the harder if Barth had been German and not Swiss. The fact that Barth was Swiss does not detract from the courage he demonstrated in the 1930's but rather should remind us how important it is that Christians have a place to be other than that defined by our nationalities.

20. For a critique of Barth's ecclesiology in relation to his social ethics, see my "On Learning Simplicity in an Ambiguous Age: A Response to Hunsinger," *Katallagete,* 10 (Fall 1987): 43–46. For a thorough comparison of Barth's ecclesiology with my own, see Reinhard Hutter, *Evangelische Ethic als Kirchliches Zeugnis: Interpretation zua Schlusselfragen theologischer Ethik in der Gegenwart* (Erlangen, Germany: Neukerchener, 1993).

CHAPTER 3

Why Truthfulness Requires Forgiveness: A Commencement Address for Graduates of a College of the Church of the Second Chance

As will become clear, the "college" in this title is Goshen College. I was honored by being asked to give the commencement address on April 18, 1992. Goshen is a college sponsored and supported by the Mennonite church, though non-Mennonites are also faculty and students. The address was obviously written presupposing some knowledge of Mennonite life and churchly practice. I have not tried to change that for the non-Mennonite reader, though I have added a few explanatory notes that may make references clearer. I have not tried to "translate" what I say here to a non-Mennonite audience preferring to let what seems puzzling remain puzzling.

I should make clear to the non-Mennonite reader, however, that though the Mennonites are perhaps most widely identified by their commitment to pacifism, that commitment is but part of their practice of reconciliation based on Matthew 18. So "pacifism" does not simply name their refusal to go to war, but rather is an aspect of their practice of resolving disputes and conflicts through confrontation, forgiveness and reconciliation. Put in a somewhat misleading fashion the Mennonites made the Catholic practice of penance the character of their relation with one another and the world. As a result they are not easily classified as Catholic or Protestant. See, for example, Walter Klaassen's *Anabaptism: Neither Catholic or Protestant.* (Waterloo, Ont.: Conrad Press, 1973). For a wonderful account of "The Rule of Christ" for Mennonite ecclesiology see Michael Cartwright, *"Practices, Politics, and Performance: Toward a Communal Hermeneutic for Christian Ethics"* (Unpublished Ph.D. dissertation, Duke University, 1988), pp. 298–434.

1. It is only in the context of reconciliation as a practice that the use of the Mennonite "ban" is intelligible. For rightly understood, the ban is an act of love by the community to help erring members discover that they in fact are not living in unity with the body. See, for example, Marlin Jeschke, *Disciplining the Brother* (Scottdale, Pa.: Herald Press, 1972).

2. I think it is not accidental that Ian makes his living by becoming an apprentice to a master cabinetmaker, becoming in the process a master craftsman himself. Reconciliation is no less a craft than making cabinets, as each requires a transformation of habits and vision if they are to be acquired happily. For the development of this point, see my *After Christendom?* (Nashville, Tenn.: Abingdon Press, 1991), pp. 93–111.

3. *Martyrs Mirror,* whose full title is *The Bloody Theater of Martyrs' Mirror of Defenseless Christians Who Baptized Only Upon Confession of Faith, and Who Suffered and Died for the Testimony of Jesus, Their Savior, from the Time of Christ to the Year A.D. 1660,* was compiled in 1660 by the Dutch Mennonite, Thielerman J. van Braght. It is currently published by Herald Press of Scottdale, Pennsylvania (1950). As the title indicates, the book is composed of the stories of Christian martyrs from the beginning to 1660. The book has been used since its inception as a way to give Mennonites a sense of what makes them Mennonites. Hermeneutically, the book at least suggests Mennonite insistence that they stand in continuity with the church through the ages, not so much on the basis of "doctrine," which is not unimportant, but on the basis of witness. For an excellent account of the background as well as the continued diverse use of

Martyrs' Mirror, see John D. Roth, "The Significance of the Martyr Story for Contemporary Anabaptists," *Brethren Life and Thought* (forthcoming).

4. I was told by the Egyptian Orthodox student who picked me up at the airport in South Bend that there had been no pro-war sentiment for the Gulf War at Goshen College. That is the kind of political correctness I admire.

5. The violence of the flag also embodies the moral significance of sacrifice. I am acutely aware that when many honor the flag they honor those who died in war as well as those who sacrificed their general unwillingness to kill. As a Christian pacifist those sacrifices are a constant reminder of how profoundly we have failed to help Christians be an alternative to war. Thus, good German Lutherans and Catholics made Hitler's war possible. Any compelling account of nonviolence as an ongoing practice requires how those who have fought in war remain part of God's kingdom. For further reflections along these lines, see my "Pacifism: A Form of Politics," in *Peace Betrayed: Essays on Pacifism and Politics,* ed. Michael Cromartie (Washington, D.C.: Ethics and Public Policy Center Publication, 1989), pp. 133–41.

CHAPTER 4
The Democratic Policing of Christianity

1. For a wonderful challenge to the presumption that there is less "religion" in America today than in the past, see Roger Finke and Rodney Stark, *The Churching of America, 1776–1990: Winners and Losers in Our Religious Economy* (New Brunswick, N.J.: Rutgers University Press, 1992). Finke and Stark argue that the "churching" of America has remained fairly constant in numbers. What changes is the churches to which people belong. The "decline," so often announced, in fact is the shifting of membership from established denominations to more energetic new denominations. The authors suggest that you can be pretty sure a denomination is on the decline when its ministry gets a retirement fund. Finke and Stark make no normative judgments about such shifts in the "religious market." I admire their self-restraint, in particular because it illumines the ideological, which is to say Protestant, character of those, such as Martin Marty, who write about American religious history.

2. Harold Bloom, *The American Religion: The Emergence of the Post-Christian Nation* (New York: Simon and Schuster, 1992), p. 32.

3. Ibid., p. 49.

4. Bloom describes himself as "an involuntary believer in the American Religion," but he obviously prefers gnosticism to Judaism and Catholic Christianity. Nowhere is Bloom's own gnosticism more apparent than in his assumption that religious criticism begins with the question: "What is the essence

of religion?" His answer is that religion arises from our apprehension of death (ibid., p. 29). He thus exemplifies the ahistorical, and thus apolitical, characteristics of gnosticism. Accordingly he embodies his profound observation that the irony behind the American Religion, which is nothing if not a *knowing,* is it "does not know itself" (ibid., p. 263).

5. Leander E. Keck, *The Church Confident* (Nashville, Tenn.: Abingdon Press, 1993).

6. I confess that I appreciate Keck's candor in this respect. To say the title is not appropriate to mainline churches is to say "I like things the way they are, even if I cannot justify the way things are." Such a view is not unlike Richard Rorty's defense of democracy having priority over philosophy. See, for example, Rorty's "The Priority of Democracy to Philosophy" in *Prospects for a Common Morality,* ed. Gene Outka and John Reeder (Princeton, N.J.: Princeton University Press, 1993), pp. 254–78. The issue, of course, between Keck and myself is that we, unlike Rorty, are part of a tradition that believes our politics must be faithful to God. Thus, appeal to "the way things are" must be part of the normative display of that tradition. I obviously am not convinced that Keck's appeal to the mainstream is a sufficient display of the church's faithfulness. I find it interesting that Keck's response, as well as many others' responses to *Resident Aliens,* concentrates on the title rather than the material convictions and practices that Willimon and I indicate create the churches' alien status in a liberal culture.

7. The commonplace assumptions embedded in the Bernadin quote beg for analysis that they seldom receive. For example, why is it assumed that "pluralism" adequately describes American society? From what perspective does that description work and in whose interest? As John Milbank and Ken Surin have argued, the very description "pluralism" often assumes a hegemonic position meant to domesticate genuine conflict. Equally problematic is the notion that "religiously rooted positions" can be "translated" without becoming something else in the process. Such a view of translation abstracts language from the practices intrinsic to any language that is doing actual work. For example, see Alasdair MacIntyre's critical comments on the idea of "translation" in his *Whose Justice? Which Rationality?* (Notre Dame, Ind.: University of Notre Dame Press, 1988), pp. 370–88.

8. Constantinianism can be distinguished from democracy, but given the American developments, democracy has become a form—at least if Bloom is even partially right—of Constantinianism in a non-Christian key. In that key, democracy is a form of theocracy in which the new priests, that is, social scientists, rule in the name of "the people."

I am acutely aware that what I am calling democracy is a complex historical process involving different and even antithetical influences. The attempt to distinguish those factors—for example, the rule of law—is useful for any attempt to qualify the liberal narrative. I leave to others that task.

I am indebted to Professor Greg Jones of Loyola College, Baltimore, and Professor Rusty Reno for their comments on this essay.

9. The current discussion of multiculturalism obviously bears on these issues. The incoherence of liberal attempts to come to terms with multiculturalism is nicely illustrated by Amy Gutmann's introduction to *Multiculturalism and the Politics of Recognition: An Essay by Charles Taylor* (Princeton, N.J.: Princeton University Press, 1992).

10. I am indebted to Professor Barry Harvey of Baylor University for helping me see this. His paper, "Theology, Insanity, and the Public Realm: Public Theology and the Politics of Liberal Democracy," *Modern Theology,* 10, 1 (January 1994): 27–58.

11. Too often in the name of the "public," theologians accept the liberal distinction between the private and the public in which the primary practices of the church are relegated to the private. Therefore, in the name of being responsible to the "wider polity," the church accepts a relegation of her own politics to a subordinate position.

12. Nathan Hatch, *The Democratization of American Christianity* (New Haven, Conn.: Yale University Press, 1989), p. 5.

13. Walter Rauschenbusch, *A Theology for the Social Gospel* (Nashville, Tenn.: Abingdon Press, 1917), pp. 174–75. Susan Curtis quotes Rauschenbusch's explanation why he rarely wrote about God, "The God of the stellar universe is a God in whom I drown. Christ with the face of Jesus I can comprehend, and love, and assimilate. So I stick with him." *A Consuming Faith: The Social Gospel and Modern American Culture* (Baltimore: Johns Hopkins University Press), p. 86.

14. Janet Fishburn explores this tension in *The Fatherhood of God and the Victorian Family* (Philadelphia: Fortress Press, 1981). See also Susan Curtis's chapter, "American Families and the Social Gospel," in her *A Consuming Faith,* pp. 72–127. She observes that when the social gospelers began to recognize the deficiencies of the Protestant churches for the support of family life, they turned to secular agencies. "These Protestants joined in the development of the political culture of progressivism in the hope that the state could become an instrument of Christian leadership. But when social gospelers themselves tried to occupy the bully pulpit of American politics, they sacrificed the independent authority of their religion to the social dynamic of the state. In this way the social gospel became a gospel of social salvation, and the authority of Christian religion was absorbed into the authority of secular culture" (127).

15. For a further exploration of the continuities and discontinuities between the Social Gospel and what we now call the Religious Right, see the chapter

"A Christian Critique of Christian America," in my *Christian Existence Today* (Durham, N.C.: Labyrinth Press, 1989).

16. Walter Rauschenbusch, *Christianity and the Social Crisis* (Louisville, Ky.: Westminster/John Knox Press, 1991), p. 14.

17. Walter Rauschenbusch, *The Righteousness of the Kingdom* (Nashville, Tenn.: Abingdon Press, 1968), p. 80.

18. Reinhold Niebuhr, *The Children of Light and the Children of Darkness* (New York: Charles Scribner's Sons, 1944). All pagination will appear in the text. The themes that Niebuhr developed in this book, however, already had been articulated in his *Moral Man and Immoral Society* as well as the second volume of *The Nature and Destiny of Man*.

19. Richard Reinitz, *Irony and Consciousness: American Historiography and Reinhold Niebuhr's Vision* (Lewisburg, Pa.: Bucknell University Press, 1980), p. 97.

20. In his *Reinhold Niebuhr: A Biography* (New York: Pantheon Books, 1985), Richard Fox notes that many of Niebuhr's liberal friends liked the "somber tones and tempered hopes" of *The Children of Light*, "but wondered with Harvard historian Arthur Schlesinger, Jr., if the part about God and sin was really necessary" (225). As we shall see, there was no doubt in Niebuhr's mind that a religiously grounded humility was necessary to sustain democracy.

21. Reinhold Niebuhr, *The Self and the Dramas of History* (New York: Charles Scribner's Sons, 1955), p. 198.

22. This became the cardinal commitment of Paul Ramsey's thinking about democracy. Protection of the individual was for him the religious presumption necessary to sustain a good society. Ramsey, however, maintained that it is exactly the commitment to the individual that constitutes the good in common.

23. It may seem harsh to accuse Niebuhr of an anti-Catholic bias, but he was unrelenting in his criticism of the "Catholic theory of the church as divine institution," which "lends itself particularly to the temptation of confusing relative with eternal values." *Essays in Applied Christianity,* selected and ed. D. B. Robertson (New York: Living Age Books, 1959), p. 200. In response to V. A. Demant's claim that if he had to choose between church and secular movements of justice, he would choose the church "because the essential content of the Body of Christ is a more ultimate thing than the most perfect system of social justice," Niebuhr confesses that he is "shattered" since he holds Demant in such esteem. Against Demant, Niebuhr asserts the "Protestant principle" that the church is not to be identified with the Kingdom of God. I think one simply has to conclude that Niebuhr must require Catholics to become Protestant if they are to be actors in democratic societies.

24. I realize that Niebuhr is often grouped with the turn to neo-orthodoxy,

but that was certainly not his own self-understanding. By associating him with Protestant liberal theology, I mean to suggest that Niebuhr thought of Christianity primarily as a provocative account of human existence that could be known apart from the church. In that sense he represents a profound, but nonetheless gnostic form of the Christian faith. Michael Wyschogrod contrasts the tendency of Christianity toward "spiritualization" with the Jewish presumption that Judaism is "not first a set of ideas but an existing people on whom commands are imposed and from whom ideas are generated but whose own being is the existential soil from which every thing else emerges." *The Body of Faith: Judaism as Corporeal Election* (New York: Seabury Press, 1983), p. 69. While I have no doubt that Wyschogrod is right to denote this temptation as a general one in Christianity, it is just a temptation that is particularly hard to resist when Christians think they must think for everyone in the interest of ruling. Protestant liberalism is perhaps the purest form of this temptation.

One of the interesting aspects of contemporary Christian thinking about politics is how many, both of the right and left, want to use Niebuhr as a justification for democracy, but yet maintain a more Catholic stance about the church. I suspect Niebuhr is right that you cannot have it both ways.

25. *Prospects For A Common Morality,* ed. Gene Outka and John Reeder (Princeton, N.J.: Princeton University Press, 1993), pp. 93–113.

26. Humility interestingly enough becomes an extraordinary weapon to quiet debate by Niebuhrians. Anyone who challenges the fundamental structure of their assumptions automatically becomes "authoritarian."

27. I do not mean to suggest that attempts to understand the complexity of this entity called America are not important. I suspect, however, that history is a more appropriate forum for the explanation of these matters than the social sciences that have so fascinated Christian ethicists. History at least has in its very character the necessity of exposing competing narratives.

28. *The Priestly Kingdom,* pp. 151–71.

29. This essay was first written for the 1993 Interfaith Community Forum, sponsored by Drew University, on the theme, "Religion and Democracy: Are They Compatible?" I am grateful to Professor Peter Ochs and my fellow presenter, Michael Wyschogrod, for their stimulating questioning.

CHAPTER 5
Creation as Apocalyptic: A Tribute to William Stringfellow

1. In his *My People Is the Enemy: An Autobiographical Polemic* (New York: Holt, Rinehart and Winston, 1964), Stringfellow tells of his life as a lawyer in Harlem. We sadly lack a biography that does justice to this extraordi-

narily complex man. For his own reflections on "biography as theology," see the preface, *A Simplicity of Faith: My Experience of Mourning* (Nashville, Tenn.: Abingdon Press, 1982).

2. William Stringfellow, *Free in Obedience: The Radical Christian Life* (New York: Seabury Press, 1964), p. 51.

3. Ibid., p. 62.

4. Lugwig Wittgenstein, *Culture and Value,* trans. Peter Minch (Chicago: University of Chicago Press, 1980), p. 56e.

5. Ibid., p. 37e.

6. William Stringfellow, *An Ethic for Christians and Other Aliens in a Strange Land* (Waco, Tex.: Word Book, 1973), p. 63. Stringfellow dedicated this book to Thomas Merton.

7. L. H. LaRue, "Constitutional Law and Constitutional History," *Buffalo Law Review* 36, no. 373: 401. For an extended account of American constitutionalism as a moral tradition, see H. Jefferson Powell, *The Moral Tradition of American Constitutionalism: A Theological Interpretation* (Durham, N.C.: Duke University Press, 1993). Powell argues that the justification of constitutionalism as a restraint on state power has, as part of the general crisis of liberalism, come to an end. As a result, "contemporary American judges do not impose the rule of reason on Caesar, they *are* Caesar" (p. 11). Stringfellow, of course, could not benefit from Powell's account, but he would not have been surprised by it. See in particular his account of the law in *A Simplicity of Faith,* pp. 127–33.

8. For my (Hauerwas) explicit reflections on the implications of this account of the law, see my "Christian Practice and the Practice of Law in a World Without Foundations," *Mercer Law Review* 44 (Spring 1993): 743–51.

9. Stringfellow, *Free in Obedience,* p. 52.

10. Ibid., p. 63. For Stringfellow's extended reflections on the power of death, see his *Instead of Death* (New York: Seabury Press, 1963).

11. Stringfellow, *An Ethic for Christians,* p. 97.

12. Stringfellow, *Free in Obedience,* p. 69.

13. Stringfellow, *An Ethic for Christians,* p. 106.

14. The loss of the importance of apocalyptic by mainstream Christians results in their inability to understand developments such as Jonestown or the Branch Davidians in Waco. Of course, liberals simply view such "cults" as bizarre and as confirmation that all religion is crazy. I suspect, however, as we come closer to the year 2000 that this society will produce an increasing number of such apocalyptic groups—and we will be equally at a loss as how to understand or respond to them. Just think how dumb it was to surround the Branch Davidians with an army. Such a strategy could only confirm their view of the world—which I might add I take to be closer to the truth than the presumption of most liberals. The tragedy of such groups is how they manifest the

failure of Catholic Christianity to teach people to be eschatologically formed. For my extended reflections on Jonestown, see "On Taking Religion Seriously: The Challenge of Jonestown," in *Against the Nations: War and Survival in a Liberal Society* (Notre Dame, Ind.: University of Notre Dame Press, 1992), pp. 91–106.

15. Stringfellow, *Free in Obedience*, p. 114.

16. Ibid., pp. 43–44.

17. Ibid., p. 38.

18. Stringfellow, *An Ethic for Christians*, p. 119.

19. Ibid., p. 107. I think Stringfellow would have found Václav Havel's *Living in Truth* (London: Faber and Faber, 1986) equally compelling.

20. Stringfellow, *An Ethic for Christians*, p. 145.

21. Ibid., pp. 147–48.

CHAPTER 6
Can a Pacifist Think About War?

This chapter is based on a paper that was commissioned for a conference on the ethics of war and peace in which various tradition/perspectives—that is, Catholic natural law, historical peace churches, Islam, Judaism, Feminism, political realism—were asked to report their traditions position on a range of questions. For example, we were asked to state our traditions position on such questions: (1) How are war and peace understood within the tradition on which you are reporting? (2) Is there a presumption within the tradition against war? (3) What grounds for war (if any) are recognized within the tradition? (4) How does the tradition deal with the question of resistance to political order? (5) How does the tradition handle the issue of motive, in contrast to just cause? (6) Does the tradition recognize prudential or moral constraints on the conduct of war once it has begun? (7) How does the tradition understand the connection between initiating and conducting war?

Such questions appear innocent, but in fact they are shaped by the presuppositions of just war theory. Accordingly, they appear as if they can be asked by anyone from anywhere. That the "historic peace church's" witness would be compromised by accepting such questions as simply "givens" simply was not considered. I accordingly wrote my essay trying to subvert the methodolgy of the conference. I was successful to the extent that the organizers of the conference, with the best will in the world, found my paper unacceptable for their proceedings. So much for dialogue. Interestingly enough, the other participant who had trouble responding to the conference's agenda was the Muslim.

1. Steve Long, *Living the Discipline* (Grand Rapids, Mich.: Eerdmans, 1992), p. 66.

2. Paul Ramsey struggled long and hard with the Methodists over such inconsistencies. He notes that his suggestion to change the wording to "We believe that war is *ultimately* incompatible with the teaching and example of Christ" failed to carry the day in the 1972 draft the Committee was drafting. Nor would the Committee change the next sentence to "We also support those persons who choose *in erring conscience* to serve in the armed forces." *Speak Up for Just War or Pacifism* (State Park: Pennsylvania State University Press, 1968), pp. 9–10. Methodists have never been long on consistency.

3. As I shall argue below, even to know what constitutes violence and/or war, one already must have been made part of practices that are nonviolent. What must be resisted are suggestions that "we" all know what violence and/or nonviolence is abstracted from particular communities' histories.

4. In my "The Difference of Virtue and the Difference It Makes: Courage Exemplified," *Modern Theology* 9 (July 1993): 249–64, I argue that only a person shaped by the courage of the martyrs—that is, courage that is according to Aquinas exemplified by patience and endurance—would be capable of reasoning wisely about just war. Too often just war is presented as if it makes no difference what kind of person or community is using the "criteria."

5. This is an unpublished book that can be obtained from Cokesbury Book Store, the Divinity School, Duke University, Durham, N.C.

6. Roland Bainton, *Christian Attitudes Toward War and Peace* (Nashville, Tenn.: Abingdon Press, 1980).

7. Ibid., p. 14.

8. John Howard Yoder, *The Politics of Jesus* (Grand Rapids, Mich.: Eerdmans, 1972), p. 97.

9. John Howard Yoder, *The Original Revolution* (Scottdale, Pa.: Herald Press, 1971), p. 29.

10. John Howard Yoder, *Nevertheless: Varieties of Religious Pacifism* (Scottdale, Pa.: Herald Press, 1972), p. 124. In a later edition Yoder expands his account to include even more varieties.

11. Reinhold Niebuhr *Moral Man and Immoral Society* (New York: Charles Scribner's Sons, 1960), pp. 43–62.

12. Yoder, *The Original Revolution*, p. 121.

13. In an unfortunately unpublished paper, "*Tertium Datur:* Refocusing the Jewish-Christian Schism," Yoder suggests "when we look at Jesus with the glasses and the glosses of the lessons of the centuries we see that his pacifism is anti-Jewish. Yet if we read him again from the start, and especially if we admit as a learning help the parallel history of our sister community, diaspora Judaism, then we have to say that the pacifism of Jesus is Jewish, nothing but Jewish and altogether Jewish. Only in a Jewish context could his kinds

of reasons, that kind of attitude toward the enemy, toward violence, toward suffering, toward the ultimate saving purpose of an all powerful God add up to the ethic Jesus teaches. Through the centuries the pacifist behavior, and the rationale for that behavior, read into the record of post-Constantinian Jews are far closer to the ethic of Jesus than the behavior of Christians in those same later times and places" (39). Yoder's account of Jewish pacifism is but part of a much larger project that explores the relationship of Judaism and the Anabaptists.

14. Yoder, *Christian Attitudes,* p. 125.

15. I am thinking in particular of neoconservatives such as Michael Novak, who like to think they are Calcedonian Christians, yet political conservatives accept the presuppositions of liberalism. No one has better seen this contradiction than John Milbank in his *Theology and Social Theory* (Cambridge: Basil Blackwell, 1990). It is not at all clear that just war theory is commensurate with the essentially agonistic presuppositions of liberal social science.

16. Nor would I deny that women were no less warriors by their support of men who did the "fighting." As Jean Bethke Elshtain powerfully demonstrated in *Women and War* (New York: Basic Books, 1987), not being able to be actual warriors often only created an extraordinary enthusiasm for war by some women.

17. James Douglass, *The Non-Violent Cross* (Toronto: Macmillan, 1969).

18. Paul Ramsey, *The Just War: Force and Political Responsibility* (New York: Charles Scribner's Sons, 1968), pp. 259–60. Implicit in Ramsey's challenge to Douglass is the assumption that those who represent the just war tradition and/or theory have the moral high ground since that theory is moral discourse that is assumed to be available to anyone. Accordingly, it is constructed in such a manner that no one can be excluded from it by virtue of his particularity. Ramsey's presumption in this respect is in some tension with his own account of just war as the product of the "generous love" of the Gospel to protect the innocent. Yet Ramsey assumed such love could now be treated as a universal because "as a matter of historical fact, there can be no doubt that Christianity trained western European man in his high regard for human personality." *Basic Christian Ethics* (Louisville, Ky.: Westminster/John Knox Press, 1993), p. 246. This new edition is accompanied with an appreciative forward by Steve Long and Hauerwas that we hope indicates our immense admiration for Paul Ramsey. Ramsey wrote unapologetically as a Constantinian. He, moreover, assumed that the "results" of "love transformed natural justice" were still present in our culture to the extent that they could be treated as a virtual universal. Thus, the pacifist bears the burden of proof. Yet it is unclear, given Ramsey's own defense of just war as a principle of Christian charity, why he assumed that the pacifist was any more "particularistic" than was his peculiar brand of Constantinianism.

Toward the end of his life, Ramsey confessed that he never ceased to wonder why "so many 'post-Constantinians' in our so-called 'liberal churches' " can "(1) proclaim with joy the end of that era, yet (2) never hesitate to issue advice to states as if they were Christian kingdoms." *Speak Up*, p. 125. Ironically, Ramsey began to suggest in his last works that the only way that Christians could sustain just war reflection in our world was by being a community not unlike that necessary to sustain nonviolence—that is, that which mainstream Christians call a "sect."

I am indebted to John Howard Yoder for reminding me of presumptions behind Ramsey's questions.

19. Ramsey, *The Just War*, p. 260.

20. The characterization of Douglass's position as "humanistic" is Ramsey's view, not my own. Douglass's account remains determinately Christocentric, as he assumes, like the good Roman Catholic he is, that what Christians believe can be true for anyone. That is not "humanism" but a form of Catholic social theory meant to challenge Ramsey's (and Reinhold Niebuhr's) implicit Lutheran doctrine of the "two kingdoms."

21. Ramsey, *The Just War*, p. 263.

22. This does not mean that an account of just war cannot be developed on non-Christian grounds. See, for example, Scott Davis's extraordinary book, *Warcraft and the Fragility of Virtue: An Essay in Aristotelian Ethics* (Moscow, Idaho: University of Idaho Press, 1992).

23. As far as I know, few courses in international relations try to describe the relation between nations in accordance with just war presuppositions. The only thing that keeps violence limited is other violence. Thus, balance-of-power models are presupposed. The attempt of just war advocates to wed just war to such explanatory schemes creates, as war is said to do, strange bedfellows.

24. Reinhold Niebuhr, *Moral Man and Immoral Society* (New York: Charles Scribner's Sons, 1960), p. 179.

25. Ramsey, *Speak Up*, p. 54.

26. Ibid., p. 100.

27. Ramsey's account that "covenant" as the natural basis for community led him to presume that whatever human communities exist, they manifest incipiently God's creative intentions. He says: "Provisionally then, in our quest for the special function of Christian love, a distinction may be made between *preserving* community that already exists among men and *creating* community where none is. Wherever there already exists community of mutual interest, such community needs always to be preserved and strengthened by all manner of appeals to enlightened self-interest and calling to mind advantages shared mutually in the 'commonwealth.' " *Basic Christian Ethics*, p. 241.

28. John Howard Yoder notes that while it is hard for Ramsey to articulate for any real-world actors an obligation not to go to war, Ramsey did (1) say you

should surrender rather than target civilian populations and (2) get more of a hearing from the Pentagon than those of us who adhere to nonviolence.

29. Ramsey, *The Just War*, p. 11.

30. John Howard Yoder, *When War Is Unjust: Being Honest in Just-War Thinking* (Minneapolis: Augsburg, 1984).

31. John Howard Yoder, *The Christian Witness to the State* (Newton, Kans.: Faith and Life Press, 1964), pp. 56–57.

32. Ramsey, *Speak Up*, pp. 73–74.

33. Ibid., p. 115.

34. Ibid., p. 116.

35. Niebuhr, *Moral Man*, p. 19.

36. Ibid., p. 240.

37. Again, Yoder reminds me that while we as Christians do not derive our stance from prior definitions of "peace" or of "the state," such a methodological disavowal is not the heart of the message. By focusing as I have in this chapter on conflict with an alternative system, the other dimensions of the Gospel witness can be forgotten: (1) that violence is renounced because truth-telling is powerful, (2) that the enemy is loved and the side of the underdog taken because that is the angle of God's intervention in history, and (3) that we accept unmerited suffering as the right thing to do not only when "nonviolent coercion" can be contemplated but also when/if there is no such pragmatic promise.

38. I find it interesting that many that supported the Gulf War in the name of just war said nothing about President Clinton's missile raid on Iraq in response to the allegedly planned attack on George Bush. Even if such a plot was state-sponsored terrorism, that does not justify from a just war perspective a terrorist response, which the missile raid clearly was.

39. Yoder, *Christian Attitudes*, p. 448.

40. Ibid., p. 450.

41. Klaus Wengst, *Pax Romana and the Peace of Jesus Christ* (Philadelphia: Fortress Press, 1987), pp. 87–88.

42. The attack on "theory" in this chapter may appear disingenuous since my very antitheoretical stance can be construed as a theory. By objecting to theoretical accounts of "pacifism" as it is understood by those who hold to just war theory, I am, however, trying not only to resist letting my opponent define who I am but attempting to remind us that the "theory character" of much just war thinking is surprisingly ahistorical. It is as if just war is simply given in the nature of things. In that respect, it would be interesting to explore what differences might be present in those who speak of just war tradition rather than just war theory. Obviously, not a great deal hangs on the words "tradition" or "theory" in themselves, but the former at least indicates that just war is not a stable position but requires historical display. James Johnson's

work, for example, I take to be an ongoing critique of Ramsey's "theory" in the interest of freeing just war from its Christian roots by providing a historical account. Michael Walzer's *Just and Unjust Wars* is extremely interesting from this perspective, as he explores just war through historical examples. I take it that the examples are not meant simply to exemplify, but are intrinsic to his argument. How that set of presumptions coincides with his initial attempt to derive just war from a theory of rights remains unclear to me.

CHAPTER 7
Whose "Just" War: Which Peace?

1. Alasdair MacIntyre, *Whose Justice? Which Rationality?* (Notre Dame, Ind.: University of Notre Dame Press, 1988).

2. Richard John Neuhaus, "Just War and This War," *Wall Street Journal,* January 23, 1991.

3. John Howard Yoder, "Just-War Tradition: Is It Credible?," *Christian Century* (March 13, 1991), pp. 295–98.

4. See, for example, "The Glaspie Transcript: Saddam Meets the U.S. Ambassador," in *The Gulf War Reader,* ed. Micah Sifry and Christopher Cerf (New York: Time Books, 1991), pp. 122–33. Saddam made extremely clear in his conversation with Glaspie that he considered the fall in the price of oil to be an "economic war." In response, Glaspie said: "I know you need funds. We understand that and our opinion is that you should have the opportunity to rebuild your country. But we have no opinion on the Arab-Arab conflicts, like your border disagreement with Kuwait" (p. 130).

5. Bryan Hehir, "The Moral Calculus of War," *Commonweal* (February 22, 1991), p. 126.

6. Michael Walzer, "Morality and the Gulf Crisis," *New Republic* (January 28, 1991), p. 14.

7. Stephen Fowl, "On the Frustration of Practical Reasoning," unpublished paper, (Department of Theology, Loyola College, Baltimore), pp. 4–5.

8. Ramsey's defense of the principle of double-effect, that is, the principle that one can never intend to kill a noncombatant—though their death may occur indirectly, applied not only to issues raised by noncombatants but to the attitude that should be taken toward the enemy soldier. He notes: "The Christian must never intend to kill a man, since love refuses to allow that motive, and countenances only the intention of saving life, even one's own. To kill even an unjust man, as an indirect effect beside the intention to save one's life, would be unjustified if by any means it may be avoided. Profoundly at work in his (Aquinas) line of reasoning is what justice transformed by love requires

to be extended even to him who wrongfully attacks." *War and the Christian Conscience* (Durham, N.C.: Duke University Press, 1961), pp. 43–44.

9. I am indebted to Professors Greg Jones, David Matzko, and Philip Kenneson, and Mr. David DeCosse for their critique of an earlier draft of this chapter.

CHAPTER 9
Communitarians and Medical Ethicists: Or, "Why I Am None of the Above"

1. Charles Taylor, "Cross-Purposes: The Liberal-Communitarian Debate," in *Liberalism and the Moral Life,* ed. Nancy Rosenblum (Cambridge, Mass.: Harvard University Press, 1989), p. 163. Taylor is particularly concerned that the contrast between liberalism and communitarianism confuses the ontological issue of atomism-holism with the set of issues surrounding individualism-collectivism alternatives. These issues are obviously interrelated, but not simply so, since one can be an atomist individualist (Nozick) and a holist collectivist (Marx), but also a holist individualist—probably Richard Rorty.

This essay was written before I had the opportunity to read Ronald Beiner, *What's the Matter with Liberalism?* (Berkeley: University of California Press, 1992). His arguments concerning the liberal-communitarian debate parallel my own. For example, he notes that "liberalism itself is unavoidably a communitarian theory. It makes available a determinate set of social goods that excludes other rival goods" (p. 25). The problem, he rightly argues, is defenders of liberalism refuse to weigh and compare the worth of different good. Later, he observes that Walzer, Taylor, and Sandel, each in their own way affirm community and at the same time affirm pluralism. To expose the problem with this appeal to pluralism Beiner quotes MacIntyre's characterization of such positions as the "great pluralist mishmash of the shared public life of liberal societies." The real predicament, as Beiner observes, does not admit of "communitarian solutions, for the withdrawal into particularistic communities merely confirms what defines the problem in the first place" (pp. 30–31). That is why I am not a communitarian. I am a Christian. Beiner acutely observes: "It is surprising that commentators on the liberal-communitarian debate have not drawn attention to its religious dimension. It is hard to appreciate the full contours of the debate without being aware of the degree to which it involves a Jewish-Catholic challenge to the 'Protestantism' of contemporary Kantianism (even if some of the spearheads of this Kantian revival are themselves non-Protestant)" (p. 16).

2. It is not accidental that the subtitle of Engelhardt's *Bioethics and Secular Humanism* (Philadelphia: Trinity Press International, 1991) is *The Search for*

a Common Morality. Engelhardt, because he defends the necessity of a liberal peace treaty, is often deeply misunderstood. For example, in a new preface to a revised version of his *The Foundation of Bioethics* (forthcoming), he notes, as a "born-again Texan Orthodox Catholic," that he holds "that there is no secular moral authority that can be justified in general secular terms to forbid the sale of heroin, the availability of abortion, the marketing of for-profit euthanatization services, or the provision of commercial surrogacy, he firmly holds none of these endeavors to be good. Indeed, they are great moral evils. But their evil cannot be grasped in purely secular terms. To be pro-choice in these general secular terms is to understand God's tragic relationship to Eden. To be free is to be free to choose very wrongly."

3. Taylor, "Cross-Purposes," 169.

4. Christopher Lasch, "The Communitarian Critique of Liberalism," in *Community in America: The Challenge of Habits of the Heart,* ed. with intro. by Charles H. Reynolds and Ralph Norman (Berkeley: University of California Press, 1988), p. 183. Lasch also is one who observes that some formulations of the communitarian ideal conceive of politics not as a way of compelling people to become virtuous, but as a way of keeping alive the possibility that they will become virtuous by fitting themselves for congenial practices. The celebration of pluralism by this form of communitarianism makes it indistinguishable from liberalism. For an attempt to challenge the communitarian celebration of virtue as good in and of itself, see my "The Difference of Virtue and the Difference It Makes: Courage Exemplified," *Modern Theology* 9 (July 1993): 249–64.

5. Alasdair MacIntyre, "Patients as Agents," in *Philosophical Medical Ethics: Its Nature and Significance,* ed. Stuart E. Spicher and H. Tristram Engelhardt (Dordrecht, Holland: D. Reidel, 1977), pp. 197–212.

6. Ibid., p. 200.

7. Ibid., p. 206.

8. MacIntyre develops his account of the bureaucratic character of medicine in his "Medicine Aimed at the Care of Persons Rather Than What . . . ?" in *Changing Values in Medicine,* ed. Eric J. Cassell and Mark Siegler (New York: University Publications of America, 1979), pp. 83–96. MacIntyre notes that modern medicine is inescapably bureaucratic in its form insofar as (1) the patient only has access to the physician through a route of receptionists, secretaries, and nurses, (2) it is the role that matters, not who fills it (thus, the importance of files), and (3) the importance of face-saving and the correlative necessity to eliminate the unexpected.

9. MacIntyre notes that our understanding of medicine has been distorted during the battle over infectious disease. During the period from 1900 until very recently (1950), it was natural to think of the physician as an applied scientist whose task it was to identify physical changes in the patient and to prevent those changes through chemical or biochemical agents. One result of

this change in the physician's task is that promised cures are at odds with the three ends of medical practice that are necessarily interrelated: (1) to stave off death as long as possible; (2) to prevent suffering pain of physical disability as long as possible; (3) to promote the patient's general health and physical well-being. The problem is that these related ends fall asunder in contemporary medicine. "The chronic conditions which require treatment and the technology available as the instrument for treatment allows us to continue life in such a way as to prolong suffering or to extend disability. There may be no way to promote my well-being which does not involve bringing about my death at a certain point; it may even be better for me if I had not been born. The physician or surgeon, therefore, pledged by his oath and the tradition of his profession to pursue all three ends now is forced, especially with the chronic conditions, to make choices, choices sufficiently frequent in occurrence and sufficiently harsh in character for moral choice to have become a central medical task." "What Has Ethics to Learn From Medical Ethics?" *Philosophical Exchange* 2 (Summer 1978): 38–39.

10. I try to display the implications of such training in my *Suffering Presence: Theological Reflections on Medicine, the Mentally Handicapped, and the Church* (Notre Dame, Ind.: University of Notre Dame Press, 1986) and *Naming the Silences: God, Medicine, and the Problem of Suffering* (Grand Rapids, Mich.: Eerdmans, 1990).

CHAPTER 10
Killing Compassion

1. That most of the victims of Dr. Kevorkian have been women I do not think accidental. Doctors, even doctors like Dr. Kevorkian, become priests of the new ethic of death, giving people the permission to die.

2. Daniel Callahan has acutely depicted the relationship between the movement toward euthanasia and the imperative for medicine to cure in his *What Kind of Life?* (New York: Simon and Schuster, 1990), pp. 242–43. For a similar assessment, see my *Naming the Silences*, pp. 97–112.

3. I am aware that utilitarianism comes in many different varieties, but I think the distinction between different kinds of utilitarianism not important for the general point I am making here.

4. This article can be found in my *Vision and Virtue* (Notre Dame, Ind.: University of Notre Dame Press, 1981), pp. 111–26. My concern with the overconcentration on love as the central moral concept in Christian ethics involves not only moral issues, but Christological questions. Often, hand in hand with the concentration on love is a correlative low Christology. For example, it is difficult to account for Jesus' death if all he was about was recommend-

ing that we ought to love one another. The concentration on love as the heart of Jesus' teaching is often associated with our ignoring Jesus' eschatological proclamation of the Kingdom of God. Once Christianity is robbed of political power, all it has left to underwrite are cultural sentimentalities such as love.

5. Oliver O'Donovan, *Begotten or Made?* (Oxford: Clarendon Press, 1984), p. 11. Pagination is given in the text.

6. See, for example, Paul Wadell's wonderful book, *The Primacy of Love: An Introduction to the Ethics of Thomas Aquinas* (New York: Pauline Press, 1992).

7. One, among many, passages in Willimon and my *Resident Aliens* (Nashville, Tenn.: Abingdon Press, 1989) that most angered readers was the suggestion that Christians might contemplate the death of their children as a consequence of their children's baptism (pp. 148–49). This suggestion seemed obvious to us, given the language of baptism in Romans 5, but it seems today that most Christians assume that Christianity is about the project of making existence safe for ourselves and our children. For Willimon and my reactions to the unanticipated popularity of that book, see our "Why *Resident Aliens* Struck a Chord," *Missiology: An International Review* 19 (October 1991): 419–29.

8. For some extremely illuminating remarks on the interrelation of theory and storytelling, see Ronald Beiner, *What's the Matter with Liberalism?* (Berkeley: University of California Press, 1992), pp. 10–14.

9. Liberal theory as well as social practice is various as well as interrelated in a complex fashion. Beiner provides an adequate characterization by noting that "liberalism is the notion that there is a distinctive liberal way of life, characterized by the aspiration to increase and enhance the prerogatives of the individual; by maximal mobility in all directions, throughout every dimension of social life (in and out of particular communities, in and out of socioeconomic classes, and so on); and by a tendency to turn all areas of human activity into matters of consumer preference; a way of life based on progress, growth, and technological dynamism. This liberal mode of existence is marked by tendencies toward pluralistic fragmentation, but paradoxically it is also marked by tendencies toward universalism and even homogenization." *What's the Matter with Liberalism?*, pp. 22–23. Inherent to liberalism is the attempt to create societies and people without memory. "History" becomes an "academic" subject that serves no moral purpose.

10. For a more extensive, but still inadequate, account of the Christian practice of singleness and marriage, see my *After Christendom?* (Nashville, Tenn.: Abingdon Press, 1991), pp. 113–32.

11. In a series of publications, Steven Post has illumined this issue in an extraordinarily fruitful fashion. See, for example, his "Love and the Order of Beneficence, *Soundings* 75 (Winter 1992): 499–516.

12. This peculiar set of trade-offs creates what I call the Groucho Marx problems of ethics. Groucho Marx said that he would not want to belong to a

country club that would have him as a member. Most of us do not want a life that we have chosen—even more we fear our children living as we lived.

13. Charles Taylor, *Sources of the Self: The Making of Modern Identity* (Cambridge, Mass.: Harvard University Press, 1989). (Pagination is given in the text.) For a more critical analysis of Taylor's book, see my and David Matzko's "The Sources of Charles Taylor," *Religious Studies Review*, 18, 4 (October, 1992), pp. 286–289.

14. For a wonderful account of how the land of Palestine became holy for Christians, see Robert Wilken, *A Land Called Holy* (New Haven, Conn.: Yale University Press, 1992). Wilken notes: "The narrative character of the gospels (recording Jesus' life from birth through death) indelibly imprinted on the minds of Christians the sanctity of time. For Christians in Jerusalem, however, the proximity of the holy places made possible a sanctification of space" (p. 113).

15. In effect, vocation becomes the Protestant substitute for natural law reflection. Indeed, the natural law tradition in principle held out greater possibilities for Christians to take a critical stance toward their behavior in "the world" than the language of vocation. Honor and duty became self-justifying norms that could not be challenged, since there was no place from where they might be called into question.

16. It is not accidental, as George Marsden has documented, that fundamentalism drew on Baconian presuppositions for its reading of the Bible. See his *Fundamentalism and American Culture: The Shaping of Twentieth-Century Evangelicalism, 1870–1925* (New York: Oxford University Press, 1980), p. 112.

17. No doubt part of the story also involves the increasing belief in progress as an end in itself. See, for example, Christopher Lasch, *The True and Only Heaven* (New York: Norton, 1991).

18. Alasdair MacIntyre rightly argues in *After Virtue* (Notre Dame, Ind.: University of Notre Dame Press, 1984) that the distinction between fact and values derived not from any obvious epistemological theory, but rather become necessary to legitimate the authority of the bureaucrat. The latter depends on "expert advice," which correlatively depends on predictability, which depends on the control of "facts." Without denying that human activity is capable of some generalization, MacIntyre argues that human affairs are characterized by a "systematic unpredictability" that cannot be suppressed, even by the supervising strategies of bureaucratic liberalism (pp. 88–101).

19. These are obviously complex issues that I cannot adequately discuss in this context—or perhaps anywhere. Indeed, I am not confident that I rightly understand O'Donovan's position. At the beginning of *Resurrection and Moral Order* (Grand Rapids, Mich.: Eerdmans, 1986), he rightly castigates those who would have us choose between resurrection and creation as moral sources (pp. 31–52). Yet his fear of "historicism" leads him through the rest of the book

to appeal to the created order for moral reflection. I think he rightly senses that the eschatological character of the resurrection in fact makes a kind of historicism unavoidable for Christian moral reflection. This position is not as problematic for me as it is for O'Donovan, since I make no pretense to think about the moral life for those who do not share in the baptism made possible by Christ's death and resurrection. For a display of the difference that these theological questions make for attitudes concerning the status of animals, see John Berkman and my "The Chief End of All Flesh," *Theology Today* 49 (July 1992): 196–208.

20. Albert Borgmann, *Crossing the Postmodern Divide* (Chicago: University of Chicago Press, 1992), pp. 97–102. Pagination is given in the text.

21. In *The Peaceable Kingdom* (Notre Dame, Ind.: University of Notre Dame Press), I argued that patience, with hope, are the central Christian virtues, given the eschatological character of our faith as Christians. I am not sure I well-understood that point at the time I wrote, but I am becoming increasingly convinced that patience is the crucial Christian virtue.

CHAPTER 11

**The Church and the Mentally Handicapped:
A Continuing Challenge to the Imagination**

1. Garret Green, *Imagining God: Theology and the Religious Imagination* (New York: Harper and Row, 1989), p. 63.

2. Ibid., p. 66.

3. I think there is a profound relationship between Christian nonviolence and the joy Christians are to learn from the mentally handicapped. Each forces us to be what we otherwise could not become. For example, pacifists are often challenged with "What would you do if . . . ?" in the hopes that the Christian imagination will be extinguished in the name of "realism." Yet as John Howard Yoder points out, such a question assumes we are trapped by an inescapable determinism: "I alone have a decision to make. My relationship with the other person in this situation is at bottom one which unfolds mechanically. The attacker is pre-programmed to do the worst evil he can—or at least the evil he has fixed on his mind. He is not expected to make any other decisions or act in any other way." *What Would You Do?: A Serious Answer to a Standard Question* (Scottdale, Pa.: Herald Press, 1983), p. 14. Yet the Christian, exactly because we believe our existence, like the existence of the mentally handicapped, depends on the gifts of others to give us alternatives to such a deterministic world. For Christians, the "real world" is that constituted by the community formed by a crucified yet resurrected Jesus. That resurrection reminds us that we do not live in a world determined by violence, but in a world constituted by

God's nonviolence exemplified in the cross of Jesus. Such nonviolence is made possible by the moral skills of this community that seeks to embody the character of this God, skills that constitute cracks in the ubiquitous violence which characterizes the so-called real world. Such imagination is not fantasy if God is the God of the resurrection miracle. Just as that God will not have "peace" created through violence, neither will God have our lives made "better" through the elimination of the retarded. For further reflection on the relation of the care of the weak and nonviolence, see Philip Kenneson and my "The Church and/as God's Non-Violent Imagination," *Pro Ecclesia* 1 (Fall 1992): 76–88. I have included some paragraphs of that essay in this chapter. I am indebted to Professor Kenneson for joining me in the writing of them.

4. For a wonderful account of the ability of disabled children to lead Christian lives, see Brett Webb-Mitchell, *God Plays Piano Too: The Spiritual Lives of Disabled Children* (New York: Crossroads, 1993).

5. For a more extended account of this sense of time, see my *Christian Existence Today: Essays on Church, World, and Living In-Between* (Durham, N.C.: Labyrinth Press, 1988), pp. 253–66. The most insightful account of my views about time are made by Philip Kenneson in his "Taking Time for the Trivial: Reflections on Yet Another Book from Hauerwas," *Asbury Theological Journal* 45 (Spring 1990): 65–74.

Stanley Hauerwas is Gilbert T. Rowe Professor of Theological Ethics at Duke University. He is the author of numerous books, the most recent being *In Good Company: The Church as Polis*. He is also co-editor, with Alasdair MacIntyre, of a book series entitled "Revisions: Changing Perspectives in Moral Philosophy."

Library of Congress Cataloging-in-Publication Data

Hauerwas, Stanley
Dispatches from the front : theological engagements
with the secular / Stanley Hauerwas.
p. cm.   Includes index.
ISBN 0-8223-1475-4   ISBN 0-8223-1716-8 (pbk)
1. Sociology, Christian. 2. Forgiveness—Religious
aspects—Christianity. 3. Liberalism (Religion) I. Title.
BT738.H32 1994
261—dc20   93-44504   CIP